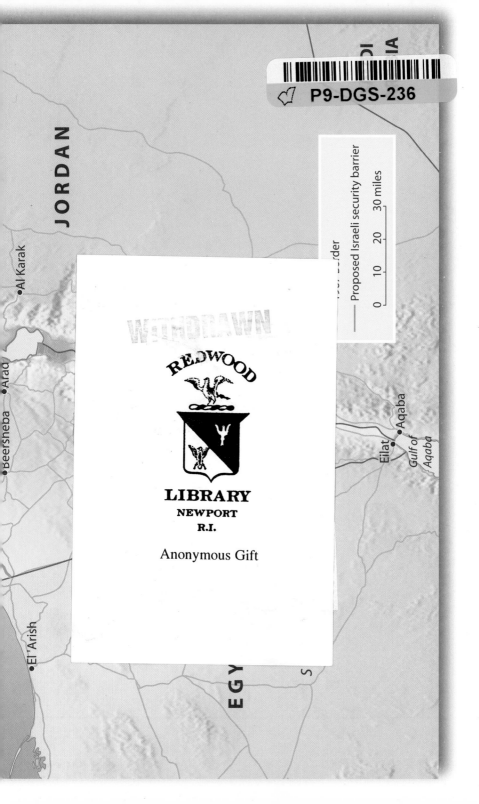

JORDAN

•Al Karak

•Arad

•Beersheba

•El'Arish

Eilat• •Aqaba

*Gulf of
Aqaba*

EGY

S

—— Proposed Israeli security barrier

0   10   20   30 miles

Also by Richard Ben Cramer

What It Takes: The Way to the White House
Joe DiMaggio: The Hero's Life
What Do You Think of Ted Williams Now?

HOW ISRAEL LOST

THE FOUR QUESTIONS

RICHARD BEN CRAMER

SIMON & SCHUSTER

NEW YORK LONDON TORONTO SYDNEY

SIMON & SCHUSTER
Rockefeller Center
1230 Avenue of the Americas
New York, NY 10020

SIMON & SCHUSTER and colophon are registered trademarks
of Simon & Schuster, Inc.
For information about special discounts for bulk purchases,
please contact Simon & Schuster Special Sales:
1-800-456-6798 or business@simonandschuster.com

Designed by Jaime Putorti
Map by Paul Pugliese

Manufactured in the United States of America

10   9   8   7   6   5   4   3   2   1

Library of Congress Cataloging-in-Publication Data
Cramer, Richard Ben.
   How Israel lost / Richard Ben Cramer.
       p.   cm.
   1. Arab–Israeli conflict—Moral and ethical aspects.   2. Arab–Israeli
conflict—1993—Peace.   3. Palestinian Arabs—West Bank—Social
conditions.   4. Palestinian Arabs—Gaza Strip—Social conditions.
5. Israel—Social conditions.   6. Israel—Ethnic—relations.
7. National characteristics, Israeli.   I. Title.
DS119.76.C73   2004
956.05—dc22   2004045354
ISBN 0-7432-5028-1

For Ruby

Contents

HOW
ISRAEL
LOST

I

Why do we care about Israel?

Why do we care about Israel? An eyelash of land around the eastern Mediterranean shore, in some spots the nation isn't ten miles wide. North to south, you can drive it in half a day—if you don't get stuck behind some Polish geriatric squinting through the steering wheel of his first automobile, putting to a new test (at thirty-two miles per hour) his life's talent, which is survival. In fact, our care must be more for that turtle-ish Jewish survivor than for the land he drives. Even if the world called the question tomorrow and awarded to the Jews, or to the Arabs, every *dunam* of land in Palestine—every hill, vineyard, olive grove and old stone house, every grain of difficult soil that's been fought over for a hundred years—the whole ball of wax wouldn't match in mass, in fecundity or natural wealth, a quarter of a province of the Congo.

No, it isn't a great rich place, nor gloriously old as a nation-state—fifty-years-and-change it has stood. Its apologists and ideologues tend to start their histories in the mist of Bible-time, to enforce an air of eternity, inevitability, permanence. But there's another story in what the Zionists called "the facts on the ground." There are still thousands of houses whose land records go back exactly for those fifty-years-and-change, and then their histories stop, blank and glaring, like the screen when a film snaps in the projector. These are the properties of "absentees"—Arabs who ran away or were chased away in Israel's birth-war of 1948. Still, there are thousands of old men in refugee camps who will show you the keys to those houses—keys they will pass on to their sons as prize and burden. And still there are the old Jewish fighters, whose preternatural vigor shows why the Arabs ran. On a research visit in 2003, I was privileged to tour the old Negev battlefields with Itzhak Pundak, a brigade commander from the '48 War. He marched me from a wrecked railroad bridge, around the Jewish sniper posts, onward to Egyptian artillery bunkers, from time to time regarding me narrowly from under handsome silvery brows. "Is this too much?" asked the eighty-nine-year-old. "Do you need a rest?"

We have never cared about Israel for her political influence—she never held sway in what Bush the Elder called The New World Order. In the U.N., for example, you wouldn't go out of your way to win Israeli approval—unless for some strange tactical reason you need an implacable majority of third-world nations against your proposal. Whatever Israel is for, most of the world opposes. This is one of the few truths embraced with satisfaction by both Arab and Jew. The Palestinians see Israel's unpopularity as confirmation of their cause. (They wuz robbed! They are victims! Their rights must be restored!) The Jews see it as confirmation of a tenet even more deeply held: the whole world is against them—no matter what they do.

In the Arab world, where conspiracy theory is even more popular than Islam (as religions, they offer identical comfort: nothing happens without a reason), it's fashionable to see the West's care for Israel—especially America's fixation on Israel—as evidence of a grand scheme for global domination. Israel is assumed to be some sort of U.S. foot-in-the-door, behind which glistens the world's wealth of petroleum. There are a couple of problems with this type of theory. For one thing, adults in the region have by now borne witness to interventions, proclamations and general buttinski from two generations of "American experts on the Middle East"—Special Presidential Negotiators, Deputy Assistant Secretaries of State, Regional Ambassadors, Plenipotentiary Envoys. . . . Hell could freeze over before these guys dominate *anything*—some, you wouldn't let 'em change your tire. The second problem is conclusive: no one can explain how America's support for Israel brings the U.S. any leverage over Middle East oil. Sometimes it makes it hard even to buy Middle East oil.

It's also fashionable for Arabs (and for some Jews) to descry within the tapestry of American politics a controlling weft of rigid steel thread—which they call (depending on who's talking) The Zionist Lobby, AIPAC, the Jewish Money Men, the Hollywood Mafia, or most simply and mysteriously: Jewish Interests. Whatever they call it, they use it to explain why the U.S. government and U.S. public cannot seem to hear, or to remember, or take into account for two days straight, the plight of the Palestinian Arabs who lost their country when the Jews took over. In this type of "analysis," congressmen and presidents (no matter their names, their parties, or provenance) are thought to snap to attention, saluting the Israeli flag, whenever Jews show up with threats or the blandishment of their hefty checkbooks. This is also nonsense.

By what lever do these U.S. Jews lift the world? With the power of their massive vote? Maybe they're two percent of the voting public. (They used to be three but they can't even get it together to make Jewish babies.) And they are, by now, the least bloc-ish bloc. The children of reliable Democrats got richer and more Republican (just like white guys), and *their* children—today's young Jews—are like totally, kind of like . . . *way uninterested.* The savants who whispered that Bush the Younger went warring in Iraq to do Israel's bidding (led by the nose—as half of them added—by that known Jew, Deputy-Pentagon-Panjandrum Paul Wolfowitz) failed to notice, or failed to point out, that the organizers of the big anti-war demonstrations were also Jews—who whipped up a fine anti-imperialist fervor with a speech by the last burning star of the radical kibbutz movement, Noam Chomsky. (They're everywhere!) . . . And the notion that Bush has to dance for Jewish money ignores so many realities that they cannot all be listed. First and foremost, the present Bush—because he is present in the White House, and pro-business—can have for his reelection effort as many millions as he needs, or wants, or could dream of. The flashiest, most-talked-about "Jewish money" comes from Hollywood, where the only true religion is hating Bush. And even the quieter monied Jews of Wall Street look like homeless next to Bush's pals in the oil bidness—pals who would just as soon see Israel go away so they could more comfortably shrimp the toes of the Arabs.

If George W. Bush derives any benefit from caring about Israel, or trying to help Israel, it is not from Jews. (No matter what a president says or does about Israel, there is some group of Jews who'll denounce him as a Nazi.) The only plausible political gain comes from his fellow born-again Christians. The U.S. Christian right believes that the Jews are *supposed* to have the Holy Land—number one, because the Bible tells them so. The Bible says, too, that the second coming of Christ will require that the Jews be "ingathered" again in Zion, which will bring on Armageddon, which will cause Jesus to return. There's also a political meeting of the minds, going back to the days when the Christian right saw Israel as a brave anti-Soviet (more recently anti-Islamic) outpost of "Judeo-Christian values."

Curiously, it's this last fuzzy reason that comes closest to answering "Why do we care?" For in the end, there is no rational benefit in *realpolitik*—either internationally, or for campaigns inside America. There is no lobby or group in the U.S. that could pressure the government to make Israel the number-one recipient of American foreign aid—three billion dollars *each year* (plus a couple of billion in loan guarantees)—and that's before you start adding in special military credits, trade preference and other backdoor deals. The only other country that comes close is Egypt—we pay them two billion to act like they don't hate Israel. Altogether, almost half of the U.S. aid dollars *for the world* shower the land for a few hundred miles around Tel Aviv. (Talk about making the desert bloom!) . . . And not just by dollars should our interest be measured. There is also the matter of attention we pay. We may spend more than five-billion-a-year in the currency of newspaper words and CNN chat; there are endless and more-or-less deep analyses in monthly magazines, in *The New Yorker*, the *New York Review of Books* and the quarterly *Foreign Policy*; it's no accident (and not without effect) that *The New York Times* covers Jerusalem better than Staten Island, or that *Redbook*, the ladies' mag, responds to its readers' new fear of terrorism by commissioning a personal essay from a mom in Israel (who also just happens to be the head of the Jerusalem office of AIPAC). The fact is, Israel sells. And we have sold ourselves on Israel. Why? Because in some measure we are all like those Christians who see and support shared values there. For decades, we've read and talked about Israel, we've backed and begirded Israel, we've paid for Israelis' first-world standard of living ... because we came to assume, somehow, *they are like us.*

The Israelis, no dummies, did what they could to foster this impression—from appointing a government spokesman who talked like he grew up in Detroit (he did), to allocating scarce shekels for the world (i.e., Western World) tour of the Israel Philharmonic. From '48 on, the most important resource of the young nation was the harrowing and latterly triumphal story of the Jewish people—which had elicited the sympathy of the world, and spurred the U.N. vote that made the Jewish state. And so, the first growth industry of Israel (even before tart Jaffa oranges found their market in Europe) was what the locals called *hasbarah*—which literally translates as "explaining," but we might call it propaganda, or spin.

From the moment a U.N. cease-fire ended the first war in the spring of '49, Israelis led the world in guided tours. Their new immigrants were living in squalid tent camps, the air force was maybe two banged-up bombers, but the government still bought fistfuls of boat and airline tickets, and hotel rooms and state-of-the-art buses, to put together freebie trips for eager Swiss or Swedish students, South African "opinion makers," Jewish "pioneer campers" from North America, young politicians and journalists from all over the world and, of course, rich Americans (who might fund the guided tours of the future with a generous gift someday). They had to get their story out—and the *hasbarah* industry attracted the best and the brightest. It wasn't just the friendly tour guides, who could explain—in their perfect Dutch or Danish, Walloon or Serbo-Croatian (language skills were the other great resource)—how the Arab armies shot deadly artillery from that hill, *right there!* (And those poor kibbutzniks who just gave us that wonderful lunch live under that threat every day, even now. . . .) There were also the spokesmen, guides and greeters for every government department, every municipality, the big Histadrut national labor union, the Israel Lands Authority, the Jewish Agency—they were all making friends, "explaining." And these guys were good! . . .

Long ago, I witnessed one tour of up-and-coming American poobahs—or poobahs-to-be—the Young Presidents Organization. And some wiseacre asked a sticky little question: *Are Israelis going to have to pay compensation to the Arabs who ran away?* . . . Now, the fact was, and is, that Israel won't pay a nickel—but the first "explanation" was palliative: *Yes, it's a complicated question . . . now, a commission is studying the fairest method . . . but you have to understand, land records under the Turks. . . .* And then, as the tour moved on, the *hasbarah* man was walking next to that fellow, and issued this pained, confidential aside: "You know, it was a terrible shame—we begged them to stay!" . . . which was a bold, but uncheckable lie. And that night at dinner (a slap-up dinner, on the cuff of course), having found out that his new friend hailed from Connecticut, the *hasbarah* professional inquired—just by the bye: *Say, how's it going with those pesky lawsuits from American Indians—aren't they claiming that half the state is theirs?*

Whatever the topic, the subtext was always the same: We are doing our best under impossible pressures. Imagine how you would feel—for we are like you. But the *hasbarah* succeeded better than even Israelis dreamed. By 1960, Paul Newman—no less—was larger than life on the world's screens in *Exodus*, as a Super-Panavision Jewish underground fighter, with the shiksa-goddess Eva Marie Saint as his home-from-the-holocaust honey. Israel was boffo! So, the message grew bolder. By the end of the Sixties, after the triumph of the Six Day ('67) War, the prime minister, Golda Meir, was asked a similarly sticky question about the rights of Palestinians. "What are you talking about?" she snapped. "There are no Palestinians."

Still, the big shift happened in the Seventies—and not from hubris but need—after the ('73) Yom Kippur War. The surprise, and surprisingly effective, attack by their Arab neighbors reminded Israelis they *could* be wiped off the map. The Israel Defense Forces, which to that point had seemed invulnerable, now suddenly looked hapless and needy. Israel dropped all her prior reserve and cast herself shamelessly as America's little buddy in the Middle East. She burrowed into every U.S. plan for the region—so deep that without her there wasn't any plan. She had to become indispensable—and the story line she put out to the Western public had to change, as well.

It had to be more than "they are like us." Now they wanted us to know that they *were* us—or standing in for us—surrounded, outnumbered (that much of the *hasbarah* stayed constant) . . . hungry for peace, but determined to fight—as the Superman serial used to say—for truth, justice and the American way. Our view of the place had to change: it wasn't just an interesting little desert land (where more U.S. Jews would live, if they weren't so damn *comfortable*). Now, all Americans had to be stakeholders in the Holy Land, partisans in its conflict. And we were! (Those were American planes—TWA—that the PLO blew up . . . and that poor Mr. Klinghoffer, who got shoved off the cruise ship in his wheelchair . . . as usual, the Palestinians undermined their own cause with thorough efficiency.)

Withal, it was more than a Middle East friendship—our enemy was theirs. For there was, underneath, a real affiliation between the American public (between citizens and subjects all over the Western World) and *this place*—which had more or less launched their sense of self. Israel began strumming this chord under Prime Minister Menachem Begin, a right-wing true believer who took power in 1977. For almost thirty years, under left-wing Labour party governments, Israel had cast herself as a modern, socialist, secular state. In the shock and dismay after the Yom Kippur War, the Labour party fell apart, and Begin marched in, bearing the Torah. In his first speech as premier, he announced with characteristic drama: "We shall not ask any other nation to recognize our right to exist. We got our recognition from the God of Our Fathers at the dawn of civilization."

Begin would put the holy back in Holy Land. And in the West—which was also swinging to the right under the whip of Margaret Thatcher, and Ronnie Reagan's homey little chuckles—the Jews of Israel were depicted as heroes. Beset by despicable acts of terror, cruelties, massacres of women and children . . . still, they hadn't budged an inch, but had managed (against all odds—against evil!) to stand in, and even to rebuild and reconsecrate their special place, which was our special place, too (whether we're religious or not) . . . because there—here—we became *who we are* . . . as Western souls, endowed by God with a right to bestride His planet. (Bestriding was Thatcher/Reaganism writ in one word.) . . . Here the promise happened—*here.*

We all belonged to this place (and Jews all had at least a sneaking suspicion that they belonged *in* this place). Here man invented God, or knew the God who invented man— and that gave us all a place to stand. This sparked a loyalty that needed no reason. It was pre-rational—from some deeper part of the brain than words could get to—or call it a piece of our collective unconscious. Whatever the name, it's not the sort of thing that mere thoughts, or daily facts, can easily grind away. . . . Which makes it the more remarkable what has happened, lately—or was it lately? This is one of those big stories that doesn't break, but just seeps into being. At some point in these latter years, Israel ground away, or gave away, her birthright of loyalty from the West.

You could see it happening in a hundred ways, little and large—when you look back, and the pattern shows. The Israeli Minister of Defense has to pack his bags and scuttle out of Europe, because he got wind somehow that he might be arrested and charged with war crimes . . . a small dispatch from London notes the departure "for Palestine" of a group of Britannic do-goods who are going to the West Bank to protect Palestinian olive-pickers against the depradations of Jewish "terrorist settlers" . . . the Canadian government cancels the tax break for some Israeli affiliated charities, because contributions (for instance, the gift of an ambulance) might be used in the occupied territories. . . .

The one that stood me on my ear (and fetched me onto this story) was in my home, America, and in my home-business, in the news columns of *The New York Times*—no less!—and not just for one day, but day after day. On the front page, two stories would be "tombstoned" (i.e., matched, side-by-side). One story would tell about the latest terrorist suicide bomb in Israel; and the other would report on what sort of killing the Israeli army did in response, in some West Bank town or Gaza. The stories were equal—no judgment and no moral distinction was drawn between them. And this from the former house organ of American zionism!

Clearly, the ground had shifted—something big was up. This book project was born to answer the question: What happened?

Maybe it was the daily dose of video, flashed around the world—Israeli tanks blasting holes in buildings, and Palestinians weeping in the West Bank or Gaza . . . maybe the deaths of some nice, well-meaning Westerners, Americans or Brits, who were trying to stop Israeli bulldozers from destroying the houses of Arabs . . . or maybe the simple realization that the Israelis sang us a song of David, when they'd long since become Goliath. One way or another, Israel lost control of the narrative that is her lifeline.

Support began eroding first—twenty years ago?—in Europe. (Israeli *hasbarah* pros dismissed this as traditional European anti-Semitism.) Americans, less burdened by knowledge of the world abroad (and perhaps less cynical in all their faiths), lingered in their loyalty until . . . these days, they don't know what to think. This, too, I see now in a thousand little ways: the fund-raiser for the United Jewish Appeal who tells me he's getting pitched out of *nice Jewish homes*— or he never even gets in the door . . . the dear old Hadassah ladies in the "assisted living" complex, who tell me they've stopped picking up the paper ("It's so terrible what you read in there about Israel, I don't even look.") . . . or the friend from my little American town, whom I tell that I'm doing a book about Israel: "No offense," she says (for she knows I'm Jewish), "but that president over there—or, it's not president, prime minister—I just don't like him, he's not a nice man!" . . . Sure, the freshet of U.S. aid still flows—but that's the government. If the American people fall off the bus, the government will follow someday soon. One thing's for sure: Thirty-five years of occupation doesn't make it smell like home—to us. . . . Or put it another way: somewhere along the line, we got the feeling, "they *aren't* like us." Or maybe we don't want to be like them. And this is just one of the ways—one big one—how Israel lost.

Where I grew up, in a suburb of Rochester, New York, there was a temple called B'rith Kodesh—which (I now know) means Holy Covenant, though I never thought about it at the time. It was just B'rith Kodesh, as normal and established a landmark in my life as the public library, which was more or less across the street. The temple had a Sunday school to which I had to go. Why did I have to go? There wasn't any why about it. I had to go to Sunday school like I had to be bar mitzvahed, like I had to get through high school and go to college—those were my jobs. And I thought even less, at that time, about what they taught us in Sunday school. It was just Jewish stuff I had to learn, like my Catholic neighbors had to learn about saints, and Latin. At least we didn't have to go to confession.

It was Bible stories, mostly—Noah and the ark, Moses getting fished out of the Nile. . . . That, and a lot of Jewish history, which mostly consisted of non-Jewish tyrants with lumpy names (like peanut brittle in your mouth)—Nebuchadnezzar, Ahashueras—who at different times in different places tried to do in the Jews. But then God showed up and smote them a Mighty Smite, and things were better till next Sunday, when the Jews were in trouble again. (It's like my friend Ilan Kutz says about Jewish holidays—they all pretty much add up to the same thing: "They tried to kill us. They didn't succeed. So, let's eat.") . . . All the stories were taught in a seamless succession, and no one made much fuss—certainly, I did not—about which ones came from the

Bible, and which from later books, or from no books at all (like that impoverished little Hanukah story, which we all pretty much recognized as a plot to keep us from succumbing to Christmas).

And the last strand in this skein of woes was Hitler and the holocaust. Maybe this was taught with a little more heat because it had happened in the time of our teachers' lives. But there wasn't any more detail than we got about the Babylonians or Assyrians. Nevertheless, this Hitler business was my favorite Sunday school story. For one thing, I knew from independent sources (a series of wartime boys' books called *The Yankee Flier*—I'd inherited the set from my uncle, and read them all at least three times) that, in this case, God's Mighty Smite had arrived in the form of glorious U.S. Air Force squadrons, and George Patton's smashing Third Army—which, I felt, put *me* on the side of the angels. . . . And the other good thing was the end of this story—the creation of Israel—which I thought had potential to keep the Jews out of hot water for several Sundays in a row.

We didn't learn much about what Israel was. The teachers seemed to exult in it mostly because it was a place to speak Hebrew—which was another excuse for us to have to learn Hebrew. We did learn that Israel was a desert till the Jews showed up and made it bloom. We had to make it bloom, too, by slotting dimes into little cut-outs on a piece of cardboard with Hebrew writing on it—each dime would buy a pine tree to make Israel green. (It seemed to me, God ought to smite up some pine trees, while I used my dime for a big Three Musketeers bar.) . . . We were taught that the Arabs tried to kill off Israel at birth, by attacking all at once—which fact was presented as a modern confirmation of all the *other* stories. ("See? They're *still* trying to murder us.") . . . And we knew that Israel was definitely innocent and excellent: Ben-Gurion, Weizmann, Yigal Allon and Abba Eban were added to the roster of good-guys—on the same page, as it were, with Abraham, Isaac and Jacob, Moses and Aaron, Queen Esther, sage Solomon, King David and a bunch of prophets. In fact, it was all one mudpie to us, straight from the Bible to Ben-Gurion—monotheism and zionism were both good isms the Jews thought up.

What I liked about Israel, apart from the fact that it was the end—last stop on the Sunday school train—was the slogan we heard every time the subject came up: *"Israel was a land without people for a people with no land."* . . . This was the tersest, most powerful storytelling—as good as all the other jingles that filled my head at the time: *See the U.S.A. in your Chevrolet . . . Winston tastes good, like a cigarette should.* (They were probably also the work of Jews.) But this was so neat a turn of phrase, and a turn of history, that it seemed to confirm for me the biggest of all Sunday school stories: the sense and economy, the goodness of God's creation. It all locked together in the end, neater than Legos—*a land without people for a people with no land.* That was what I knew.

It was a testament to my misspent school years that it was still just about all I knew fifteen years later. By that time, I

was a reporter for *The Philadelphia Inquirer,* happily at work
in that newspaper's New York Bureau. In fact, I was the New
York Bureau, which was our only bureau—we weren't a rich
paper at the time. My editor called me on the phone one day,
in December 1977, and asked: "How fast can you be in
Egypt?" I thought it was some stupid knock-knock joke. I
said: "I give up. How fast can you be in Egypt?" But it turned
out he was serious. The Egyptian president, Anwar Sadat,
had just traveled to Jerusalem to propose peace—huge
news. And now, it was announced, Menachem Begin, prime
minister of Israel, would return the visit, at Ismailiya, Egypt,
on Christmas Day. The paper had to do *something* to cover—
but what could my bosses do? They couldn't uncover something *important,* like City Hall, or the Phillies! But the New
York Bureau was already gravy—and in it was a Jew, who
would work on Christmas. "I'll be there tomorrow," I said.

For the next seven years, I was a Middle East reporter, in
and out of Israel a hundred times, and all over the Arab
world. By the end, I thought I knew what I was doing. But
what I had to learn first was the depth of my ignorance. On
that first flight to Egypt, I could tot up my certainties on two
fingers: The Jews were the good guys; the good guys always
won. I never knew that much for sure again.

And when I got to Israel, a few weeks into my new career,
my confusion was complete. Sure enough, there were the
pine trees. (I was glad of that, and they'd done splendidly.
Which ones were mine?) . . . For the rest, I was reminded of
a line old Harry Truman spoke about his opponent: "It's not

what he doesn't know that bothers me. It's what he knows for sure that's just plain wrong."

Those assholes honking at my rent-a-car, as I puzzled out some Hebrew road sign—were these the heroes of the Six Day War?

My first guide to Jerusalem, who cheated me out of a hundred bucks, and favored me with this axiom: "The good Arab it's the dead one." Was he the heritor of thirty centuries of humane Jewish wisdom?

And then I met the Arabs—live ones—and they were good: hospitable, dignified, rational, articulate and oppressed. But that wasn't the most surprising and disturbing fact that I had to work in. The true astonishment was, simply, *they were here.* They were here, their fathers were here, their grandfathers . . . for centuries!

What about the land with no people for the . . . well, you know the rest. In '48, the Jews, in fact, had no land. Okay. . . . But there was a people here!

I began to write their stories, too. Not the big picture—I didn't know the big picture. But I wrote what happened in front of my eyes, to people I had met and talked to. My newspaper was beset by protest—committees of Jews who came to complain, and try to lose me my job. "What kind of Arab apologist did you send there?" . . . "Is it really *Ibn Cramer*— is he an Arab?" . . . "Oh, we know his kind—the self-hating Jew!"

To their enduring credit, my bosses never told me about all the trouble—*for years*—which was a wonderful freedom

. . . and a kindness to me, because I would have been hurt: by that time, I utterly loved the place.

To be precise, it wasn't the place, it was the people, and their stories. For a reporter, this may be the greatest place on earth. Every day's a smorgasbord. You leave your hotel or house in the morning and plunge into a sea of talk—news, explanations, wooing, slogans, argument, imprecations, jokes . . . it's a wonder they had time to build a country, when they're talking eighteen hours a day. And what a brilliant brand of talk! Everybody you meet has a story, is a story—a big multinational, complicated light-and-shade saga. They're all articulate. (Practice makes perfect.) Anywhere you go, there's somebody who'll speak English—or any other known language. It doesn't matter where something happened— you can get anyplace in a couple of hours. . . . And it's always life-and-death.

Even stuff that doesn't matter is life-and-death. I've seen ladies jump out of their cars and engage in a screaming ten-minute argument—that ended with them *spitting on each other*—over a parking space. (On my street in Tel Aviv, during research for this book, I watched a citizen filibuster a cop and a tow-truck man for twenty minutes, until his car was finally hauled away, while he ran down the street, beating a bass-drum tattoo with his fist, first on the tow truck, and then on his own car.) It must be the hummus that gives them the energy. Or maybe it's the lamentable pressure of mere existence that spurs exertion—demands it—a decades-long stress test. But life is lived here at a pitch I never saw elsewhere.

To be perfectly honest, I should say one more thing: I may have had as many friends among the Arabs—or the Palestinians as they now should be known. I had as many pleasant encounters, conversations, meals (a lot more tea). Certainly, I found as many good stories. . . . But I lived among the Jews. And enjoyed them, and laughed with them and about them (nobody makes better Jewish jokes than Jews) . . . and probably I studied them—as a grandma will study her daughter's child—to see if and where the family resemblance would show up.

I had a couple of American friends there, Ben and Minnie Balter—friends of my parents, really—honorary uncle and aunt to me. They were Rochester folk who, in retirement, had moved to an apartment north of Tel Aviv. And I remember Benjie, when I first arrived, trying to explain the joy of the place. "See that mailman?" he'd say. "He's *Jewish*. . . . See that guy sweeping in front of his store? See the cop? *They're Jewish, too!*" That was a punchline that for him never lost its wonder, humor, comfort. I guess his generation had grown up with such an unshakable, undermining sense of being "other"—outside the mainstream—that for him it was enough (It was a miracle!) that everywhere he looked, there were Jews. It wasn't that way for me. But I think I love Jews precisely for that sense of being "other"—so many of them have it within their breast. It gives them not just the sense that they are different, but the imperative: they have to be different—because they are Jews. So, there's an earnestness about examining life (or at least living it by some rules and standards) that makes it interesting to me—or makes it seem to *matter* . . . and since this—how lives are lived—is also my study and line of trade, you could say it conforms to my own prejudice.

I love the Jews for being so ably mercantile, agile and glibly hucksterish. Every business, every cause, has a splendid slogan—or a catchy musical jingle. Tin Pan Alley is now in Tel Aviv. (During my research visits, the election jingle for Arik Sharon was so irresistible—impossible not-to-sing-along-to—I almost signed up to vote for the old bastard myself.) . . . I love the Jews for being learned. I remember sitting, one Saturday, with an Israeli Arab professor from the University of Haifa, Ramzi Suleiman. (Actually, I should identify him with the ethnic moniker that he helped to invent—he is "a Palestinian in Israel.") And Ramzi was marveling at the Jews, too: "You know, I was watching TV," he said, "and there was a panel in Hebrew—three scholars talking about the difficulties of translating Japanese poetry. In what other country this size could you find three people to discuss it?" . . . I love the Jews for being smart—and for the shameless way they show it. An Israeli who's about to inform you precisely how, where and why you are wrong (the national sport is competitive talk) will figuratively roll up his sleeves by announcing (in Hebrew, of course): "Now, I'm going to show you where does the fish pee." The first time I heard this (being a true American), I thought it must be "where do the big fish pee"—more or less like my friend in our poker game, who used to announce, when he started to win: "The big dog walks late." But no, it's not about the "big fish." It's about who among us knows—*where is the invisibly tiny hole on the fish where the pee comes out of* . . . that's what he's going to show you—knowledge!

I love the bare-knuckle brawl that is their public life. The newspapers each day are a festival of personal attack . . . with a level of personal knowledge that keeps institutions human-sized. General So-and-so screwed this other general out of a coveted district command—they've hated each other since officer college. Minister So-and-so has no choice but to take what Sharon gives him—his ambitious wife only married him because she thought he could be prime minister. In part, this *personalness* is owing to the size of the country: everybody knows everybody, or something about everybody—usually just enough to convince them, that guy is an asshole. During this last election, when the list of candidates for the Likud party was announced, I sat with a trio of ladies, who went down the list one by one and told me why each was unfit to be in the Knesset, the Israeli parliament: This one is nothing but a driver for that lady minister (and God knows what else he does for her) . . . this one left his wife for some hussy they had gone to school with (they'd never liked her, either) . . . this one, as an officer in the army, used to hit on the eighteen-year-old soldier girls. . . . Of course it wasn't a strictly fair test—because the ladies were all Labour-Meretz style left-wingers, and were honor-bound to hate everybody on that right-wing party list. That, and the fact that the Likud list was, even by Israeli standards, unusually thuggish this time.

In the spirit of strict fairness, I should confess to one more love I developed—if not a love, then at least a disposition to love—a prejudice in their favor. Like the Israelis, I came to trust and believe in the army more than any other institution in the land. For one thing, I liked the soldiers, who were wry, clever, brave, cocky, whiny about soldier-life and amazingly candid. But I also liked the institution's lack of chickenshit—covering the IDF in the field for a day here and a day there, in what must have added up to months, I don't think I ever saw anybody march or salute. A dogface soldier could call his colonel by his first name (everybody knows everybody)—or tell him he thought he was wrong. I liked the way soldiers would wonder if *they* were doing wrong—in fact, they were honor-bound to refuse an order that they thought was indecent. (This was a tradition in the IDF, going back to the underground days before statehood—it bore a grand name: The Purity of Arms.) . . . And as a reporter, I loved them for showing me who they were. I remember the first time I ran into an IDF platoon during the first (1978) invasion of Lebanon . . . and the soldiers divined that, at some point, I would be going back to Israel (surely, before they would) . . . and they lined up to write on my notepad their home phone numbers and mothers' names—so I could call, to say, "I saw your son, and he was okay." I hadn't truly understood before that the fearsome armored killing machine was really just boys—most of them scared to death, too.

Later, I saw the IDF boys do even tougher duty, when they squared off against other Jews, settlers in the rocky Sinai, who claimed that they were the real custodians of the zionist dream. The IDF had to get them out, because peace had arrived—at least a deal with Sadat . . . the Sinai peninsula was going back to Egypt. And these two groups of Jews went at each other with a zealous and personal fury. The army boys had orders, from the only general who was mule enough to get this done—Arik Sharon. And the settlers thought they had orders from God—the *imperative* to live in this desert, where He gave His law—and they had the worst insults: "Nazis!" "Gestapo!" . . . and they had God's own supply of stones with which to pile up barricades, and tires to burn for acrid thick smoke, and their bodies chained to this and that . . . and it got to be dangerous, devilish and finally a dismal business to get them out. But, they did get out. And stayed out. . . . Which is one reason I know it can still be done.

Or maybe it can't be done now. Maybe the settlers in the West Bank and Gaza are too many—near a quarter million they number, now—or too committed, dug-in, too God-struck-crazy, to be removed by any method. . . . Or maybe Arik Sharon is too old, now, and has no more will to fight with other Jews. . . . And maybe the army's different, too—boys, still, but different boys? . . . That was one reason I had to go back—to see. I had read in the newspaper: So-and-so, a photographer, was killed when a shell from a tank was fired into a crowd in Gaza. Wait a minute! *Who* fired his tank cannon into a crowd of civilians? *On what orders?* And what happened to him? . . . There were no more stories about it. Nothing happened! . . . *Nothing?* . . . Was there no more examination of how a life is to be lived? Then, that was an even bigger way, how Israel lost.

See, I thought I knew the country—but it turned out, I didn't. At least I couldn't understand how the country I knew was doing the things that I read about now. Maybe the country I knew was gone—buried under some new kind of nation, which was also Jews. But what kind of Jews were they? (What's the point of being Jews, if there's no ache of humanity left in you?) . . . And what happened to the guys I knew? As I remembered, they weren't the kind to give up.

If I had to sum up what I thought I knew—twenty years ago, after seven years' contact with Israel—I would have called it "a nice little socialist country, with one problem." The problem, of course, was the Jews' relations with the Arabs—inside the country, in occupied lands, and in the nations nearby. . . . Now, I'd say, the "one problem" (which Israelis refer to in shorthand as "the conflict") has eaten up the rest of the country.

For one thing, success at arms in the conflict, coupled with the policies of annexation and settlement, has made the country not-so-little. It's a land of major-league highways, now—a lot of new ones ("bypass roads," as they're euphemized) cut and blasted right into and through the rocky hills, so the settlers won't ever have to see any Arabs. Then, too, the long national fight about the settlements is producing, for the first time, a generation where everybody doesn't know everybody. When I told my well-connected Tel Aviv friends that I was going to a party at a settlement near Nablus, they looked at me with horrified concern—they'd never been near there, didn't know anyone "out there" (nevertheless, they knew they were assholes), and as for driving through the West Bank for a visit—*just for fun!*—they'd sooner shop for their *shabbas* cakes on Mars.

The socialist bit—that's gone altogether. When Israel became America's little buddy, she also changed over—not coincidentally, during the Reagan years—to a hard-edged capitalistic economy. You could call the operation a success: the suburbs north of Tel Aviv are a bustling hive of high-tech; there's a lot more money in the economy, now; and it's easier to do business. (You can take as much cash as you please into or out of the country; there's no more waiting list for phones—that used to last *for years*—and a cell phone you can have the same day, so you can fit right in, talking every waking moment.) But for the first time, there are also homeless people, and families who say they can't find work, or enough to eat, who were camping out in a Protest of the Hungry in a Tel Aviv park for months.

As for the "nice"—well, it's not-so-nice, now. I'm not talking just about the not-nice things that a suicide bomb does to people on a bus, or the equally not-nice effect of a missile fired from the air into a Palestinian neighborhood. Those are terrible events, but discrete—the kind of thing that CNN-chat can wrap up in a day or two. And, as a consequence, that's more or less exactly what CNN-chat covers—and never chronicles the holes left in the lives of survivors: the long fight to regrasp the sense that you are yourself and whole, after the loss of a limb; the marriages that break up after the loss of a child; the strain in a family when their house is blown up and they move in with relatives; or the effect on a boy when he looks in his father's eyes and sees, all at once, there is no hope there.

But I'm talking about even more than that—the effect on the lives of people who were never near an explosion of any sort—the effect on a whole society. For in this way, too, the conflict is not nice—in the older sense of that word—its effects cannot be nicely delimited. And after thirty-five years of occupation, after two *Intifada* uprisings, after a three-decade cycle of grim, dry determination (or resignation), followed by a few drops and then a wave of hope, followed by a bloom of elation . . . till elation is burned away again by horror, and the grimness sets in anew . . . there are no lives in Israel or Palestine that have not been heated and hardened. On the Palestinian side, there are so many lives and dreams on hold ("We are under occupation—what we can do?") that the conflict has more or less replaced life—or cooked it to a standstill. The only consolation is that everything can be (and is) blamed on Israel. Among the Jews, the effects are harder to pinpoint—and, to me, more insidious—because the whole point of Israel was to create a place where Jews could live the best life—and liveliest—in accordance with their values.

Some of the symptoms are just horribly mundane, notable only for the deadening that they effect subtly, over time—no one thinks twice, anymore, about being clumsily felt up with a beeping wand, while a question or two is mumbled ("Any gun today?"), whenever they stop for a cup of coffee, or a carton of milk at the market. . . . Some of the changes are horribly sad: it used to be such a friendly place—you could stop anybody on the street for help, all the kids wandered the country at will, and everybody picked up hitchhikers. (If it wasn't for folks giving rides, half the soldiers wouldn't have got to Israel's wars.) But now people are wary, and they don't even want their kids to go out (much less thumb a ride to Mount Hermon or Eilat). . . . And there are some effects that are just horrible, period. The latest studies show that one out of nine Israeli women lives with violence (beatings, rape or threats of death) from the male at home . . . for the first time, parents worry about violence among kids at school . . . there are, for the first time, road rage killings . . . and the kind of grisly family crimes that I used to think of (with perverse patriotism) as strictly weird-American: fathers who murder their own kids, or they kill the wife and then themselves.

Of course, you can get a lively argument (two Jews—three opinions) as to whether these sociological phenomena are really the result of the conflict. To me, it's an open-and-shut case: you can't ask two generations of your boys to act in the territories as the brutal kings of all they survey ("Break their bones," was the order to his troops from the sainted

Yitzhak Rabin, during the first *Intifada*—six years before he became Israel's martyr to peace)—and then expect those boys to come home, and live in lamblike gentleness as citizens, husbands, dads. To me, it's one of those historic turns that is so rife with rue, you don't know whether to cry or laugh: in 1967, Israel was forced into war by the conflict, by threat of violence from outside her borders. So, she made war—brilliantly—and conquered the territories where that violence came from. But then—here's the ugly turn—she decided (or she didn't decide, she just slipped into acting as if) those territories were also part of her country . . . and so, the violence she feared was brought inside the country, too. Here's another way to look at it—no less rueful, a little more human: If you had to pick one effort that was the keystone of Israel's first years (that in itself is hard—it was a country where so much was needful at once), it would be the creation of a new kind of Jew. This one would be different from the European Jews whom the zionist founders knew and derided—different from all the Jews, since the Middle Ages. This New Jew would be a farmer, a miner or a laboring man, and *tough:* no more cowering with the holy books behind the temple wall, while the Cossacks, or the Nazis, or (in this case) the Arabs rained death down on them . . . this Jew would be a fighter, a stoic, a Spartan. This, too, succeeded brilliantly, and the generation that the founders raised was the one that conquered all the lands of "Greater Israel." But this was also the generation that would never decide what to do with those lands. They didn't think they had to. They were stalwart, innovative, hard as nails—they could handle whatever transpired. Occupation—they would make a new kind of occupation, too, the best the world had ever seen—the Arabs would be grateful! . . . And it never occurred to them that they—their country, them, inside—could be affected by *being the occupiers*. No, not these men of steel . . .

For what it's worth, the scientists—sociologists, psychologists, doctors, public health savants—tend to think the rise in violence within Israeli society does have to do with the occupation, or at least the conflict. But of course, their findings can be dismissed: *What else could be expected from a bunch of left-wing dovish professors? Half of them are probably Arabs, anyway.* . . . And this, too, is part of the point—one of the things that happened to Israel. Because now, it is the conflict, and your attitude toward the conflict (Hawk or Dove; right wing or left), that is the number-one definition of who you are, and whether you're worth listening to. Facts are no longer facts, if they come from someone who's on the other (i.e., wrong) side . . . which is another loss for a country built from "facts on the ground"—or another way of saying "the one problem" has seeped into everything.

Soon after I went back to Israel, I was introduced to a lovely man, Elisha Spiegelman, the editor of the two-hour Friday-night newscast on Israel's Channel One (the state-owned channel that was, for years, the only channel). As I remembered, the big news show on the Sabbath eve—the only time when everyone was home—was the single most influential arbiter of public opinion in the country. And Spiegelman had been working for the Israel Broadcasting Authority since television started here, soon after the Six Day War. He reminded me of editors I had met in the newsrooms of my youth—the kind of guy you'd like to work for: smart and open, easy to talk to, but never easy about the truth—and plenty tough enough to take the heat (when it's really one of his reporters who caused the problem that brought the heat down). I told him I thought he must get *plenty of heat,* as the editor of the big show. . . .

"Well, I used to be editor," he said. "Then, I was fired. Then, they asked me to do the job, again."

"Why were you fired? And why brought back? What's going on there?"

"Well, we have some problems at Channel One."

"What's it about? What caused the problem?"

Spiegelman paused for a moment, maybe weighing what he had to say—or maybe weighing who was I (where did I stand, as it were). . . . "I think," he said, with a self-conscious smile, "the cause is the occupation."

I almost laughed out loud. But he was serious. "That was the first time—that was the cause—when they told us there are people you *can't interview.* . . .

"That was a Labour government, incidentally—during the first *Intifada*—and the first order was about Palestinian leaders. We were not allowed to interview them . . . so you know what we used to do? Man on the street. But we'd be on the street when the faction leaders came out of their office, and we'd put their words on, that way. We'd say, 'We didn't know it was a leader! We were just talking to people who walked by!' . . .

"You know, during the eighties, when we had film of the PLO meeting in Tunis—where they said they were changing their aim, and going for an independent state of their own—we got a direct order from the general manager: 'No sound allowed.' We could only run the film to show the picture—no words!

"Then other orders started coming down. It started with the Arabs, but it spread, after that. We were not allowed to interview [the extremist anti-Arab Meir] Kahane—while he was a member of the Knesset! The High Court overturned that order. . . . And then, Tommy Lapid, the head of the Shinui party—you know who he is? . . ."

(I did know. He was, at that moment, headed for a huge election victory, and a deal thereafter with Arik Sharon, where he would bring his members of Knesset into the government in exchange for becoming the minister of justice.)

". . . When Tommy Lapid was the general manager, he was the one who said we should be a zionist television—not objective. He now presents himself as the liberal leader of the upper middle class. . . ." If we hadn't been in a nice café, Elisha would have spat.

There was one more effect of the occupation he wanted to mention—that was cheap labor. When the Palestinians were pouring in to work for whatever wages were offered, Israel got addicted to cheap labor in every industry. Now, that addiction had infected the news business. ("It's the same, it started with the Arabs," he said, with a short laugh. "Then it spread back to the Jews.") At his station, at the private TV stations, and now at the newspapers, too, there were few staff workers who had union wages and union protection. Most people were hired as independent contractors or on personal service contracts—and they did what was wanted by management, or they were gone. The owners and managers were hiring their own political protégés and ordering the rest to toe the line—or else. "They have no way to fight," Elisha said. But he was still fighting.

"We're still trying to do a fair job as journalists. We're running between the drops. We use material that was already broadcast abroad—like a Bob Simon piece for *60 Minutes.* Or we let the people in the street say what we want to say. Then, we say, 'We're only quoting!' "

Still, his problems were getting worse. Channel One was losing market share (a good excuse for management to make changes). . . . All the stations (his, too, reluctantly) were now in the business of all-night marathon newscasts CNN-style ("Let's go live, now, to Fred Furrowbrow, who's at the scene.") from the site of every terrorist incident—aided by the government's new *hasbarah* tactic, to show the world, as lavishly as possible, the Jewish victims of terror. "Nobody wants to do it," Elisha said, 'but you look at the ratings, it's very high." . . . There was a good story about a refusenik—a kid who refused to serve in the army—who was on a hunger strike in jail. And he was the nephew of Sara Netanyahu, wife to the right-wing former (and maybe future) prime minister, Bibi Netanyahu. Elisha couldn't touch that story—wouldn't even bring it up with his latest boss, a Likud crony by the name of Yosef Bar' el—there weren't going to be any refuseniks on Channel One. And Elisha was in enough trouble already. The orthodox religious would no longer talk to him for his Friday-night show. He used to tape them before the Sabbath, and run a line beneath the talking head, assuring viewers that the interview had been conducted on Thursday. Now, that wasn't good enough. The fact that his show was on (that TV was on!), when God commanded rest, was a *desecration*—in which they would not participate—and he was an Enemy of God. The settlers all hated him because of his left-leaning secular lies. "If you say they built an unauthorized settlement, then they call you a liar because they say they got their authorization from God, three thousand years ago." If Elisha ran a story on Arabs—or put anything on the air about Arabs—that did not take proper account of "their murderous nature," then he was an apologist. And a story that chronicled with any dispassion what the army did to the Palestinians in the territories would brand him clearly as an enemy of the state. "They say to me, 'You're using our television to attack us?' "

Besides that, his cell phone was ringing. He listened for a moment, and said into the phone: "What are you, a kid—and you think we'll have a monopoly on this story? . . . So, think how you'll treat it properly for this week. And we'll talk when I get back." You could see on his face, as he folded up the phone, he was going back soon.

But he had one thing to add—about those army stories. To tell the truth, he didn't like to run them, either—didn't even like to read them in the papers. "Because I am ashamed of myself," he said. "The army is doing this in my name. And it's my child. My boy is a soldier there, and doing similar things. So I don't read it, now. Because I get shame."

I felt sorry for him as he hiked up his coat and walked into the rain, headed back to his office. But his troubles were soon diminished. A few weeks after I talked to him, he was fired again.

Dan Halutz kept his job. He is a major general and commander of the Israeli Air Force (IAF). When I went back to Israel in the autumn of 2002, General Halutz had made himself more famous than a general ought to be, with an interview that appeared in the newspaper *Ha'aretz*. The Jerusalem correspondent for my home-state paper, Peter Hermann of *The Baltimore Sun*, counseled me as soon as I got to the country: "You'd better read that interview. It's unbelievable."

The sad part was, it wasn't unbelievable—just the reverse. I believed that General Halutz told the truth—or tried to. He was sincere. In fact, he articulated thoroughly and well the attitude that Israel *must have* to do what she has done. It is the only attitude that explains the facts.

In the case that spurred the interview, the facts were pretty grim. It was an operation in Gaza to assassinate Salah Shehadeh, the leader of the military wing of Hamas, the most successful Islamic resistance group. The Shin Bet, Israel's secret police—on any given day, they know better than anyone else what's going on in Gaza (they know, just for example, about *ten times more* than Yassir Arafat)—was aware that Hamas had given Shehadeh a new hideout apartment in a neighborhood called Daraj. They knew the neighborhood was packed with civilians. (There are no neighborhoods that aren't packed—Gaza is, by official count and bar-none, the most crowded place on earth.) They knew Shehadeh's three-story cement and block building was cheek-by-jowl with others of similar height and density. Nevertheless, on the night of July 22, 2002—almost midnight (good sleeping time)—an American-made F-16 streaked over Gaza and dropped onto Shehadeh's apartment house a bomb weighing one ton.

Two thousand pounds of steel and explosives is a serious bomb. Shehadeh's building crumbled to a killing crush of rubble. He was dead in an instant. His bodyguard was with him—he was dead. Shehadeh's wife, Leila, was with him—she was dead. Their daughter, fourteen-year-old Iman—also dead. In the days that followed, various *hasbarah* pros would try out the story that the IDF hadn't known that other family members were present. "There was no intent on harming civilians," said Israel's minister of defense, Benjamin Ben-Eliezer. "According to the information we had, there were not supposed to be civilians in his vicinity, and we express sorrow at the harm to them." It was the honest man, General Halutz of the air force, who would tell the army radio channel (but not till a year later) that the military, and the government, knew Shehadeh's wife was there—they decided to drop the bomb anyway.

But the list—also dead—didn't stop with Shehadeh's family. His building was filled with families. And the neighboring buildings (also severely damaged) were filled. The IDF never issued a list (or even a count) of the dead. But two days after the bombing, Gush Shalom (the Peace Bloc) listed them (and their ages) this way:—there was Salah Shehadeh, and also:

1. Leila Shehadeh (41)
2. Her daughter, Iman (14)
3. Zaher Nassar (37)
4. Muna Fahmi Hewaiti (30)
5. Her child, Subhi (4)
6. Her child, Mohamed (3)
7. Mohamed Al-Shawa (40)
8. His son, Ahmed (?)
9. Iman Hassan Mater (27)
10. Her child, Dunya (5)
11. Her child, Mohamed (4)
12. Her child, Aiman (1)
13. Ala Mohamed Mater (11)
14. Dalia Mater (6)
15. Dunia Rami Mater (2 mo.)
+ 150 Wounded

The same day that list first transpired, the death toll was hiked to seventeen—after the discovery of two more dead children, buried under broken concete. In all, fifteen of the dead were civilians, and eleven were kids.

By the time those names were published, the residents of Gaza had held the predictable (and predictably fierce) mass-funeral-cum-demonstration, with calls for revenge and vows to make the blood of Jews flow equally—no, even more!—in response to this terror. "We will chase them in their houses and in their apartments," said the Hamasnik political chief, Sheikh Abdel Aziz Rantisi, "the same way they have destroyed our houses and our apartments." From international capitals (even from slumbrous Washington) a predictable round of denunciations had been launched—the Swedish foreign minister actually used the words "a crime against international law." Inside Israel, the who-struck-John was in full flower, with on-scene reports from Gaza, long analyses in all the papers, instant polls that showed (surprise!) that people were upset, and *hasbarah* on every side to surround and cauterize this ugly boil. The army bigwigs blamed the intelligence (*Children?* Who knew?) . . . while unnamed "intelligence sources" said the poop was plenty good. The government promised a full investigation . . . while the chief of government, Prime Minister Sharon, called the bombing "one of our most successful operations." Meanwhile, the peace agitators, Gush Shalom, were trying to popularize the slogan "How can you sleep?"—which slogan was spray-painted at night onto the cars of some pilots.

Still, it all would have blown over—as so many other incidents, similar in kind if not in particulars, had blown over before . . . replaced on the news channels and in the papers by a new outrage—or perhaps by reprisals for this outrage—in what those *goyishe* foreign ministries like to call "the tragic cycle of violence." Nobody knew this—it would have blown over—better than the boss who ordered this bombing, Arik Sharon. He'd decimated his first Arab village (at least the first one we know about)—burying men, women and children under the rubble of their houses—*in 1953.* That was a place called Qibya—and the hand-wringing over that operation made this stuff look mild. Sharon more or less invented Israeli army assassinations when he was the military chief in Gaza, more than thirty years ago. People didn't like that, either—or said they didn't. Then, as minister of defense, twenty years ago, he presided over the biggest massacre in IDF history, in the Sabra and Shatila refugee camps of Beirut. (Of course, the IDF didn't do the killing—their Lebanese Christian little buddies did.) And when *that* story came out, there was hell to pay. An official blue-ribbon national commission looked into that one, and recommended that Sharon must not serve anymore as minister of defense— *never again.* . . . So, he didn't. He got elected prime minister instead.

Anyway, this one would have blown over, too—and soon enough. Except, then, Gush Shalom started writing letters to Israeli generals, warning that their actions *were being watched* . . . and information on any crimes would be forwarded to the International Criminal Court at the Hague. And that little gambit was too much for Dan Halutz. Israelis—Jews!—ratting on the Jewish armed forces? That was, in his eyes, nothing short of sedition . . . and that's why, one month after the bombing, he sat down for an interview with the journalist Vered Levy-Barzilai, for Israel's premier paper, *Ha'aretz:*

Ha'aretz: "*Are you suggesting that members of the Gush Shalom group who made those comments should be placed on trial for treason?*"

Halutz: "We have to find the right clause in the law and place them on trial in Israel. Yes. You wanted to talk to me about morality, and I say that a state that does not protect itself is acting immorally. A state that does not back up its fighters will not survive. Happily, the State of Israel does back up its fighters. This vocal but negligible minority brings to mind dark times in the history of the Jewish people, when a minority among us went and informed on another part of the nation. That must not happen again. Who would have believed that pilots of the air force would find their cars spray-painted with savage graffiti because of a mission they carried out."

"*Did you speak with the pilots whose cars were spray-painted?*"

"Yes. An agitated pilot came to see me. He asked himself, and me, whether this was a nightmare, a horrible dream that he was about to wake up from, or reality. The truth is that I didn't know what to tell him. We both sat there, stunned and hurt. The only thing I was able to say, finally, was that he shouldn't pay attention to marginal phenomena. To me, these people aren't even marginal. They are outside the margins of the State of Israel." . . .

"Will anything in the procedures, the decision-making process of the IAF or its operational performance change because of what happened?"

"Definitely not. Nothing will change and there is no reason to change anything." . . .

"There were several direct references to you as a war criminal. How did you feel about that, and will you think twice before making a trip to Belgium?"

"I am sorry to disappoint the Belgians, but of all places in the world, I never had the particular intention of going to their country. More seriously, though, we operate according to an extremely high moral code. And since that is what guides us, I don't think that there is any court to which we have to give an accounting. There is no such court. Personally, I have a deep feeling of justice and morality. And as for how I feel—I feel just fine, thank you. I really meant it when I told the pilots that I sleep very well." . . .

Halutz said pilots often need information from their command desk, or intelligence, to know what they are bombing.

"But this time, the opinion that is supposed to assist you made you fail?"

"Made us fail? By what yardstick? Who are the people who claim that and who decided the criteria? I assert that everything that happened prior to the mission passes my moral test and is rooted very deeply in the 'envelope.' After all, who and what are we talking about here: about a person who was the very archetype of the personification of evil. A dictionary that wants to define the term 'terrorist' could just enter his name. He killed more than a few, more than a few dozen, members of the Jewish nation."

"So that is the legitimization for the liquidation, but what about the innocent people who were killed?"

"The result consists of two parts. First, a perfect positive result because we hit the person. The second result, for which we said we were sorry, is that uninvolved civilians were hurt."

"Innocent civilians, don't you mean?"

"I deliberately say 'uninvolved civilians,' because we know for a fact that even the greatest terrorists are sometimes cloaked in a civilian guise."

"But you will agree, of course, that at least the eight [small] children and infants were innocent?"

"Of course."

"And they were killed because you acted on the basis of inaccurate intelligence information?"

"The intelligence was very accurate. Sometimes, though, you have no control over all kinds of things that take place in a space that is hidden from view. In retrospect, it turned out that I simply did not have part of the information; it changed in the course of the mission."

"And you do not regard this as an intelligence or other failure?"

"No. The decision-making process was right, balanced, proper and cautious. The problem lay in the information,

and the information changed. I reject all the criticism in regard to this operation—pre-, during and post. Within the pa-
rameters of my moral values, the fact that uninvolved
civilians and innocent children were killed is very saddening.
I am sorry for that. But it did not stem from a professional
problem."

*"The decision to use a one-ton bomb was criticized.
Wasn't the choice of that weapon a mistake?"*

"No. Professionally, and in retrospect, too, it was the
most correct decision. I have no problem with all kinds of
people and journalists asking these questions, but I am in
favor of letting the professionals give the answers: For a half-
ton bomb to achieve the effect we wanted, we would have
had to drop two of them, because of the calculations of the
chance that one of them would miss altogether. That was a
decisive consideration. So the operation decision was correct. As for the intelligence information that changed—anyone who waits for 100 percent certainty in every case will
probably never act. The attempt to look for guilty people
here is shameful. I do not see anything resembling the moral
level of the soldiers of the IDF anywhere else in the
world." . . .

*"If you had known in advance that there were fifteen or
seventeen people in the building, including children, would
you still have ordered the bombing to go ahead?"*

"I am not willing to answer a question like that, and certainly not to cite numbers. I am ready to discuss the question
of principle: Is there a situation in which it is legitimate to

strike at a terrorist when you know that the operation will exact a price in the form of casualties among civilians and un-involved people?"

"And what is your reply?"

"I have no doubt about it. The reply is positive. Against a person who has perpetrated, or who is known for certain to have a plan for what is called mega-terrorism, my reply is cat-egorical: yes. How many people? I don't know. I will be able to give that answer at the moment of truth. Let's go back to the suicide bombing in the Park Hotel in Netanya on the eve of Passover. Let's say we would have known about this terror-ist in advance and would have trapped him in his house—would it have been legitimate to strike at him even if there were other people there? My answer is yes. How many peo-ple? I don't know and I am not ready to state a number. I re-peat again that I am very sorry about innocent children who are killed. But anyone who sets out to murder children in Is-rael has to take into account that children are liable to be killed in his surroundings. . . ."

Halutz said he cannot subscribe anymore to the IDF tra-dition called "The Purity of Arms."

"In my eyes, that is a fundamentally invalid concept. Weapons are not pure. They are not intended to be pure. A pure weapon is not a weapon. Maybe it was once a weapon, but it has been turned into a pruning hook. By the same token, I am sorry to have to announce that there are no clean wars. I don't know of a person who is capable of waging a clean war." . . .

Halutz said a pilot who objects to a certain mission as indecent should bring up his objections in the pre-operation stage—"in order to be persuaded."

"And if after all that he still doesn't accept the order?"

"Then he can get up and leave the squadron."

Refusal to perform a mission, he said, "is not part of the rules of my game." And neither is a lot of worry or emotion about what happens after the bombs hit.

"Is there a format within the system that makes it possible for the pilots to do emotional processing?"

"Why emotional? Anyone who needs help, of any kind and in any area, will get it. All the mechanisms exist, including psychological help. Only people who have emotional problems need to do emotional processing." . . .

"Still, you have also gone through a difficult month. You and the IAF came under attack, and from the media everywhere. Who strengthened you?"

"I don't need strengthening, I am a strong person. Or let's put it this way: To this day, I have not needed external strengthening. I know how to cope with things by myself. In this case, I had no doubt, and certainly there was no need for strengthening from anyone. And I very much hope that in the future, too, I will not encounter situations that will make me need such help. What is this obsessive preoccupation with feeling?"

"A pilot drops a bomb. A bomb kills people—sometimes those he planned to kill, sometimes not. Isn't it legitimate to ask a pilot what he feels after he releases the bomb? Can we

expect him to ask himself that question, and is it in fact asked in the IAF?"

"No. That is not a legitimate question and it is not asked. But if you nevertheless want to know what I feel when I release a bomb, I will tell you: I feel a light bump to the plane as a result of the bomb's release. A second later it's gone, and that's all. That is what I feel."

What happened to Israel is, standards changed. The fact that Halutz kept his job—after he told the world that Israeli pilots don't care, or shouldn't care, or *can't care,* if a few Arab babies more-or-less are "also dead"—that was one sure sign. In the old days he would have been gone so fast, his head would be spinning. He wouldn't have had time to pack a bag, before his exciting "promotion to new duties"—say, as General Chief of Procurement—buying aircraft parts in France. . . . Not because he told an untruth. (Clearly, he told the truth.) And not because his attitude was incompatible with the air force job. (His attitude was compatible—exactly— with the air force, and with his fellow IDF generals. Nobody got to be general—even back in those days—by acting like Mother Teresa.) . . . But Halutz would have been gone because it was the stated policy of Israel to attempt to live in peace with her neighbors—and this would not help. He would have been gone because it was the stated policy of Israel that noncombatants, even Arab noncombatants, *would not be harmed*—even if Israeli soldiers were endangered to protect them—and what Halutz said did not reflect that policy. He would have been gone because Israel held herself to a certain standard—maybe an unfair standard, and maybe a standard often unmet—but, like Hebrew National, she answered to a Higher Authority.

Actually, it was exactly like the hot dog company—she *advertised heavily* that she had to meet a higher standard—and maybe it was half ballyhoo. But the key fact was, that was the way her people wanted the nation to be seen. The zionists were not just ideologues, but idealists. There was an earnest and continuous national discussion about how their society *ought to be,* and leaders were expected to be exemplary. The public would make exceptions for fan-favorites, like Moshe Dayan—whatever he did was all right—and personal peccadillos were not the issue. (Any schoolchild in Afula or Ashkelon can tell you about the high-ranking Israeli diplomat who was found dead, tied down on a Paris hotel-room bed, with two girls—or by some accounts, a girl and a boy. Those stories were simply enjoyed.) But in public behavior—in the name of or for the state of Israel—the standard held, and people expected not to be embarrassed. Now, they don't expect much, at all.

Nothing shows the change better than the underlying cause of the carnage in that Gaza apartment house—the policy of assassination. How did a nice Jewish state decide to go into a business like that? . . . Well, as in so many other bad businesses, she didn't decide—not openly—she just slid in. And, like other bad businesses, it started with Arik Sharon. Thirty years ago, as head of the southern command, he considered it his mission to stop any trouble in or from the Gaza Strip—so he decided to stop the troublemakers. He built a small secret unit called Rimon—that was the Hebrew word for the pomegranate fruit, and soldier slang for a hand grenade. At first, Rimon would simply *get* troublemakers killed—by telling some enemy faction, or enemy family, where the troublemaker could be found, at a certain time . . . and if they had to, of course, they would supply a gun. But sometimes, you couldn't rely on the enemy clan—in which case, the Rimon boys (dressed as Arabs, speaking Arabic) would take care of business themselves. Then, they would leak the news, somehow, that some unidentified Arab enemies had bumped off this bad guy—not that anyone was watching too closely.

The first time the government came out of the closet—admitting (if only with a wink and a nod) that they'd put a hit on some Palestinians—was in the early 1970s. One of the first operations was revealed because Golda Meir wanted her voters to know that the state had hunted down and "put to justice" the Black September commandos who had kidnapped and murdered eleven Israeli athletes at the 1972 Munich Olympics. In '73, a team of Israelis, led by the top commando, Ehud Barak (in drag for the occasion, with a long dark wig and false breasts), slipped ashore in Beirut and gunned down three PLO officials in their apartments. And assassinations were more frequent after 1982, when the Israelis once again invaded Lebanon—they would keep advisers and operatives in the country for the next twenty years.

Still, assassination was sporadic, and case-by-case—a special remedy for special circumstances, until the year 2000 and the outbreak of the second *Intifada*—with attacks inside Israel, and suicide bombings. The prime minister at that point was that old drag queen, Ehud Barak. In November 2000, he ordered a hit on a Palestinian leader named Hussein Abayat, a member of Arafat's Fatah team—but nothing complicated this time, no commandos or costumes. The IAF simply flew in a gunship and hit Abayat's Mitsubishi with antitank missiles. Simple as pie—he was melted onto his car seat. That started the wide-open assassination business. And it started the list of also-dead: two ladies in their fifties, who happened to be standing near Abayat's car, were also-charred-to-death . . . nevertheless Barak vowed to continue the policy. He never got much chance. He was voted out in favor of Arik Sharon—and then, the policy went wholesale. The number of dead in Israeli assassination attacks—just since the second *Intifada* began—has climbed to more than two hundred and fifty. About a hundred and fifty were targets. A hundred or so were simply in the wrong place when the assassination went down.

But wait—that's another thing. They aren't assassinations. Once the IDF got into the business more or less every week, the professional *hasbarah* men started tinkering with the wording. So, then, these attacks became "targeted killings"—which phrase caught on. It sounded surgical. But after a while, everybody knew this wasn't surgery, more like slaughter—so, the wording changed again. It wasn't killing at all. The new idea was these guys weren't actually people, but "ticking bombs"—about to blow up and kill more Jews. They must be defused! . . . So, the IDF now announces the demise of selected Palestinians as "focused preventative actions." . . . Anyway, no one asks anymore (notice, Halutz was never asked) about the policy of killing suspected evildoers—on their way to doing the evil—and without the niceties of arrest, arraignment, trial, argument, evidence . . . without any public proof at all.

The underlying principle (or lack thereof) is the rule of law. In the old days that was, perhaps, the one tenet on which you *couldn't* get an argument in Israel. When I first got to know the country, the only institution that was more august than the army was the High Court of Justice—the Bagatz, as Israelis refer to it, by its acronym—equivalent to the U.S. Supreme Court. There were jokes about it, sure—how the justices would tortuously examine how many angels could dance on the head of some pin—still, everybody wanted his pin considered. . . . But now, the Bagatz has taken a dive—and the issue, once again, is the occupation.

On the topic of targeted killings, the court did consider a petition brought by a Communist Arab member of the Knesset, Muhammad Baraka. The lawyer for Baraka argued that since the Israelis control the territories, the security forces could make arrests, and put the suspected criminals on trial. (The Israelis have made hundreds of arrests—it can be done.) But one of the justices, Mishael Cheshin, broke in to yell at the lawyer: "My son goes into Area A. I don't want his life to be endangered!" . . . The lawyer fell back to an even more basic point: "Who is to decide who is a terrorist?" The presiding justice, Eliahu Mazza, snapped: "Certainly, not the court. . . . As far as we know, the IDF has information about those it attacks." So, that was that—let the army decide. The court denied the petition.

One more example: In order to hold on to the West Bank and Gaza—and to dissuade any locals from doing terrible things to fight the occupation—the security forces *punish collectively.* Say, a kid from a village near Jenin sneaks across the Green Line, into Israel proper, for the purpose of blowing up some Jews—or he tries to sneak across the Green Line, and is caught. The security forces will show up in his village and, at the very least, knock down his house. Except he's a kid, so it's not really his house, but his father's, or his grandfather's, or an uncle's house. In fact, if it's like most Palestinian families, it's the whole extended clan's house, with apartments for uncles, cousins, married sisters . . . it could be forty or fifty people's house. And they didn't even know that young Ahmad, their cousin—or whatever this kid is—had lost all hope of doing anything else, and had sneaked off with dynamite strapped to his belly. So, should they lose their house?

It's a made-to-order Bagatz issue. In fact, since the occupation is The Question in Israel, everything about it comes up in a case at the High Court—or it could, if the justices will hear a petition. Torture by Israeli secret police (is that okay if it's meant to forestall future terror attacks?) . . . Arab land taken by the army for "security zones" (who decides—and whose security?) . . . water rights (should the Arab farmers go dry because the new settlement on what used to be their land has decided to grow tomatoes?) . . . But here's the Bagatz swan dive again: in the case of collective punishment, the justices agree that collective punishment is at least arguable. (In fact it's prohibited by the Geneva Conventions, but to the High Court of Israel, the Geneva Conventions are just arguable.) So the Bagatz used to require the army to give a notice of demolition—forty-eight hours—so the affected family could go to (an Israeli) court and at least make a plea that they shouldn't be made homeless. Most of the time, the court would give a green light to the army, anyway—but at least there was a chance for review, under the rule of law. The army didn't like that. If they gave notice, a crowd could gather. People could throw stones, or set booby traps. The generals insisted the security of Israel required *immediate* demolitions. (Jews could get hurt knocking down those Arab houses!) . . . And so the justices ruled that these punishments were justified for the security of Israel. And then, with the coyness of a schoolgirl, the members of the court further reasoned that they, as learned justices, were not experts on security. The experts on security are the security forces! And since it's the security forces knocking down the houses . . . well, you get the drift. Let the army decide if notice should be given. End of case. End of Bagatz.

The big problem is, nothing spreads faster than a few little exceptions ("just in this case" . . . "under the circumstances") to the rule of law. It's like the ban on interviews at Channel One—it starts about the Arabs, it spreads back to the Jews.

So . . . there's a Sunday morning train from Haifa to Tel Aviv, the cars are packed with soldiers returning from a Sabbath with their families. Beautiful kids—tall, healthy, clear eyed, well spoken—they are the triumph of the nation . . . except they're having a lively technical discussion about shooting a ricochet . . . in case you should happen to shoot, you know, a lady, a little kid, or someone old . . . and they're simply not *labelable,* believably, as a terrorist—and if there's an investigation . . . but you can show that your bullet hit the cement *behind* the also-dead ("No, next to them is better—it won't bounce if it's straight in behind them") . . . well, then, no problem—it was just an unlucky ricochet. The discussion ended with general agreement: It doesn't matter, these days—there's not going to be any investigation.

So . . . it's election time and Ariel Sharon is running for another go-round as prime minister. He's way ahead. ("There's no one else" is the way people say it.) . . . Except then, he runs into a problem—a story in the papers: it turns out, he screwed up the spending for his *last* campaign, and he, personally, had to pay back a lot of money, but he didn't have the money . . . so he took some money as a "loan" from a guy in South Africa—an old pal of his, a guy named Kern. Unfortunately, Kern (pal or not) is still kind of a foreigner, which may make it kind of illegal for Sharon to be taking money from him . . . like *a million-and-a-half dollars*—which is transferred all over the planet before it lands in Sharon's pocket, *secretly.* . . . Now, I'm thinking back to the first time Rabin was prime minister, and it was discovered that his wife had an illegal bank account—in foreign currency—twenty thousand dollars in Washington. Rabin couldn't take the heat. He had to resign. So I'm asking around—inquiring of Israeli experts— do they think Sharon is going to have to step down? It's a mark of their kindness, no one laughs in my face . . . Within two days, the stories in the papers have shifted to a new topic: who was it leaking that nasty stuff about Sharon? Sure enough, a lady is found—deputy-assistant-prosecutor-something—and her head is in the noose. Sharon cruises on to victory.

It was Sever Plotzker, the distinguished economics correspondent for Israel's largest paper, *Yediot Ahronot,* who finally answered my question—why Rabin had to fall on his sword for twenty grand, and Arik Sharon can take a million and a half. "The standards have changed," Sever said. "These days, clean does not mean one hundred percent clean. Thirty percent dirty is still clean."

And for the next big burdensome question—*why* did the standards change—I had to ask Liora Nir. God gives the heavy burdens to those whose shoulders He made to bear them, and Liora is one of His real *shtarkers.* She used to work in the government press office (under that spokesman who came from Detroit)—but she quit when the big bosses, Menachem Begin and his defense minister, Arik Sharon, decided to drop bombs on some apartment houses in Lebanon. She's done fine, ever since, as a brilliant student of Israeli society. Her sharp eye on her countrymen has made her, at present, the inventor, proprietress and CEO of a TV channel that shows *telenovelas*—month-long South American romance dramas (subtitled in Hebrew, or course)—because she figured what Israelis needed was a cheap, available and emotional escape. It's the hottest channel on cable TV.

"What changed the standards?" I asked her, and her answer was simple: "We changed. It's us. . . . Do you know the word *booshah*?" she asked. "It means shame. Gradually, we lost *booshah*."

"Why? You mean the soldiers?"

"The soldiers—it starts there. Everybody is a soldier, and being a soldier means the territories. 'Make sure they don't get through. Make sure the grandmothers don't hide anything under their skirt. They'll trick you. They hate you. Make sure they don't get over on you.' It's a very demoralizing and corrupting experience.

"You have to numb yourself. The only way is to harden yourself. And that cannot stop at the Green Line. And it can't stop with the Arabs. You have to make a buffer against what you see. And you carry that with you.

"But it's not just the soldiers. We all were corrupted. I'm not talking about a few rotten apples. That's always. But it's what does the system do when it finds a rotten apple? These days, it's nothing. People are not shocked anymore."

Liora said attitudes changed because lives changed— or maybe it's vice versa, chicken and egg. But everything changed, since she grew up in what her old boss, Zev

Chafets, that Israeli-American spokesman, used to call The Era of High Zionist Certainty.

"In those days there were two principles: number one, whatever was not allowed was forbidden." (If you wanted to do something, and it was good for the state, and you were well enough connected—like, for instance, you had a Labour party card—the government would give you a special permission.) "Number two, you worked for the good of the state, and the state would take care of the public." (The standard of your worth was not your big career, or you made a lot of money. If you made money you hid it—poverty proved decency. Your worth was measured by what good you did for the zionist society.)

Liora said the shock of the Yom Kippur War knocked the first stones out of the wall of certainty—for instance, the biggest boulder of belief—that the government knew best. By the 1980s, the rock slide was an avalanche. "The world changed. The idea became: 'Take care of yourself.' You could be a good citizen by being a happy citizen—you could make money, people started flying to America, back and forth, starting businesses—'privatization.' The society started to be about individuals, the cohesion started breaking apart. After the '73 War, Rabin [the old-school zionist fighter] called the people who ran to America *'nefollet memushot.'* I don't know how you'd say that in English—something like 'the fallout of muck.' A few years later, they were the Best and the Brightest—Rabin's son is in America, now. It's the opposite of the Kennedy line—ask what you can do for your country."

So . . . now the long trend of privatization, atomization, individualization has come together with the hardening— the buffer that has to be built against the bad things Israelis have to do or see . . . except for the most part they don't see—day to day, they don't have to look . . . because that's a collective problem—not their doing—they're busy with their job, taking care of Number One . . . and that stuff "out there" is *so disappointing*—where is it written they should have to feel terrible? . . . And one more thing—a new thing, the latest thing:

They tried! . . . This is not just the hawks now, but all the Jews—down to the old peaceniks—they are convinced in their hearts that they elected a prime minister, Ehud Barak, on a platform of peace . . . and in the year 2000, Barak went to Camp David, to sit with that wonderful Bill Clinton (Clinton the Israelis would elect today, in a heartbeat!) . . . and Barak offered that scumbag Arafat everything he wanted— or everything he could legitimately want—anyway, a country: *Barak tried to give them a state!* . . . And what did that scumbag do—he said, NO! And then he started a war—a second *Intifada,* where he sends children to blow themselves up, to kill our children. So . . . to hell with them. We tried. Now, whatever happens is their own fault. Let them take up their problems with Arafat.

This is also the latest and greatest reason that standards changed—or there are no standards (under the circumstances—just in this case). . . . Because it's not their fault. They *can't* make peace. They have no partner for peace. . . .

That's the reason Halutz keeps his job, or Sharon can take a million or two—because the Jews think they need a Halutz now, they need a Sharon. (And they don't need a Spiegelman to give them static on their own TV.) . . . And if things inside their own country are getting worse—if it's their own society that's hostage? . . . *Well. We'll deal with that later. This is war!*

Liora Nir said it this way: "What you see is the conflict. It's in impatience. It's in aggression. It's in the rejection of anything different. Look, Israelis were never soft. But their hearts—this is a generalization, of course—but you could always push a button somewhere, and touch their hearts. Now . . . I don't know."

The only winner in this deal—in thirty-five years since the Six Day War—is the conflict itself. It's the blob that ate Cleveland. It changes hearts and minds.

Remember that old brigade commander from the 1948 War of Independence? I went to see Brigadier Itzhak Pundak for a long talk. He knew the Palestinians well—knew how to get along with them, and how to make it worth their while to get along with Jews. While Pundak served as the military governor of Gaza, in 1971–72, he made sure that Palestinian men had work, old people had health care, kids had schools and playgrounds. And the Gaza Strip was placid, almost progressive: some refugees actually moved out of camps and into real houses. The population actually went down! . . . And Pundak knew Arik Sharon, too. That was the same time Sharon was running the southern command, inventing his secret assassination units (and claiming it was he who pacified the Gaza Strip). In his memoir, published in the year 2000, Pundak recalls Sharon as a disgraceful officer—a liar, cheater, a swindler and suck-up, a killer and a coward. Sharon's policies impeded progress in Gaza—made a generation of enemies—and policies like them brought on the *Intifada*. . . . So I went to ask Pundak how those policies could be reversed. How could Israel move toward peace?

"Look," said Pundak. "This is a different country because our enemy made it a different country, not because we made it a different country. Arafat could have had ninety percent of the land, just like that, in the deal Barak offered him. And he didn't, so what does he want? He went on to start a war, a very dirty war against children and women, in the streets and in the restaurants. So first we have to win the war—and we will. . . . My advice is, any Jew who doesn't have nerve should leave this place." Incidentally, I asked the old brigadier: *Who was he voting for?* . . . "Sharon," he said. "There's nobody else."

I went to the northern seaside town of Nahariya, for a talk with Smadar Haran. Hers was a famous name in Israel when I first knew the place, because on a Sabbath night in April 1979, four Palestinian terrorists came in a rubber boat from Lebanon, beached in Nahariya, and invaded the apartment of Smadar and her family. Smadar's husband and her four-year-old daughter, Einat, were grabbed by the terrorists right away. They were taken two blocks away, to the beach,

where the father was shot to death in front of the little girl—
so that was the last thing she'd see. Then, one of the gunmen
smashed Einat's head against a rock with his rifle butt until
she was dead, too. Smadar was hiding with her two-year-old
daughter, Yael, in a crawl space over the bedroom, while two
terrorists noisily hunted through the apartment—they knew
there were more people there. Smadar kept her hand
clamped over her baby's mouth—one sound, and they would
be killed. Police finally came. Two terrorists were killed in a
shoot-out. Two were captured. Smadar was discovered and
helped out of the crawl space. But her baby was dead, too. In
the effort to hide, she had smothered her child.

Now, I went to see Smadar not for the details of the crime
against her, but for what she did after. To me, she was exemplary. Soon after the attack, she was interviewed on Israeli TV,
and she wasn't interested in blaming the government for its
failure to stop terror. She wouldn't blame police for their
delay. She wouldn't blame the Arabs! . . . People were so
upset about that—the IDF's chief of staff, Ezer Weizman, accused her of "undermining the morale of the nation." . . .
What really upset the Jews was something else she said: she
was asked what she felt, while she was hiding, and she said she
felt like her mother must have felt, because her mother was in
the holocaust. And thirty years later, Smadar, her daughter,
was going through the same thing. That was taboo—it drove
people *nuts* . . . because the whole point of Israel, the tough
Jewish State, was supposed to be 'never again' . . . and what
was she telling her countrymen, now? That there was no

point? Nothing had changed? Or they'd got themselves into the same fix? . . . I admired her for more than what she wouldn't do—blame—but for what she would do. She wanted to *live*. Her mother's response to the holocaust was to live—to come to Israel, to live a long life and build something new. And that was Smadar's answer, too. She is Smadar Haran Kaiser now—remarried—and she made a new family. She still looks like that twenty-something mom who was on TV the first time—a few wrinkles around her eyes, now, but laugh wrinkles. She still lives near the beach in Nahariya—she would not be driven away. She doesn't want to be a famous victim. She will not be a victim of any sort.

We sat at her kitchen table, so I could ask her how the country had changed. Her husband, Yaacov, a psychologist with offices attached to the house, came in to greet us and ask what we wanted to drink.

Smadar was telling about Yitzhak Rabin inviting her to Washington, to accompany him to the White House, where he would shake hands with Arafat, and they would sit down to talk peace. At the last minute, Smadar backed out. She couldn't shake Arafat's hand. She told Rabin, "You're the politician—you have to do it. I don't." But Rabin did say, that day at the White House: he had come to make peace in the name of Smadar Haran.

"Now, it's not the same," she added. "Barak tried to give them everything. Arafat's answer was to start killing . . ."

"Wait a minute," I protested. "Are you telling me now that Israel's the victim?"

The husband, Yaacov, broke in with an announcement, by way of answer: "Now I am going to make a coffee," he said. "But let me leave you with one small sharp question. Do you think it is possible that we are unconditionally hated?"

"You mean, *the whole world is against us*?"

He shook his head, not in denial, but to brush away my objections. His voice got hard. "Look. Let me tell you something. To Hitler we were the appetizer. First was the Jews, and then he wanted to be emperor of the world. We are still the appetizer—now for radical Islam. And if, God forbid, if Israel will have to kneel here, in front of terrorism, there will be no place safe. . . . Unfortunately—unfortunately and horribly—we are a school. We are a laboratory—and you are watching us. And when the United States has to fight against terrorism—fighting in the cities, targeted killings—your methods won't be so far from ours."

Maybe he's right. Maybe they are all right . . . and they are like us, or we are like them—or no better than them, certainly. Maybe we would do the same, or worse—maybe anybody would. . . .

I remember another interview—this one with Ron Ben-Yishai, the veteran reporter on the Israeli army beat. And I was wailing about the killing in the territories—asking Ron: *What got into his boys?* . . . But he seemed not to be listening. He interrupted with a little smile. "Congratulations," he said. "Your CIA just pulled off your first targeted killing."

And that was true enough. That day, a CIA predator

drone had fired a missile onto a car in Yemen, and fried six Al Qaeda guys. (Anyway, we said they were Al Qaeda guys. . . .)

Maybe it's also true, the old Bible prophecy—"Israel will be a light unto the nations"—in this case, a lurid mercury-vapor security light. Our CIA confers with the Israelis on how to pull off proper assassinations. Our Homeland Security toughs study at the Shin Bet's knee. Now, as the *Jewish Daily Forward* reports, the Bush administration is sending legal experts to consult with Israelis—on how to justify the killings. (Israelis have done a lot of good work on that.)

We are learning in the grim lab of Zion. It's one more reason—surely the ugliest—why we must care about Israel.

II

Why don't the Palestinians have a state?

Let's start out with a short inventory of where things stand in Palestine. It is the first measure of where things stand that this tale needs to be told: one trick the Palestinians never learned from the Jews was how to take control of their own national narrative and employ it for their own aims. As a consequence we simply don't know their story—about which lack the majority of Palestinians will profess amazement and dismay . . . and still never reason for one moment about the cause, preferring instead to explain this away (as everything else is explained away) as a consequence of overwhelming zionist power—in this case, propaganda power.

The first and most basic fact, which has endured, now, for more than ten years, is that the Palestinian territories are "closed." As a newspaper reader, I always thought of that word in the sense of "closed off from Israel"—which was more or less how it was billed by the Israeli *hasbarah* batallions. The idea was (as they explained) that Israel couldn't trust the Palestinians from the West Bank or Gaza to come into Israel and work anymore. So, now, alas, the evil and ill-advised terrorist attacks essayed by some Palestinians would deprive the great mass of Palestinians of their best chance for livelihood. And there was in that explanation—as in all good *hasbarah*—a dollop of plausible truth. (It made even more human sense if the *hasbarah* pro would cop—as most did—to the punitive element of closure: *We'll see how brave they are when they can't put food on the table.* . . .) And this much is surely true: more than a hundred thousand Palestinians from the territories used to earn wages in Israel every day. Now, for the most part, they have been replaced by Romanians, Moldavians, Colombians, Uruguayans, Philippinos, Thais or Taiwanese . . . and life in the West Bank and Gaza has grown poor to the point of desperation.

But it is also true that "closure" is a much more complicated, pervasive and punitive policy than that. It doesn't mean simply "closed off from Israel"—more like closed to the world. The Gaza Strip, for instance, is completely fenced off, not only from Israel, but from Egypt (Israelis control that border crossing) . . . from its own seacoast (Israelis bar or control all approach or egress by water—including local fishermen) . . . and even from its own airport (Israelis control that, too).

On the West Bank side, Israel is building a "separation fence," which is not really a fence, but a massive concrete wall—about twenty feet high. This Great Wall (at least the part already built) is itself fenced off with barbed wire and security roads on both sides, and studded with pillbox guard-posts for its full length, which is to be more than two hundred miles. It will cut Palestine in half, north to south—except, it's not really close to half. If the Palestinians somehow succeeded in their stated aims—getting Israel to give up all the land conquered in 1967, and going back to the 1948 armistice line (the Green Line, as it's called here)—the new nation of Palestine would still take in only twenty-two percent of Mandatory Palestine, that is, about one-fifth of the land from the Jordan River to the sea. And now, with this new wall, Israel is effectively seizing more. The wall isn't being built on Israeli land, but on land newly taken from the Palestinians. For most of its length it runs far to the east of the old Green Line—so it effectively makes Israel bigger. Where it runs near Jewish settlements it juts out to wall those settlements into Israeli control . . . where it runs near Palestinian villages, it walls off the village land from the village—or, in the case of seventeen villages (so far), it has walled off the village altogether, into a new kind of no-man's-land between the wall and what used to be the Green Line.

Israeli *hasbarah* contends this is not an attempt to set a new border as a "fact on the ground"—just another way to cut down on terror attacks. But then, the head architect, Ariel Sharon, announced an expansion of the project: a new section of the Great Wall will connect the two (north and south) ends . . . with more wall—another wall—to be built *on the east side* of the Palestinian territory, along the Jordan River . . . in other words, between the Palestinians and the nation of Jordan (where there are no terrorist infiltrations, or none that get anywhere near Israel) . . . which would completely encircle the West Bank territory (as Gaza already is completely encircled) . . . creating a perfect ghetto.

And even that is not the end of the policy of closure. For the ghettos of Gaza and the West Bank are also sliced by closures *inside*—with a filigree of checkpoints, barricades and roadblocks that can prevent a Palestinian (any Palestinian) from moving between, say, Nablus and Hebron, or proceeding unmolested from Bethlehem to Ramallah, from Khan Yunis to Gaza City, or . . . well, they can't go anywhere. Even when the Israelis announce "a withdrawal" of their troops from some Palestinian town, that doesn't mean the checkpoints *around the town* are withdrawn. So, Palestinians aren't any less imprisoned—their prison just got bigger. These internal closures have an economic effect that is just as serious as the closure from Israel. A worker from Bethlehem who can't get to his job in East Jerusalem soon won't have a job. The same is true for a Palestinian who's selling a product instead of his labor. If he can't get to his customers, and they can't get to him . . . do we really need to ask, *How's business?*

The statistics are mind-numbing: no one in the developed world can truly understand what these numbers mean.

For the period of 1994–1996, the World Bank figured "the annual costs of closure and permit policies at about eleven to eighteen percent of GNI [gross national income] in the West Bank, and thirty-one to forty percent in the Gaza Strip." After a total closure in March and April 1996, unemployment among Palestinians (or severe underemployment) was estimated at sixty-six percent.

In the year 2000, when the second *Intifada* began, the situation got much worse: in the first four months of the uprising, the number of Palestinians living under the poverty line increased by fifty percent. The cause was not only the loss of work in Israel. A constant and total closure killed off all Palestinian manufacturing. (Machinery, parts and raw materials all have to come *from Israel.*) In addition, one hundred eighty-one thousand trees were uprooted from Palestinian farms, and three-point-seven million square meters of croplands were destroyed. . . . So, after three more months, the poverty figures had doubled again: two-thirds of all Palestinians were living under the poverty line—in the Gaza Strip, that figure was eighty-one percent. And here is the official definition of poverty: a household of two adults and four kids, with consumption that averages less than $2.10 a day.

Here are some effects on a more human level—facts and impressions that stuck with me. For the first time, I heard stories of Palestinian suicides—not suicide bombers, just suicides. . . . For the first time, I saw malnutrition among Palestinian children—and heard teachers who told of kids who couldn't come to school (even when schools were allowed to open), because they were hungry, or the family was hungry—and children of eight years old go to work . . . For the first time in my working life, I violated every good rule of journalism and, at the close of an interview, fished into my pocket and offered all the money I found there to the man I had just interviewed. (And to our mutual embarrassment, he took it.) . . . And here's the statistic that I understood best: Gasoline comes from Israel. Gasoline requires cash. So in Gaza, the price of a donkey had risen by five hundred percent.

To my mind the noneconomic effects are worse—because they attack the grace and glue of Palestinian society, which is honor. In fact, the manner of Israeli occupation seems designed to eliminate honor—and its absence is shame. No one can stand for twenty minutes at a West Bank checkpoint—one little cog in the machinery of "closure"—without seeing humiliation heaped upon the population . . . and shame for both the occupied and the occupier.

What is a checkpoint? That little question is the heart of the matter, because it is whatever (and wherever) the Israeli army, or the Border Police, say it is that day. Some of the roadblocks on the big roads into Jerusalem have the air of always and forever, with booths for the soldiers and sandbagged half-tracks dug into position to blow away offenders . . . and the soldiers there may have a workaday calm, as they glance in your car, and ask for your papers (or maybe not), showing no more fear or hostility than a passport stamper in the airport. Then again, they might be nervous that day, and you may be stopped there for hours. . . . There are many checkpoints much grubbier and catch-as-catch-can—a bunch of barrels or plastic barricades in the road—or simply a truck, or a half-track—with a command spray-paint-scrawled in Hebrew on a scrap of plywood (if there is any sign at all) . . . to STOP HERE, or SHOW I.D. . . . or maybe it's the one word that implies obedience to any command—TSAHAL (Army)—and as for what you're supposed to do, the soldiers will make that up as they go. If you're a Palestinian, you must stop—that much is for sure—even if no one tells you to stop, or tells you anything at all. (If you pay no heed and just move on, you could very well be shot.) You must stop if you are on foot, or driving . . . or if it is cold or hot, or raining like hell . . . you stop, even if your kids are hungry and crying in the backseat . . . or a load of your family farm's tomatoes is rotting in the sunshine . . . or your wife is moaning in labor on her way to the hospital. You must stop if the soldiers are having lunch and simply cannot be bothered. When they do take an interest, sometimes the Israelis want to see a permit for your travel, and if you don't have one, that could be another several days of obeisance and waiting at an Israeli police station. Sometimes, the soldiers want to take your I.D. card and "check it"—either against a printed list of evildoers, or they radio your data to the secret police, who will, after some delay, figure out whether you are interesting. Either way, you cannot move until you get your I.D. back. Sometimes, you are invited to sit on the stony dirt, or mud, where many others may be sitting already—sometimes, for hours. Sometimes, the soldiers stop you twenty-five feet away and gesture with their weapons toward your shirtfront—which means that they want you to bare your torso—any explosive belt there? Sometimes they want to look at other parts of you, or feel you, whether you be male or female . . . and sometimes you must undress—more often if you call attention to yourself, or indicate annoyance with these procedures. I know of one school headmaster, a dignified elder man, who passed the same checkpoint on his way to school every morning, and was made to undress—not once but often—and stand naked while his students passed by. This was richly humorous—that old man was (formerly) so conscious of the honor of his position.

The simple rule is, there are no rules—or no rules that were the same rules yesterday. You must watch and obey—that's what it's about. The function of the checkpoints is to show who's boss. I had a friend in Tel Aviv, a Russian new immigrant and a soldier, who tried to explain to me (very kindly in English, his third language) why it was important to stop some people, even if they weren't planning anything criminal. "Because the bad attitude—you know? If they are acting like they are the good, and we are the bad one. Then, you must show them control."

I had another friend in Ramallah, a Palestinian man—could it be, he's actually near fifty years old now? (When I first met Ghassan Khatib, he was the president of the student association at Bir Zeit University.) Anyway, we're all adults, now—and his mother, alas, is something more than that. She took sick. So, Ghassan had to visit her, in Nablus. He couldn't wait to apply for a permit from the Israelis—so he had to go around them. . . . How bad could it be? Ramallah to Nablus couldn't be more than thirty miles—maybe forty minutes by car. . . . But of course, he couldn't take his car, or even a taxi. Instead, he would travel the homeboy way—begging rides where he could, till he got near a checkpoint, and then he'd leave the road, and cut through villages, fields or wadis, to go around the checkpoints—a lot of people do it. Terrorists, for instance, never go through checkpoints. . . .

Anyway, he made it through. (He was there, and telling me the story, wasn't he?) By the time he got near Nablus, he had traveled by six separate conveyances, and a lot of time on foot. But he didn't have to deal with the Israelis—except once. He was walking on a path through a wadi, a dry riverbed, when his progress was stopped by a high mound of dirt and stones. Ghassan climbed in his city shoes—scrambled to the top—and when he got there, he stopped dead. At a distance of about twenty feet, there was another mound with an Israeli armored personnel carrier perched on top, and its big-gun muzzle was pointing at his chest. An Israeli soldier called out a command—but Ghassan doesn't speak Hebrew. The soldier made motions with his hands, as if he were hiking at the sides of his shirt. Ghassan just stood still. The soldier said, in Arabic, "What are you, shy?" Ghassan said, "No. I am ashamed. It is a shame." The soldier made the motions again. Ghassan made no move. There was a stand-off. . . . It could have been the end of his journey—or his life. In the event, the soldier only shrugged—looked at Ghassan as if *he* were weird—and waved him around the APC with the barrel of his submachine gun. Ghassan walked on, to Nablus and his mother. And the trip to see her took him only four hours . . . which was lucky, because he was a busy man. He was the (new reformist) minister of labor for the government of Palestine.

A lot of these stories don't come out lucky. Yusuf Abu Awad caught some bad luck at the checkpoint outside his village in the hills near Hebron. This was back in the autumn of 2000. It was about seven in the evening. Yusuf and a friend were coming home from work. Yusuf was the sort who was always working—that day he'd been driving an excavator. When he could, he worked with logging equipment for the Israeli forest managers of the Keren Kayemeth. (They were the people who used to take my dimes for the pine trees.) On that night—November 16 was the date—Yusuf had to drive straight home, because his brother Ghazi was going to meet him there, so they could pick up another brother from work. (The only people with families more omnipresent and obligating than Jews are the Palestinians.) . . . But, of course, to get home, Yusuf had to pass the checkpoint.

He wasn't even quite there—still a couple of hundred meters away from the checkpoint on Highway 60, the main drag that leads from Hebron to Bethlehem and Jerusalem—when six soldiers, three from the left and three from the right, appeared on the road and commanded him to stop. Who knows what their plan was—some sort of new proactive policy? Check them before they get to the checkpoint? Yusuf didn't know why—the town had been quiet—but, of course, he couldn't ask. They ordered him out of his car. They took I.D. from him and his friend. They ordered him back in the car. He sat. . . . So far, there was no luck involved, except maybe good luck—he could speak Hebrew.

Maybe that was not good luck. One of the soldiers started throwing stones at the car. There was no way to know what got into him. Maybe he was returning the favor that some kids had shown him at some prior time. Or he'd had a bad day, his wife was on the warpath—who knows? Bad luck. Yusuf jumped out of the car. It was a rented car. It would cost him a fortune to fix all the dents. "What are you doing?" he called out in Hebrew. "Why are you causing trouble? Stop it!"

"Shut the fuck up, son of a whore. Get back in the car and I don't want to hear a sound from your ugly voice."

"I'm not the one talking bad. You are the one with the ugly talk." Yusuf got back in the car. But he couldn't let it drop—he was still protesting: "You want I.D., we gave you I.D.! There is no curfew. There's no demonstration. You're the only one throwing stones!"

"Shut up, motherfucker, or I'll shoot you right now."

"You want to shoot, go ahead! You are the sonofabitch who's causing the trouble."

The soldier shot from a distance of about four feet. His gun had bullets that enter the target, then explode. Later, in the morgue, Yusuf's face was perfectly all right, but the top of his forehead, crown of his skull, and his hair were simply gone. He was thirty-one years old. He left a wife, aged twenty-five, a daughter of six and a son of five.

According to eyewitnesses, an officer arrived in a jeep, and in a hurry. He screamed at the soldier: "What are you, crazy? Why'd you have to shoot him down? What could he do to you?" He ordered the other soldiers to take the shooter's gun, and put him in the jeep. But when Yusuf's family (with the help of the Israeli human rights group B'tselem) filed a complaint, and investigation ensued, it emerged that Yusuf was accused of trying to take the soldier's weapon . . . so, of course, the shooting was self-defense. Why would a single unarmed man with no prior record of violence—or even re-sistance—suddenly confront a well-armed troop of six sol-diers, and try to take one of their guns? . . . Well, the army can't be expected to explain every little thing. A spokesman said it was possible that Yusuf was one of those sad cases, with deep (and previously hidden) psychological problems.

Here's where things stand in Palestine: an Arab population of more than three million—an educated and cultured peo-ple—is being abased. These are the last Palestinians to cling to their homeland. (There are more millions all over the world—a diaspora weirdly reminiscent of the Jewish dias-pora, and the "Jewish Problem" that Israel was designed to fix.) These are the Palestinians who wouldn't run, or couldn't, or would only run so far. It is their vow—and their triumph (if it may be so called)—that they'll stay, despite everything.

Everything is pretty much what they're up against now.

Economically, they are being driven—steadily and by apparent plan—to a preindustrial subsistence. Any of their lands that their captors desire may be taken—for military purposes, for settlement, or a security zone, or a road, or a fence, at any time. Through most of this occupation, nothing the Palestinians built was permitted or legal in Israeli courts—so nothing was built for good. The Palestinians are basically an unarmed people—with no military force that deserves the name (no armor, artillery, warships or aircraft)—that is in daily confrontation with one of the world's best armies. Moreover, that opposing army serves a policy that is designed to hinder and embitter daily civilian life, the simplest rights and duties of human existence: going where one needs to, making a home, raising a family, or making a living. And if a Palestinian opposes these hindrances with too much vigor, with violence, or too noisily, his property may be forfeit, or his freedom, or his life, without meaningful restriction and often without price.

Politically, as a people and cause, the Palestinians are supported by a hundred nations. This plus five shekels will buy coffee in Jerusalem—if it's a day the Israelis let them go there. For most of the years since 1948, the Palestinians put their faith in the bellicose support of their "brother" Arab nations—vows to "redeem the sacred homeland" (by bathing it in the blood of Jews), and ornate pan-Arab plans to wipe "the Imperialist Zionist Entity" (the word *Israel* was taboo) off the face of the planet. The vows and plans weren't worth much, either. . . . It is a big part of the reverence for their fighters (and unwillingness to criticize the commandos, holy warriors, martyr-bombers—whatever they call themselves, and no matter how stupid they are) that Palestinian history is marked and driven by a peculiar shame: For fifty years, while they lost their land, they never really fought for themselves. They weren't equipped (who would do *that?*) and didn't seem to know *how* to fight. Just by way of example, in the 1967 War—which lost them the last twenty-two percent of their homeland—the Israeli troops who arrived to conquer and occupy Nablus were astonished to meet no resistance at all, and to be greeted by welcoming thousands (the whole town turned out to cheer), until one Israeli soldier tried to take away a gun being toted by one resident. Only then did the Palestinians divine that these were not Iraqi troops.

No one in Palestine is waiting, now, for rescue by Iraqis or anyone else. In fact, there is no Palestinian who hasn't come to understand that "support" from the governments of the Arab world—all the official wailing about the plight of Palestine—is mostly to shift attention away from those governments' failures at home. Every few years, even now, the Arab chieftains will convene in emergency summit to pledge aid (these days, with dollars—billions of 'em) for Palestine. A lot of that money never arrives. And as for arms, tanks, planes, troops—well, that's simply not in the cards, now. The superpower who used to arm and embolden the Arabs (Palestinians, like most of their "brothers," put great stock in Soviet might) doesn't even exist anymore. Now, the Palestinians are counseled to heed and trust—as broker between them and the Israelis—the other superpower, America, a nation they attacked and offended, who was and is the main bulwark of their enemy, and who wants for the Palestinians (if truth be told) nothing more than that they should shut up, and stop complicating U.S. policy.

So, who will champion Palestine? Well, there is the Palestinian people's own government—not that anyone ever asked them if they wanted such a government—led by the president (apparently for life) and chairman of the Palestine Liberation Organization, Yassir Arafat. It is also almost ten years, now, that Mr. Arafat's government has held sway in Palestine—which is roughly the same stretch of time that the chairman-and-president has ever been in Palestine. By 1993, when he had led the PLO for a quarter-century, Arafat and his podgy cadres had been exiled not only from the sacred homeland, but also from every neighbor of Israel. He was consigned (for God's sake, *across an ocean*) to cold storage, and well-merited obscurity, in Tunisia. Then, Yitzhak Rabin decided to make peace . . . and after that, it was just like *Sleeping Beauty*: Rabin kissed Arafat (actually, it was a handshake on the White House lawn), and Yassir awoke, sprang to life, and pronounced himself ready to wed.

It hasn't been a fairy-tale marriage. Rabin was killed for that kiss—shot to death by a religious assassin at a peace rally in Tel Aviv. And Arafat, who arrived to a hero's welcome in Gaza and the West Bank (maybe they thought *he* was the Iraqis), brought with him a gaggle of thugs and thieves, whom he soon installed as the Government of the Palestinian Authority, and who showed themselves, like locusts, notable only for their numbers and how much they eat. The Palestinians (the local ones, I mean) call these ravenous newcomers "The Tunisians"—but not to their face. The main governmental business is repression of "disloyalty." And if you should happen to run into a Tunisian (if they're not being chauffered by in their gleaming automobiles, or entertaining themselves in their new villas)—if you should happen to *run afoul* of one—or be denounced to him, or to the secret police, as a potential political rival, or an economic competitor to some Tunisian monopoly, or (worst of all) as a collaborator with The Jews . . . then, you're toast. They are worse than Israelis.

Arafat was recalled to Palestine to give his people a state of their own, and a government that was for them. He went back to sleep, instead. He attends (latterly from the bombed-out ruins of his own headquarters, imprisoned more or less by Israeli tanks) only to his own power and perquisites, which he considers the same thing as government. His stuporous insularity left open the entire field of leadership, to be filled by Islamic holy warriors. And the nation he was supposed to father is stillborn—though he didn't even know that. After he signed, with Rabin, a Declaration of Principles (which was just an invitation to more years of haggling—*if* he minded his p's and q's), it was a year before his advisers could convince him that he hadn't got a state, yet. Arafat had read only the parts about him being boss. (That information came from Mahmoud Abbas, who was—too late, it turned out—

finally installed as prime minister with the mission of pulling Arafat's chestnuts out of the fire.)

And here is a grand historical fact—the oddest and saddest of all. This is the closest the Palestinians have ever come in their aspiration for a nation of their own. It's the sort of bleak consolation that reminds me of a Palestinian joke. As the wounded man said to the dying one in the next hospital bed: *"Well, that's the peace process!"* . . . Of course, when you ask Palestinians why they may be the last people on earth to get a country, the answer is one word—Israel. But the Kyrgyz have a country, the Tajiks, Uzbeks, Turkmen, Georgians . . . they also had a little one-word problem—Russia—but they made it through. For God's sake, even the unlucky Kurds may get a country before the Palestinians. Why? . . . Was there a reason the world thought it could put the Jews in Palestine—atop the Arabs there? . . . And why is the last twenty-two percent of Palestine the site of the longest occupation by force in modern history?

It is the joy of visiting in Palestine that you will be received with graceful kindness, and with a dignified duty-to-guests that has disappeared from more modern places. No matter the circumstances of your host—even in the rudest tin-walled house of the most troubled family in a refugee camp—you will be welcomed and bidden to sit comfortably in the best room, often lined with chairs, or sometimes with pillows on the floor, where you sit cross-legged. Tea will be served, and perhaps a soft drink to follow, or coffee, or fruit that your host may cut into slices, which he offers to you from a plate or straight from the blade of the knife, while you talk. If you finish one drink or dish, another will arrive—maybe dates or figs, nuts or honeyed sweets, and more tea—till mealtime, when, of course, you are invited to stay.

Your host will inquire as to your health and well-being—not once, for that would be perfunctory, but several times, to indicate that this is his concern. If you have come to find out about a certain event, a story or situation, and other people may be able to help you, a son will be dispatched, or a neighbor's son, to bring the other people who may be of interest. A brother or a close friend may also arrive to lend honor to the occasion. Anybody else who appears is invited to join the circle for tea—and though they may have no knowledge of the subject under discussion (and do not speak, so as not to burden the conversation), they will shake hands all around and stay for an appropriate time, so as not to dishonor the host or guest. You may stay as long as you like. (I have often been invited to spend the night—my hosts worried for my safety at dark checkpoints.) But if you must leave, you may find that your host leaves with you, to assure himself that you are safely on your way home, or to your next destination.

These kindnesses are not simply good manners. And they have nothing to do with who you are, or your standing in the world. They are about your host's own view of himself—his duties and dignity. Islamists contend that these duties of hosting (and all other Arab graces) are enjoined by the Koran and evidence of the goodness of the One True Faith. But I have been as kindly and assiduously hosted by Palestinian Christians—and by Druze families, as well. Kindness and generosity to strangers are cultural requirements for an Arab man, a chunk of the bedrock of both self and society. This is the highest imperative—a matter of honor.

It is easy for a Westerner to enjoy the Palestinian sense of honor—so old-fashioned and charming, so exotically foreign. I have heard two generations of Israeli press officials complain—*"Yeah, yeah, sure, I know: they're so nice! They're so polite!"*—as round after round of Western correspondents is wooed and won to sympathy for the Palestinian cause. But it is hard for any Westerner (impossible, it seems, for Israelis) to credit honor as imperative. When superior force—the law or the army—or common sense, self-interest or even personal safety come to conflict with honor . . . then, honor will win. Honor is trump. That's one reason there is no peace. Any peace deal that does not accord with honor cannot be accepted—and if it is imposed, or accepted perforce, it cannot endure. In fact, without an awareness of honor, nothing can be made to stick—and nothing can be understood.

The one requirement of Arab honor that Israelis do know and talk about is the matter of "honor killings." This has to do with the females of a family, if one is discovered to be unchaste. If, for instance, she has sex before marriage and gets pregnant . . . even if she is raped, even raped by a member of her family (that happens, too) . . . or if someone in the community testifies to her lewd behavior, or there is simply too much talk—unbearable rumor—about her behavior . . .

then, her own father or brothers may kill her, "to whiten the honor of the family." Israelis talk about this because it confirms for them the brutality of Arab society—or even the beneficent effect of their occupation. (Said Brigadier Pundak, the old Gaza governor, "We had to put a stop to that!") . . . Brutal it is. But there is more to be learned from it than that simple fact.

What it confirms is that honor is collective. An individual Arab is adjured to proper behavior *for the honor of the family*—which contributes to the honor of the larger clan, and the tribe (all related and allied families). The roots of "honor killing" go back beyond the days of the Prophet, to centuries when Arab tribes wandered the desert, and increased their size and sway, their wealth and access to land and water, by raiding rival tribes for their sheep, camels and women. More women meant more wives, more sons—which meant more fighters and more land, water, cattle, wealth. The tribe survived by reserving for itself—exclusively—the breeding capacity of its females. . . . And honor killing endures because Palestine is still a tribal society—despite the new, higher level of education, worldliness (and satellite TV) . . . despite an overlay of anachronistic Stalinist rhetoric ("The Arab masses," and blah-de-blah-blah) . . . despite their plaint and plea that the world must now reckon with them as one people, and a nation—they have trouble thinking or doing as a nation, themselves. So far, the history of their struggle (and particularly their leadership) could be written in one line: Every man for himself—and his kin.

Once you recognize honor and kinship as bedrock for the Arabs of Palestine, a lot of nagging mysteries—some of them hoary with age—make a sort of sudden sense. Why did so many Arabs run away in 1948? Well, the wholesale flight didn't start until after a massacre at the Arab village of Deir Yassin—a slaughter by Jewish fighters that the new State of Israel did not cover up, but picked over and probed in overt self-examination. Men, women and children killed! There were even allegations of Arab girls raped by the Jewish fighters. When word of that *dishonor* got around, other villages simply emptied out. . . . Why could the Arabs not fight for themselves? Why was there no Palestinian army-in-waiting (as the Jews had their underground Haganah) when the 1948 War broke out? In fact, there were Arab militias, but they'd been raised to defend their clans, and they were no match for the Jews' new national army—especially when clan leaders used their wealth to depart, for the safety of *their* women and kids. . . . (Maybe that question itself is unfair: when I asked an august Palestinian professor, Sharif Kana'ana, why the Palestinians had no army-in-waiting, he said there was no point trying to equate the 1948 Arabs and Jews. "The Palestinians were in their home. Why should they have a plan? That's like asking someone whose house was broken into, *'Why didn't you have a plan? Why didn't you have a knife in your hand?'* ")

Honor and family also shed light on some up-to-the-minute mysteries. How can it happen (as the Jews so often ask) that a Palestinian mother *celebrates* at the funeral of her son, a suicide bomber. *"How could a mother be like that?"* the Israelis wail (for that Joy-of-Dead-Jews is the stuff of their nightmares). They have to keep a simple explanation at the ready: "They're animals." . . . "Human life means nothing to them." . . . Even more empathetic Israelis—even peaceniks! (well, that's too small a sample: let's say former peaceniks)—are willing to settle on explanations that have nothing in common with their own experience of how people (and parents) are: "Well, it's just different, when we have one child or two in a family, and they have twelve. They'll just make more children!" . . .

But it is never said—in conversation, on TV, or in the Hebrew papers—that the mother of a "martyr-bomber" has no choice. It is a matter of honor. . . . In fact, the honor of a woman and her family is all (and almost only) about her sons. It is her duty and destiny to produce sons for the tribe— which is why, after she gives birth (say, to a first-son named Khaled), her own name will forever recede, while she is called by her kin (and by her neighbors, and every shopkeeper) Umm Khaled—Mother of Khaled. (That's also—as Americans ask—why all those Palestinian commandos show up in the papers with those wacky names—impossible for a proper Yank to keep straight—*Abu This and Abu That.* "Abu" simply means "Father of.") . . . The mother of a suicide bomber may mourn and cry for her son forever. But if she isn't seen at his funeral, making the sound of joy—a high trilling noise from the back of the throat, the same sound she would have made at his wedding—then she would not be seen to accept the honor of his death for the family. If she would not tell the TV cameras, when she's interviewed afterward, that she is proud of her dead son—that she would give all her sons—then she dishonors her whole tribe's struggle, and her family, altogether. She would be stripping the honor of her kin, of her name, of her own life (and her son's) . . . it is unthinkable.

One more mystery to illumine: in the spring of 2002, when suicide bombs were blowing up Israelis every week, and the government had to *do something,* the IDF encircled and attacked Arafat's seat of government, his compound in Ramallah—and blew it to smithereens. But they didn't blow it up and walk away. They kept the siege. They went into the compound, and through it (or through what used to be the compound)—and carted away, hauled across the Green Line, truckloads of paper—the entire recorded annals of the Palestinian Authority. The only items from this pilfered cache that the Israelis publicized were records (and there were plenty) that implicated Arafat in support of suicide bombings, or armed conflict against Israelis. That was part of the Israeli campaign to discredit Arafat as a "partner for peace." . . . But there were more records—tens of thousands of pages—that told a larger story: letters to Arafat from Palestinians all over the territories (and some from refugee camps in Lebanon, Syria or Jordan), requesting aid, emergency funds, support for the family, for a son's education, or a wedding . . . notes from officials—major and minor— requesting or recommending jobs or little payments for this or that family, and for reasons that often didn't need to be written (Arafat would know the family, of course). . . . For instance, this note from a West Bank official, Hussein Sheikh, who addresses Arafat by his *nom de guerre*, Father of Amar:

> *In Honor of the Warrior President,*
> Dear Brother Abu Amar, May God Protect Him,
> I request that you be so kind as to allocate financial assistance in the sum of US$ 2,500 for the following brothers: Raed Al-Karmi, Ziad Muhammad Daas, and Amar Kadan.
> With thanks,
> Your son, *Hussein A-Sheikh*

On the bottom of the same page, Arafat's instructions, in his handwriting:

> *Ministry of Finance / Ramallah—The sum of US$ 600 shall be allocated to each of the aforementioned.*

These thousands of notes—and the fact that Arafat personally approved every expenditure over two hundred fifty dollars—actually cleared up a number of little mysteries. For one thing: What does he do every day? . . . The answer is, he greases palms, every day and all day. Arafat never takes a day, or even an hour, off. He doesn't have friends. He doesn't read, doesn't see movies, probably never has seen a play, or gone to a concert or a museum . . . Arafat doesn't do *any-*

thing except Palestinian politics—and this *is* Palestinian politics.

These papers also answered the question: What does he do with the money? When the Israelis remit tens of millions in taxes they collect from the occupied lands, or the Arabs actually do pony up and send a few bucks (or a few millions)—how come nothing gets built? . . . Well, there is no money left for stuff like clinics, streets or schools . . . not after the PA pays forty thousand government employees (mostly "clerks" who never had training, and don't actually know how to do anything—but each one has a family, now beholden to the Chairman) . . . and then there are about forty thousand more involved somehow in "security" (a lot of other heads of families who are, by the grace of the Warrior Prez, dressed up with uniforms and salaries, and serve under officers who are officers because they're clan leaders) . . . and then, Arafat doles out a few thousand dollars more—or tens of thousands, daily—in little *baksheesh* that rewards or buys (or, at the very least, rents) more loyalty. . . .

What these documents answered, in sum, is the big question of how Arafat keeps his perch as the chairman and president, the father of his not-quite, never-quite nation. He is the shrewdest operator and most shameless manipulator of his people's sense of loyalty, honor, family, clan and tribe that ever was.

Here's one big question that's harder to answer: if two generations of scholars—Western, Arab and Israeli—have dis-

cerned in Palestinian society the primacy of honor and family
. . . if the Israelis have not only a warehouse full of the PA's
documents, but thirty-five years of secret police investiga-
tions in the territories (not to mention more than fifty years
of living as neighbors with the Palestinians of Israel) . . . why
would the IDF and the government of Israel act like they are
the only ones who don't get it?

Why would a series of Israeli governments—every one
with the stated aim of making peace, or at least living in
peace with the Palestinians—maintain (and enlarge) the network of settlements on Arab lands, continue (and increase)
expropriations, confiscations, punitive destructions—and assassinations? Why would successive governments elected to
"put a stop to terror" ratchet ever tighter the vise-grip of closure and a system of checkpoints guaranteed to humiliate
and embitter the captive people?

This is not rocket science. The Israelis' own studies show
that the most common reason for suicide bombings (or for
those who are caught as they attempt suicide bombings—the
ones who get it done aren't available for surveys) is an incident in the bomber's past—a brother who was killed, a father
arrested, a mother or sister disrespected by soldiers. . . .
Every expropriation, every house demolition, every midnight break-in by soldiers who ransack a home in a search for
suspects or weapons . . . every insult at a checkpoint, every
shove with the stock of a rifle, every strip-search of an elder,
is likelier than not to produce a future "martyr"—or two . . .

that's why one *Ha'aretz* correspondent in the territories called the checkpoints, "factories for suicide bombers."

But it's easier for Israeli pols to crow about the "hundreds" of terror attacks they forestalled by "strong measures." It's easier for them to blame all the killing on Arafat—who must be "taught a lesson" by each successive Israeli premier. They can say it's all caused by the money paid to a "martyr's" family—from Arafat, from the Islamic movements, or even from Saddam Hussein . . . or they can say— easiest of all—that "those animals" simply hate Jews.

Still, here and there, one sees hints that the Israelis aren't as clueless as they seem. I had lunch in Tel Aviv with a truly big wheel, Yaakov Peri—these days, he's chairman of one of the nation's big banks. I was asking him about the effects of the occupation, and what Israelis do to keep it in force. "I think our policies," he said, "are making for Israel another two generations of enemies." And Peri is hardly some lefty Dove-Bar yahoo. Before he went into business, he ran the organization that Palestinians fear most—the hyperefficient secret police, Shin Bet.

Indeed, there are further hints the Israelis know exactly the effect of their "strong measures"—and they always have. It was Moshe Dayan—the biggest wheel of all, and the guy who conquered Greater Israel—who counseled about the occupation: "The one thing you cannot do is humiliate these people." Maybe the Jews know all they need to know about Palestinian honor—i.e., enough to use it, to make exile the only option. Didn't they know enough—even by 1948—to publicize Deir Yassin?

I wasn't quite sure where we were headed. Safwat Diab, my host, friend, guide and interpreter in Gaza, delivered us without much explanation to a market square in the Jabalya refugee camp. We parked in a wet crater. Nothing is paved there. Everything is broken. This appointment, visit (whatever it was to be), started the same way most visits start—with a climb up several flights of gritty stone stairs, taking care not to tread on chunks of loose concrete. Most buildings in Gaza seem half built, or half demolished—hard to tell which. At the top, we entered an office, which was also standard issue: a desk with a table abutting it at one end, and a number of fellows already seated, chatting over tea.

There were no tip-offs as to the function of this office—but there were some signs of import: There was the poster of the grand mosque—the Dome of the Rock, in Jerusalem—which is the official postcard symbol of the Palestinian struggle. There was a serious platter of almond cookies and honey cakes—someone had laid out money to make this meeting go. And there was the man at the head of the gathering, behind the desk in a big chair. His name was Zeid Zaki Zeid, and he was—you could see it in one glance—no one to screw around with. He wore a squarish gray suit, and you could tell it wasn't padding that filled out the shoulders and chest. His skin was a beautiful café au lait. His close-cropped gray hair emphasized the broad bullet-dome of his head, and profuse gray brows hooded dark eyes that didn't change shape when he smiled. He looked like James Coburn, when Coburn looked really tough. (Maybe that's why he felt so familiar—like I knew him from some past life.) He was introduced as the head of the Local Committee for Jabalya Camp. But when I asked what the Local Committee did, Zeid simply said that they "take care of local problems."

It dawned on me only slowly that this visit was a measure of protection for my friend, Safwat, and me. (I guess we *were* a local problem.) It was important to show that my inquiries in the refugee camp were sanctioned—not "disloyal." I had been asking around quite a bit. There was a time, early on, when I thought this book would begin in Jabalya camp—with an incident in history that few people knew about. It happened in 1971, when Arik Sharon was commander of the south, and one day he sent bulldozers to this camp and began to knock down houses. In those days, Western correspondents merely drove through Gaza (if they got there at all) on their way to Sinai, the Suez Canal and Egypt. The big story, then, was the conflict between nations—Palestinians weren't in that league. So the incident was never widely reported. But to my mind, that day changed history.

Up to that time, the refugee camps were off-limits to the IDF. They were treated more or less like territory of the U.N.—whose agencies were the only ones that did anything for the Palestinians displaced in 1948. Now, Sharon was announcing, with his bulldozer blades, that this was his territory, too. He was mowing wide boulevards through the camp—where only twisty alleys had separated the houses before—so his tanks could get in there . . . and to my mind, he was announcing, too, that the Israelis were in Gaza for keeps.

I had asked in Israel about this event—got a lot of stories (all different, of course). The old governor of Gaza, Brigadier Pundak, said that what Sharon did was just a small part of his own grand scheme to eliminate the camps altogether. He wanted to move all the refugees out of their cinder-block huts—both as a gesture of humanity and for strategic purposes. (No more refugees would mean no more right of return, and an end to their claims on their old lands in Israel.) In fact, Pundak said, he did resettle thousands of families—out of the camps and into "quite decent houses!"—till the government told him there was no money for that sort of thing, and his grand scheme shriveled. . . . The historian Meir Pa'il, who knows the IDF inside and out, said Sharon was not announcing new policy, or any change in the government's decision on Gaza. The whole problem was, there was *never any decision.* Everybody more or less assumed that the territories conquered in '67 would be traded back to the Arab nations in exchange for a treaty of peace. The man who'd conquered all that land, Moshe Dayan (going into Gaza was his personal decision), shucked off the great question of the territories—for years—with a shrug and a single sentence: "I'm waiting for a phone call." (The Arabs must have lost his number.)

So, now, thirty-five years after that war, more than thirty years after Sharon mowed down those houses, Gaza and Jabalya camp were still in Israeli hands. There were the boulevards—thirty years on, for the first time, the U.N. had just managed to pave them. And I was asking around the camp. . . . "Yes, they came in the night," Zeid Zaki Zeid said, as if this had happened last week. "They told the people they have to leave their house within twenty-four hours, and they put a red X on the house with paint. The next morning the bulldozers came, army green bulldozers, and a lot of soldiers in jeeps and on foot. . . ." To Zeid, it *was* like it happened last week—or last week, the same thing was happening, just in a different place. . . . "It's a copy of the picture that happened in Jenin," he said, referring to half-a-camp mowed under by the Israelis in retaliation for the Passover suicide bomb of 2002. For him, it was seamless succession of Palestinian victims—like my Sunday school stories about the Jews. "This was 1970, and now we are in 2003, and nothing has happened—the same. . . .

"Yes, many of the people fought. But they were carried by the soldiers and thrown in the truck. And while they looked at their house it was destroyed. Some went to stay with other parts of their families. The ones in the trucks they threw to the desert, into Egypt, to El 'Arish." (The Israelis also say some families were "relocated" onto Egyptian soil. But when the Sinai went back to Egypt—in Sadat's peace deal, 1979—the Egyptians threw those refugees back. Sadat never even asked to take back Gaza.)

Now, the gray, balding man on Zeid's left chimed in: "This was another forced exile for the Palestinians, after 1948." At that point, it came clear that Zeid had invited the other men in the room, to help him deal with the foreign visitor. (And at that point, I figured out why I felt I had met him before. He was like the machine politicians I'd met as a young reporter, in Baltimore. They were also tough guys in their field, but so desirous of acquitting themselves respectably when an educated visitor came to call. Zeid—now I knew—was a ward boss for the Arafat machine.) . . . The balding man, Muhammad Abdel Rahman Abu Rukba, was a member of the Local Committee, and clearly a man of respect. He also had a gray suit on, but softer than Zeid's, with a sweater under the jacket—professorial he seemed, as he fingered his worry beads. His high forehead had a spot at the crown, like a darkened callous, that marks a praying man— good Muslims bow their foreheads to the ground five times a day. When he spoke, it was to reinforce Zeid's seamless line—fifty years of steadfastness in the face of murderous Israeli assaults. He told of his cousin, Hassan, who was in an Israeli prison, back in those days when Sharon was commander of the south. The Israelis took Hassan out of prison, took him around the Jabalya camp . . . and then, at the edge of the camp, they shot him dead, in front of a crowd. Why? "Because he was thought of as an activist, and they brought him back to the camp to point out who else was active in the resistance. He wouldn't squeal, so they killed him in plain view. They wanted everybody to see."

Of course, Abu Rukba said, they knew Sharon well before that—knew all about him. "Since 1951," Zeid said, "when he destroyed the houses and the people of Qibde . . ."

(The town is on the map as Qibya, and Sharon's unit—in retaliation for a commando attack in '53—did knock down the houses, with a lot of folks still in them.) . . . "We know about his unit called the 101," Abu Rukba was saying. "And the Rimon [Sharon's assassination squad] was here in Jabalya . . ." They were trading Sharon lore back and forth—like a responsive reading in church. In duet, they launched a story—clearly often told—about Sharon in the 1980s, as minister of defense, with his chief of staff Rafael Eitan—they were touring bases in the West Bank. . . .

I lost track in the middle of the story. They couldn't see Sharon as I did, as an old man who is out of ideas: a one-trick pony who has no clue what to do now—save to do what he has always done, try to hit the Arabs so hard that they will never utter a peep again. He's a man who is never so at ease—so much in control—as when something big has just blown up, and Israel, after its time-honored method, is about to wreak a terrible retribution. (At last—something he *knows* how to do!) . . . My mind was racing back to those days in the 1980s, when I was under Sharon's guns, trapped in the siege of Beirut, as Sharon's artillery and aircraft pounded the city to a pulp, day after day, and for months. It was horrendous—no fresh food or clean water, no power, no gasoline—but a field day for a reporter. I walked the city every day, walked for miles, down to the bunkers of the PLO fighters in the south part of town. I got to know them pretty well. We'd sit amid sandbags, filth and flies, smoking my cigarettes and drinking their tea from dirty glasses, and they told me they were fighting for Palestine—they *insisted*—like they were at the gates of Jerusalem . . . while I knew they'd be lucky if they even stayed alive in Beirut. Sometimes they grew testy with me (and testy men with guns can be nerve-wracking) because I was American, and America supported this Zionist siege. (At one point, Ronnie Reagan's Navy actually started lobbing in shells from an old battleship—why, I never figured out.) The PLO boys would shout at me in awkward English: "WHY AM'RICA HELP ISRA'IL?" Finally, one day, testy myself, I snapped an answer back. "Because we are Israel's friend. And if you had a friend who was good to you, like we are good to Israel, you'd *be* in Palestine!" It probably wasn't true—I was just trying to make the Soviets the issue, instead of me and my country. But I was amazed to find it worked like a charm. We were instantly friends again—and I used that line a dozen times. What I figured out, over months, was the answer gave them honor. It allowed them to see themselves as steadfast in struggle not just against Israel, but against the world's superpowers. It explained (or explained away) the dreary fact that they were getting their ass kicked. . . . When honor comes into conflict with facts— once again, honor is trump.

". . . Sharon and Eitan caught this man and they killed him right there—slit his throat. The Israeli officer who told about this said the man made the sound of a sheep who is slaughtered. . . ." In the office in Gaza, the Sharon lore was winding up. He was a murderer—pure and simple—and honor was served.

I asked a few questions about suicide bombers: How did it happen that kids decide to blow themselves up? Was it true that money for the family was a lure? Was it true they mostly had problems at home? . . .

Answers to these queries came from a man on my right, who hadn't spoken much before. It seemed that Zeid had brought him in to serve as our summit's sociologist. He had a beautiful name—Hassan Ahmed Abdel Aziz Aziz—and he was, all around, a peach of a guy. Actually, more like an avocado, which was the color of his splendid suit. The undergarment (in linen of that lustrous green) was a long *galabeya*—the Egyptian-style robe, buttoned up the front—with punctilious white embroidery on the facing strip for the button holes. Over that, he wore an impeccable suitcoat of the same green linen—and over *that,* an avocado cloak with an applique strip of gold embroidery around the back of his neck. Topping it out was the traditional white headcloth, with a halo-ring of woven black goat hair to hold it in place on his pate. (I was not surprised to learn, he used to be a tailor.) He was called by the others Abu Ramsi and, these days, at age sixty-four, he was a professional consultant in *sulha*.

Sulha is the Arabs' traditional method for resolving disputes—it's about making peace. Say, your neighbor's trash is (in your opinion) misplaced, and it is fouling your fence . . . or his tree has grown up over your garden wall and is inhibiting your horticulture . . . or your wife has run away, back to her kinfolk, and says she will not return . . . or your son will not heed your wishes as head of the family . . . then, you need a *sulha* man. You and your antagonist call him in, or go to visit at his house, and each party will relate his grievances. It requires a jeweler's eye for justice, a reputation for probity—and the gift of gab—to work as a *sulha* professional. But in the best of circumstances (or the easiest cases), the *sulha* man will succeed in dividing rights and duties equally among the parties, everybody will see justice in the settlement he proposes and all will go home with honor restored. Needless to say, Abu Ramsi was an expert on Palestinian society. He had seen the gamy inside of a lot of homes.

Families, he said, have less control of their sons now. "The father is dominant when boys are young," said the *sulha* man. "When they grow up and get education—rising education is a big change, along with TV: kids get their own ideas now—the son doesn't have to listen to the father. It is hard for a father who has grown up a son to take over—and now that son is martyred. But the sons can also blame the fathers. They say, 'You should have stayed! There are still people in our old village, and nothing happened to them! You left just because of rumors . . . you left without struggle! Now, it is our turn.' "

I asked about the mothers—specifically, one mother; Israelis talk about her, because not only did she say on TV that she was proud of her dead son for the Jews he'd killed, but she made a video with her son *before* his killing spree—she knew all about it in advance, and urged him on to martyrdom. Yes, they knew her, Zeid said—she lived nearby, in Shijaya. But they talked it over for a moment in Arabic, and no one could remember her name—not even her son's name (so we could ask how to find her, as Mother of So-and-so). Abu Rukba and Zeid talked between themselves—who might know her—someone in Shijaya? . . . The problem was, her martyr-son was not one of theirs. He didn't die for Arafat's Fatah party. He was a Hamas kid (each martyr is claimed—and buried—by some party) . . . so none of their Fatah pals, or PA colleagues, would know the family. For the moment, they just called her Mother of Martyrs.

In the meantime, Abu Ramsi was telling me—with some precision—what George W. Bush should do, if he wants to make *sulha* between Palestinians and Jews. "We have examples in *sulha*," he said. "If you are brothers and you fight, you divide it. Bush has to understand what kind of problems each side is facing, and then give each his part, and support them to be equal. If there is equality there is justice, and there will be neighborhood established. Exchange will be facilitated. The matter of the population must be studied—this should be the basis for the division of the land. People have to see the justice of the solution. Also, Bush must help with projects that improve the living in this land—so people will have pleasure with this time—"

I interrupted to ask about something I'd often heard in Israel. All the Jews who ever talked to me about *sulha* maintained that the Koran forbids making *sulha* with infidels. (It was another proof to them that a real peace is impossible). Abu Ramsi said that was not the case: *sulha* is not a religious idea or function—it comes from tradition that antedates

Islam. In fact, a long and satisfactory peace reigned for centuries between the Arab tribes and the Jews who wandered the same desert. . . . The real problem, he said, is that Israelis have never understood honor. Without it, indeed, *sulha* is impossible.

"What the Jews do not understand is, first, they have to *apologize*—for taking the land, for dispossessing the Arabs and brutalizing the Palestinian people. Because without the restoration of honor, then you cannot move on to the division according to rights."

I nodded comprehension, but I didn't speak—didn't want to sound rude. The only thought that occurred to me was: "Don't hold your breath."

The sad fact is, almost everyone holds his tongue in a place like this, where "truth" must conform to honor instead of the facts. Either that, or they learn the hard way to keep quiet. You could say this, too, conforms to my own prejudice (and to my chosen way of making a living), but it seems to me that Palestinians are doubly imprisoned: first—or, let's say, foremost—by Israelis . . . second, by their own sticky web of proper lies. It's even temptingly neat to argue (at least to advance the proposition) that the one bitter bondage will not end—cannot end—without the other being broken, too.

One example from recent history: in the latest negotiations for peace—first at Camp David, then in a Sinai town called Taba, in the year 2000, under Bill Clinton's aegis—Israeli and Palestinian teams had the whole shootin' match figured out (and all nicely typed on good White House paper, with a copy for the Nobel Committee, and *everything*) . . . until Yassir Arafat read a paragraph or two, then fanned through the rest with his thumb, and said: "I don't want it."

The big sticking point was the "Right of Return"—or, as Israel calls it, the "Refugee Issue." It's about Palestinians who left their homes (in what is now Israel) during the war of 1948. Should they be allowed to return? Of course, the Israelis don't want 'em—they need more Arabs like a hole in the head. And on the other hand, the Right of Return has been a nonnegotiable Arab demand, going back, well, to 1948. To be sure, fifty years ago, that was important. Palestinians had only recently left their homes. They wanted to go back, they were trying to go back. But now, their old houses are gone—or they've been filled with Jews for three generations. Half of the old villages are gone altogether, plowed under for farmland or (more recently) paved over for new development. How many Palestinians would want to go back, now, to live as strangers among the Jews?

No one knew. So a bright and brave pollster, Khalil Shikaki—he runs the Palestinian Center for Policy and Survey Research—took the exceptional step of *asking the refugees* . . . big mistake. He found that only ten percent were interested in exercising their Right of Return. When his findings were published, a bellicose mob descended on his center, smashed up the office and pelted him with eggs. They were thugs recruited for the job by the Arafat machine. A leaflet (amazing that, in their "spontaneous fury," they managed to print up a leaflet . . .) accused Shikaki of "selling himself to the U.S. dollar" and "deviating from the consensus of the Palestinian people." It called for the PA to crack down on "mercenary academics [who] spread their poison among our people"—and to put "such people . . . on trial for high treason."

One more example, a little more famous: in the autumn of 1999, nine noted intellectuals, two former mayors and nine members of the Palestinian parliament signed a petition called "Cry of the Homeland," denouncing oppression and corruption in Palestine. It was a document that ached with love of country and disappointment with what Arafat had wrought: *"The Palestinian Authority has adopted a modus operandi of graft, corruption, humiliation and exploitation of the Palestinian people. Indeed, the Oslo Agreement now looks like a mere selling out of the homeland in return for some corrupt and corrupting elements within the PA getting rich. . . ."* The hope was, this document would be signed by thousands—as manifesto and a mandate for change. Instead, the PA "security forces" arrested the intellectuals. The ex-mayors were placed under house arrest. And the Palestinian Legislative Council empowered a special committee to monitor opinions and statements by its members, so the PA wouldn't suffer such insult again. The nine members who had signed were censured, and the PLC voted that Arafat should be immune from criticism—after all, he is the symbol of the Palestinian people.

A thuggish government can prosecute speech-crime,

even thought-crime—and hard truths (too easily) can be scoured from the papers and broadcast news. But they can't be stopped. Palestinians may be doubly oppressed—but no one can make them stupid. As reporters in the old days learned in Eastern Europe, you can always hear the real news in the jokes. Dr. Sharif Kana'ana—that distinguished anthropologist who warned me of equating Jews and Arabs in '48—has studied jokes in Ramallah since 1988. His collection is a monitor—like an EKG graph—of the Palestinian heart.

When he started collecting, the first *Intifada* had just begun. Palestinians were—at last!—taking up arms (at least rocks) against their troubles, and the jokes had a jaunty confidence: *A woman was about to give birth, but she couldn't get to a hospital—her village was blocked off by Israeli soldiers. Finally, they took her to their military hospital—and there, she gave birth to twin boys. The first boy's head emerged from his mother. He looked around—and saw soldiers everywhere. "Ahmad!" he cried to his twin brother. "We are surrounded! Bring some stones!"*

When that *Intifada* led to the Oslo peace process, and to creation of the Palestinian Authority, the jokes had a new tone and topic: *A PA policeman asked for leave, but his officer didn't want to grant it. "See that donkey over there?" said the officer. "You can have your leave, if you can make that donkey laugh." The policeman walked over, and whispered to the donkey, who began to laugh. "Not enough!" said the officer. "Now, you must make the donkey cry." The policeman whispered again, and the donkey cried. "Get that donkey out of here!" yelled the officer. The policeman whispered, and the donkey ran off. "Okay, okay," said the officer, "you can have your vacation—if you tell me how you got the donkey to obey." The policeman replied: "First I told him I worked for the PA, and he started to laugh. Then I told him I have a wife and three children, and make only eight hundred shekels a month—so, he started to cry. Then I told him, I could also get him a job, to work for the Authority—he ran away."*

In Ramallah, last year, the big news was the opening of a new Turkish bath—that, and the power struggle between Arafat and his new prime minister, Mahmoud Abbas. The jokes showed which way the wind was blowing: *Abu Amar [Arafat] and Abu Mazen [Abbas] went together to the Turkish bath. They stayed for an hour to talk over their differences. When they got ready to leave, the owner gave Arafat his bill for twenty-five shekels—Abu Amar paid. Then, he gave Abu Mazen a bill for fifty shekels. "Wait a minute!" Abu Mazen said. "You only charged him twenty-five!" The bath owner told him: "Yes, but you were so much dirtier."*

The *Intifada* jokes have grown darker, too . . . like the one about a man whose son asks him for two shekels—cab fare back and forth to the checkpoint, to throw stones at the Jews. *"Here's one shekel," the father says. "Anyway, you'll come back by ambulance."*

I liked Kandil for his jokes, right away. They weren't jokes on anyone in particular—just about the funny things people do—Arabs or Jews, it didn't matter to him. He was almost fifty years old and he'd kept his eyes open: you couldn't get any cheap baloney by him—no matter whose brand it bore. Kandil came from a Palestinian village (a hick town, even by West Bank standards), but somehow learned to get along anywhere. He wasn't fancy—he'd spent most of his working years as a laborer who rose to a foreman's rank in Israel. But he seemed to me illustrative of the biggest change I've seen in Palestine over twenty-five years.

Except for a tiny elite, Palestinians used to be bumpkins in the Arab world—*fellahin* (farm laborers), or maybe the children of *fellahin*—and mostly dispossessed, out of the swim, the objects of humor, or pity at best. That shoe doesn't fit anymore. . . . With a big assist from the Israelis (i.e., in the squeeze of the long occupation) hundreds of thousands of men had to travel the world to work—in the Gulf, North Africa, Europe or the States . . . and for the young, in recent years, no jobs meant the only good choice was education— and they took it. Kandil never got anywhere near a college— except maybe to sweep the paths—but he's got plenty of that new sophistication. Like a lot of his countrymen, without a passport of any sort, he is a citizen of the world.

As a matter of fact, that's how I got to know him. I wanted to ask about his Iraqi teeth. I'd heard the story secondhand (Kandil told a friend of mine at a party) and it was a fantastic yarn. I'll try to tell it briefly here, more or less as I heard it. . . . It happened in the mid-'90s, when things weren't so bad in the West Bank. Kandil and his wife and kids were all doing

fine—except for his teeth. They were getting loose, or starting to hurt, then one would fall out . . . a misery! And Israeli
dentists wanted fifteen thousand shekels (between three and
four thousand dollars) to fix them. Even West Bank dentists
wanted serious dough—eight thousand shekels (almost two
thousand dollars). So Kandil tried his luck in Amman, Jordan, where he had cousins—he might get a deal. But that
was just as bad, or worse (the equivalent of twenty-five hundred dollars)—no deal . . . and he resigned himself: he
would have to kiss his poor teeth good-bye.

Then a cousin in Amman said, "Look what I've got!"
and she handed him a business card from a dentist in Baghdad. Kandil said, "What are you, crazy? What do I have to do
with Iraq?" . . . "What have you got to lose?" she replied.
"My father will pay for the phone call." So Kandil called
to Iraq. . . .

To make a long story short, he could get the job done in
Baghdad, along with eighteen-hour taxicab rides back and
forth from Amman, and hotel rooms, and food—along with
everything—for the equivalent of three hundred bucks. In
Baghdad, he found that the Iraqi dinar (the whole economy)
was so shot up from the first Gulf War that nothing in the
great bazaar seemed to cost anything! So, the first time he
went back home, he loaded up his taxicab with handicrafts,
embroideries, beautiful brocades—treasures that would
fetch a *fortune* in Palestine. . . . And with that fortune (and
with a taxicab full of coffee—you couldn't get coffee at any
price in Baghdad—except, after that, at Kandil's price), he

went back to Baghdad for more teeth-work. There, he started loading taxis with treasure for the trip to Amman and Palestine—even though he wasn't going back, himself. How could he leave? He was wet in a river of money! (His Palestinian customers were selling to the Jews, who were selling to Europe—no one could get enough!) . . . And any time he mentioned that he was from Palestine, the Iraqis hugged and kissed him in a transport of solidarity. The dentist, for example, cut his price in half for his "brother"—until Kandil brought him one of those posters of the Dome of the Rock (cost him one shekel, twenty-some cents, at a shop in East Jerusalem), and the dentist forgot the last half-price that he was *going* to charge. The teeth business ended up costing zero—though the work went on for months. . . . And so, Kandil had to extend his visa: he went to the Ministry of Interior in Baghdad, where there was a lovely young woman who helped him. So he asked her to dinner. But that didn't comport with her modesty. If he wanted to feed her, he could bring food to her family's house. So he loaded a taxi with food—food in the trunk, on the seats, on the roof—then two taxis. He had a lamb slaughtered. Why not? He was rich as Nebuchadnezzar! And he went to the house with the food— which was pretty much a proposal of marriage—which was accepted. Kandil had his wife and grown children in his village. Except now, as a good Muslim man, he had another wife in Baghdad. And then, of course, she had to have a house—so he got a nice house, and a fridge, a TV, some good furniture . . . *Kandil—King of Iraq!* . . .

Anyway, it seemed to me, here was a man to know in modern Palestine. I was also asking at a moment when the world had Baghdad on the brain: George W. Bush was about to come calling—and I thought maybe Kandil could tell me how the Iraqis would react. . . . Kandil very kindly hiked across the hills and fields to sneak into West Jerusalem—he insisted we should meet at a Jewish restaurant, which I took as another thoughtful gesture: he must have thought that would be easy for me. I thought it couldn't be easy for him— though he didn't look out of place, in his workman's cap, and his tight leather jacket (as tight as the Israelis wear theirs) . . . he talked a very good Hebrew, too. Still, he was speaking in a near whisper, his eyes always scanning the room. I asked if he wanted to go somewhere else—I meant, of course, to an Arab place—but he just shook his head, and murmured: "No, it's not that . . ."

I asked how he came to know his way around Jews, and he told me a bit of his history. When he was a boy, the West Bank and his village were part of the Kingdom of Jordan. So, twice a week in his elementary school, there was religion class—on Islam, Christianity and Judaism. There, he learned that Jews had horns and tails. They walked on all-fours and ate human flesh, like regular people ate lamb or chicken. He did well in that class—always got ninety percent or better on the exams. . . . But when he was twelve years old—June 1967—a war broke out (all of a sudden, and for causes, to him, mysterious) . . . then (just as suddenly), it was over . . . and Jewish soldiers were in his world.

Anyay, his father, called them "The Jews." Kandil thought they might be Syrians, or Egyptians . . . because he checked out the backs of their pants—he'd peek behind them, every chance he got—and he couldn't see their tails. . . . Maybe Iraqis. . . . It turned out, the first one he talked to *was* Iraqi, an Iraqi Jew who admired the pita bread that Kandil was eating. (It was the village kind, fresh-baked and toasted to a crisp bubbled brown on a fire. Kandil's mom used to make batches of 'em—as the soldier's mom probably did, too.) They ended up sharing the bread. The soldier talked Arabic in a personable way, and didn't seem to want to eat Kandil . . . so, they got friendly. It was probably the first full-grown person who ever talked to Kandil like that—as the Arabs say, "by four eyes"—one guy to another. And not just a grown man, but a soldier with a gun! It was almost too heady for a twelve-year-old to handle . . . Kandil stole every pita bread he could find in his house to bring to the Jews.

That's the kind of kid he was—not the stealing part—he was so hungry to know the wider world. People forget now (when, for years, they have equated the Israeli presence with constriction), but when the Jews first took over on the West Bank, it *was* like a fresh world—modern, monied, and suddenly *so large.* I'm not talking about any high-flown concept of Western freedoms, or the winds of change—nothing that airy . . . but after a few weeks, when the curfews were lifted, the limit of their old lives—the fence that used to be like the Edge of the World on medieval maps—and the bunkers and sandbags, machine-gun nests and minefields . . . were gone!

And beyond lay the land of bedtime stories—the old places of the good life—Jaffa, or Ramla, or Haifa . . . or a hundred different villages with names that were only on the old maps now, but real and alive in their households, still—more real than anything in current life. Now they could go there! . . .

Within days of the curfew coming off, Kandil was nosing around that Green Line. And a couple of days later, he was over the line—and in a new world. He'd walk into Israel, mostly to the nearest town, which was called Mevasseret Zion. They had a real soccer field—just for kids to use!—all level, and with no stones in it. There were Jewish kids who were friendly, and they always seemed to have candy or gum, and later on, they had cigarettes—he learned to smoke. Kandil would go every day after school, sometimes alone, sometimes with friends—enough to play a game of football against the Jewish kids. And after that, Jewish boys would take him home for something to drink, and he met their parents. It wasn't long before they offered him work—maybe half a lira (that was the currency in those days) to clear brush, or move some stones. Then, he had friends and money in his pocket, too—Mevasseret was something like heaven. And if, that evening, his parents asked where he had gone after school, he'd say, "just playing with some kids . . . ," because he knew there was something illicit about how he felt in that town.

When Kandil was fifteen years old, he got home one evening and his father told him: "Some people came today to ask for the hand of your cousin . . ." Kandil knew exactly which girl his father was talking about. She was almost his age, and he knew without thinking there was something between them. He never passed her house in the village (half the families there were cousins of his clan) without looking for her on the balcony. And when she was out there, and saw him, she'd run inside and lock the door . . . Kandil waited in silence for his father to tell his opinion. "Of course, I was against that," his father said. "I said her hand should be kept for you."

"Great!" Kandil said. "When am I going to get married?" But there were many things to do before that could happen. It was a big family, and once powerful. His father's grandfather had been *mukhtar*—an appointed mayor—during the Turkish times, and had ended up (as so many clan leaders did) owning vast lands and most of the cash in his village, which stood near the road from Jerusalem to Tel Aviv. In '48, the bulk of the family's land was lost—three thousand five hundred *dunams* (some eight hundred acres) were taken for Kibbutz Shalavim. But the family was still well off, with more than two hundred sheep and goats, cows for yogurt and cheese, and money-making plum trees near their "new" village, which was in the hills, a bit closer to Jerusalem. That was one reason Kandil had to marry within the clan. There was honor to be served, and the family's position to be maintained. That's also why there had to be a big-league party, with the whole clan—hundreds of guests, many animals slaughtered . . . a bigger party still, because there were two clans in the "new" village and, of course, they were rivals. . . .

Anyway, he was halfway through his sixteenth year before he was married, and the head of his own household—which also meant, of course, he had to start his working life in earnest, too.

A Jewish man from Mevasseret got him his first job, hefting crates of milk and yogurt onto trucks at the wholesale market for the big Israeli dairy, T'nuva. Then, Kandil hooked on with the municipality of Mevasseret, sweeping, gardening and hauling trash for the Jews who lived there. After four years, another Jewish man asked him if he wanted to work in the Dead Sea area—there was a job at the nature reserve of Ein Fashkha. It was 1973 when Kandil went down, took a look—and it was beautiful—a park and spa with walking paths and mineral pools carved into stands of papyrus . . . he would work there for more than twenty years.

He was hired just for guarding and gardening—keeping the paths free of papyrus, and picking up trash that visitors left behind. But his Hebrew was good, and getting better, and the bosses promoted him early and often. One day, they told him: "Dress up smart. You're going to the city." The same company that ran the spa also ran the pool at the Hilton Hotel, on the beach at Tel Aviv. Kandil would train there for three months as a lifeguard. Then, he trained another three months as a lifeguard for the sea. When they brought him back to the spa at Ein Fashkha, he would guard the Jewish kids in the pools. The work was easy, and he got along fine with Jews. Other Arabs were the ones who gave him trouble. ("What are you doing back here, after they kicked you out?"

snarled one fellow worker, an Arab from Nazareth. "You think you can just stroll back in, and take the work?" . . . The Jewish manager overheard, and yelled at the guy from Nazareth: "Why are you talking to him like that, instead of welcoming him back? You're fired!")

A secretary at the nature reserve helped Kandil learn to read and write Hebrew. Soon, when the manager left for vacations, he'd leave Kandil in charge—and Kandil made sure there was some good surprise when the boss returned. He wouldn't just keep the paths free of papyrus—he'd make a new path, or a new pool. Kandil became more or less the manager's manager, in charge of the whole place. And he was making sixty-five hundred shekels a month—more than fifteen hundred dollars! How could he leave a job like that? . . .

People in his village said he ought to leave it, during the first *Intifada*. His bosses got him a permit to come into Israel for work—that wasn't the problem. But he wasn't paying honor to the national struggle: when kids who threw stones were being shot, how could he still work for the Jews? . . . Kandil wasn't much for politics. He liked the idea of a country called Palestine—seemed to him an idea with justice—but not at the cost of his family's well-being. One of his sons had bad health problems—the boy couldn't do much of anything, except make kids of his own, whose support, of course, fell to Kandil. So, he kept working.

That sin seemed to be forgotten, right away, once the Oslo peace process started in earnest. Arafat came back, the PA was installed—on a flood of money, for a year or two.

(Building contractors in his own village were pulling down ten thousand shekels a month!) And nobody cared who worked where. But when Rabin was killed and all that turned sour—the martyr-bombings started up, and closures—no one had a job anymore . . . and Kandil stuck out like a man on a flagpole in a bad wind.

Men in masks came to his house and warned him to quit working for the Jews. But he knew who they were—they were from his own village—and he didn't listen. One night, they left a Molotov cocktail at his door, with a book of matches. His wife got scared and begged him to quit. Another night, someone drove past in a car and shot at the house. He had no choice. . . . He wrote a letter to his bosses, and said he couldn't make it to work anymore. They said, if he could give them a couple of weeks, they would find a replacement, and they'd put him on a pension—after all, he'd worked there for twenty-three years.

So, by 1996, Kandil was without a job, too. He took a few construction jobs—at least, while people were still building on the West Bank. Or he'd sneak into Israel and fill in as a laborer for the Jews. It wasn't that bad—he had his time to himself. . . . That's how he found the time to get his teeth fixed—and to become the King of Iraq!. . . .

Kandil was away on a job when a man named Musa—a well-known man from the neighboring village—told Kandil's sons that he wanted to talk to their father. This was already the springtime of 2001, and Kandil had a new routine established: his sons told Musa to come back at six-thirty, and he would find their father at home. . . . "Look, Abu Hassan," said Musa, when they sat down that evening, "everybody knows you, and so you have nothing to worry about. But the people from the police service in Ramallah would like to talk to you. You should go tomorrow, and have a coffee with them."

The next morning, Kandil traveled to the famous compound in Ramallah (it was still intact at that point). At about ten thirty, he handed his I.D. card to the man at the desk, and said he'd been asked to come in for a talk. There was no coffee. There was no anything—he sat on the stairs till four-thirty, when they told him the chief didn't have time that day. They gave him back his I.D., and told him he should come back tomorrow, which he did. He arrived at the compound (Arabs call it the *Muqata*) by ten A.M.—that was May 2, 2001—but he sat on the stairs again till six, or six-thirty in the afternoon, when at last they came for him. Three men in civilian clothes took him up to the third floor, and into a small room, where they beat him without mercy for the next three hours. By ten that night, they picked him off the floor, trussed his hands together behind his back and trussed his feet. Then they hung him from a hook, head down, with his mangled face about a foot from the floor.

The next day, the beating started in the morning and went on all day. Or on and off all day. When the cops would get tired of beating him, they'd hang him on his hook and go drink tea. Everyone who came in hit Kandil. People who came to visit the guards—friends who just stopped by for tea—were invited to Kandil's cage, to hit him, or kick him. Then, the cops would show their friends how the real pros do it, with a thick doubled-up electric cord—twelve-gauge or ten-gauge—that was like getting hit twice-at-once. And every time they used the cable on him, blood would come out. That was his blood on the wall. . . . In the evening, they brought in a man Kandil knew—or, like everyone in Palestine, he knew about him. Ayesh Rashid was a guy the Fatah militia arrested during the first *Intifada*—in 1988 or '89—he was accused as a collaborator with the Jews. They were going to put an ax in his head, but he raised his hands in self-protection, so his hands were chopped in half, all the fingers were gone. That second night, they brought him to Kandil's cage, to warn him: "Tell them whatever they want."

But they didn't *ask anything*. No one talked to him at all, past grunting when they hit him, or cursing him on the floor while they kicked at his head. For sixteen days, no one asked anything—or told him anything—they just beat him. He would have said whatever they wanted—would have made it up, if he could—he didn't care to be brave. But there was no chance to tell the truth or a lie. He didn't know what they wanted. He didn't know why he was there. He didn't know why or how he was still alive. . . . On the fourth or fifth day, they brought him a paper—nothing on it, just a blank sheet of white paper—and they told him: "Name, family name, and signature." Kandil wrote down his name, and signed.

His family was asking for him every day. On the weekend, six days after his arrest, they were told to come with a change of underwear. But when they got to the *Muqata*—his father, one of his sons and his brother-in-law—they weren't allowed anywhere near Kandil. A guard took the fresh clothes—underwear, pants, shirts, socks. "We don't know where he is," he said. "But don't worry. We'll find him and see that he gets it." . . . Kandil could have used a change: his cage was maybe two meters long, less than a meter wide—and no water. When he was hung up, there was nothing to do but piss into his own clothes. But he didn't get the fresh stuff for weeks, until they took him down from his hook, one morning, and told him he had to take a shower, and shave. They ordered him to clean up his cage, and scrub the blood off the walls. Some of it was dried on forever—someone else's blood. Then, they took him down the hall (the cage next door had blood even on the ceiling!) . . . to another room, a bigger room, with windows—wide open against the smell—and he had to sweep that up, and bring three chairs.

Two Red Cross ladies made appearance at midday. One was a German, the other an Arab who translated. They gave him soap, toothpaste and a little towel. But the guards already had told Kandil, he was not to open, or even touch, anything they gave him. They also brought him ten cigarettes—the first he'd had in a month—and he smoked those, no matter what the guards would do. He smoked them all while he talked to the ladies—the guards could do nothing while they were present. The Red Cross was giving the PA sixteen dollars a day for each prisoner—that kept the jail in business.

The money was supposed to pay for food for the prison-ers—meat and dairy products, bread, fresh vegetables and tea or coffee. Instead, the *Muqata* jailers fed each prisoner a daily ration of one-quarter pita bread, a quarter-tomato, a quarter-cucumber and a quarter-egg. The Red Cross also de-livered to the jail five packs of cigarettes for every twenty prisoners, every day. Each prisoner was supposed to get five smokes a day. But Kandil never got one—the guards sold the cigarettes out on the street. And he never saw anything like a meal—except when the Red Cross came. Soon after the ladies arrived, a tray was delivered to the interview room, with meat and fried potatoes, vegetables and tea. (Of course the cops had told Kandil, he couldn't touch that, either. When the ladies departed, that food was for the guards.)

The ladies couldn't do much for Kandil. Their only func-tion was to find out where each prisoner was, and inform the family. They asked Kandil's name and age (forty-six) . . . did he have children (he had grandchildren!) . . . where was his home—did he rent or own it . . . did the family need help? . . . The guards had also warned Kandil not to say too much—or to say nothing at all—name and age, that's all that was required. But he talked to the ladies for three hours—told them he didn't know why he was there. And he showed them the marks on his body from the beatings. The German lady started to cry.

The Red Cross would come once a month. Apart from that, Kandil's jailers did as they pleased. He soon figured out that a new squad of guards would come on duty every two hours. The worst beatings came at the beginning and end of each shift—because officers or other cops were present, and every guard had to show how avid he was for the work. . . . He learned all the guards' little hustles—which ones, for example, would sell the olive oil and fresh food that families brought to the compound. (None of the prisoners got any of that food.) . . . He learned the rules of the place—if you could call them rules. Each week, you got a disposable razor (another Red Cross requirement), but you had to pay the guards ten shekels if you wanted to use it. (The unused ones they could sell on the street.) But after you used it, you had to put it back in its plastic package (even the used ones, they could sell for a half-shekel or so)—and God help you if your razor wasn't stored right, or couldn't be found. (The commander himself had the profit from this hustle.) One prisoner's razor went missing—a policeman had taken it—and all one hundred ninety-six prisoners were marched to the yard, stripped and searched. It was wintertime, already—and that day was a freezing rain that was half-ice when it hit you—but the prisoners stood naked for several hours, and a platoon of motorcycle cops was called in to beat them with truncheons and pipes, while every article of their clothing was searched. Finally, the cop who had taken the razor came running out: "Oh, I found it, under a table!" . . . The commander punished that guard by stripping him, in the freezing rain, and making him buy a cola and a pack of smokes for every man in the motorcycle unit. (He'd caused them extra work, after all.) . . . One prisoner made the mistake of suggesting that one cigarette should go to each prisoner, too. He was made to stand naked in a one-square-meter cage for five days.

It went on day by day, for months—the beatings and the cold and filth, and near starvation—and no one told him what he was charged with . . . until one day (it was just after a Red Cross visit) an important man, a top prosecutor, came with two aides in tow, and he sat down in the interview room, across from Kandil.

For the occasion, Kandil's feet were manacled with leg irons, and his hands were bound in front of him with plastic shipping tape—lest he harm the prosecutor, who was from an important family, and a personage in the PA.

"Now I want you to tell me the truth about what's written down on these papers." He had a sheaf of documents in front of him—putatively Kandil's confession.

"There is no truth there. All I did was sign a blank piece of paper."

"Look, your signature is here. You signed this."

"I didn't write anything in there. I never signed anything except a blank page."

"Okay, you didn't sign those sheets . . ." said the prosecutor—let's call him Ashraf. Meanwhile, he stood, took off his suit coat and draped it over a chair. The two aides set upon Kandil, beating him with their fists while he sat at the table. Ashraf dug into his briefcase and came out with a cable. Then, he came around and joined in, whipping Kandil across the back of the neck.

But Kandil didn't speak—he didn't offer to own the confession. Ashraf stopped whipping him, and busied himself stripping insulation off the end of the wire. The two goons yanked Kandil's hands onto the table, pinioned them and smashed down on the heel of his palms, with a long stick that looked like a shovel handle. "Still didn't sign?" Ashraf murmured. He plugged in the cable, and touched the bare end to Kandil's neck, and then, the base of his spine.

Kandil jerked right out of his chair and landed on the floor, unconscious. He didn't know how long he was out. When he came to, he still couldn't move—he was rigid with the pain and shock. But he heard the voice of Ashraf—still there—in a heated conversation with another man whom he addressed as "Doctor."

"What are you, crazy? . . ." This was the doctor's voice. "You give him more electric, you're going to kill him."

"So what?" Ashraf said. "So a dog has died. . . . Can't you get him up? . . ."

The doctor had to stay for an hour before Kandil could move enough to get off the floor. And his hands weren't working. The doctor said he must try to move his hands. He manipulated Kandil's fingers, gently probed the palms—well, mostly the right palm. . . . Kandil had to use his right hand to sign a paper attesting that he was in good health. And the doctor couldn't leave until he'd signed, too. Kandil was doubly sworn to be in perfect condition.

He never did own up to that "confession." But he found

out what was in it. Four or five days after his shock treatment, the deputy commander of the prison had Kandil marched into his office, and ordered him to read the prosecutor's documents aloud—"so I can understand what all you've done." The deputy was actually a guy Kandil had gone to school with. So this was personal humiliation. And for the occasion, the deputy had invited five guests—two from his own family, three from the area where Kandil lived—so Kandil's shame would go public, just as surely as if he'd printed the "confession" in the newspapers.

It turned out that Kandil had secretly been involved in the famous kidnappings of Mustafa Dirani and Sheikh Abdel Karim Obeid—two Hezbollah bigwigs who had disappeared from Lebanon more than ten years before. (Of course, it was well known that Israel snatched them—but the question that bedeviled the Palestinian Revolution was: *Who had ratted them out?* Now, at last, that canker could be healed.) . . . And Kandil had also arranged the kidnap of twelve soldiers from the Jordanian Legion (that would clear up a long-running dispute between the PLO and the monarchy in Jordan) . . . and he'd also masterminded the kidnap of an Egyptian soldier from the Sinai, near the Gaza border, at the town of Rafah (the PA could not forget its Egyptian brothers) . . . and also, he'd murdered two boys from the hills near his village . . . and he had also been the informant who dropped the dime on twenty-five separate Palestinian activists whom the Israelis killed . . . and also, he was the informant who had turned in two gangs of smugglers who were bringing in weapons from Jordan . . . and *also*—he had fired a gunshot at a member of a powerful family in his village.

When he read that last charge, Kandil knew who had ratted *him* out—or how he'd ended up in that hellhole. It was the rival clan in his own village. One of their cousins had been shot at—and their honor required that someone pay the price. . . . But, of course, he wasn't invited to explain that, or to explain anything. When he finished reading, he was taken back to his cage, and hung upside-down again. As the deputy commander remarked to his guests, this was the kind of case that needed constant watchfulness from the security service. Kandil, after all, was a dangerous man. As he had spoken clearly, in his own voice, he was nothing less than an officer, with the rank of major, in the famous Israeli commando unit, the Duvdevan! (They had heard that with their own ears!) . . .

And when Kandil heard his own voice reading that charge . . . (A major! If he'd really been informing for the Israelis, he would've had a car, and a half-million in the bank! Now, he couldn't help his sons with half a loaf of bread.) . . . he knew his life was finished. He would hang on that hook forever—watching the roaches crawl over his food, his quarter-cucumber, for hours each day, till they took him down to eat it . . . freezing in his cage through the night, begging God for sleep to take away the ache of his latest beating, the moaning from other prisoners nearby, the noise of gunshots outside the *Muqata* (What was all that shooting for?) . . . then, to be wakened at dawn by a new shift of guards, who had to beat him worse than the last shift, or worse than yesterday . . . until, one day, they would slip up—an *accident,* or accidentally-on-purpose—and whip him until he bled too much, or they'd kick his back till his kidneys gave out, or put a boot right into his brain. . . . And they'd say: *What a shame* that the informer died from a medical condition, before they could prepare all the proofs for his trial— but (We thank Allah!) at least, we have his confession. And we have cleared up many terrible crimes! . . .

But he was still alive—though half his weight, just bones under his gray jailhouse skin—on March 28, 2002, when the beatings stopped. He was hanging in his cage all day—everything stopped: the food, the shouts, the orders—nothing! He didn't see a guard all day. None of the prisoners knew what was happening . . . but the shots outside had changed to big explosions—bombs or cannon shells—something tremendous. And it went on without stopping—all day and night. . . . Then, the next night, March 29, about seven P.M., he heard it: *Hebrew!* . . . The Israeli army had destroyed the *Muqata,* and the soldiers were searching through the wreckage of the compound that night.

There were one hundred ninety-six prisoners, and Kandil was the last to be found. He was screaming his throat hoarse in Hebrew, calling to them . . . but his cage was behind a door-behind-a-door, and they didn't get him off his hook until the other prisoners told the soldiers, they'd missed one. All the prisoners were taken by trucks to an Israeli camp—they didn't get there till four in the morning—

and there, even Kandil couldn't believe what happened. At four-thirty in the morning, in the rain, soldiers came with food—and every prisoner got two rolls, one with cream cheese and one with yellow cheese, and a yogurt—fresh in its own container!—and a fresh bottle of clean mineral water . . . *and an orange . . . and five cigarettes!* . . . He had never tasted anything so delicious.

And then, when daylight came, they brought tents and bedding—everybody got a mattress and two blankets for their cot . . . and breakfast! There was matzoh (unleavened bread for Passover), and white cheese, tomatoes, peppers, *five more cigarettes* and tea. And they raised the tents, that morning, to keep out the rain, and made their beds . . . and then, lunch—there was chicken schnitzel, along with the matzoh. (Matzoh, Kandil decided, was better than the finest lamb.) . . . And it went on like that, every day—or for ten days—until the Israelis told him he was free, and he could go home.

A year later, Kandil was still amazed: "If only a tenth of the Palestinians behaved like the Israelis behaved . . ." he said. "I want you to put in the book: 'I don't wish on any-body—not even the ones from the other family—ever to fall into the hands of those animals.' . . . You know, I used to be for a Palestinian state. I was in favor. Now, I want the Israelis to wipe them out—send them all to Hell."

Kandil's troubles are far from over. If conditions improve for the PA, he knows the security goons will come for him again—and this time, they'll kill him. Why should they want him alive? . . . In his village, no one will talk to him now. It is well-known that he is suspect—"disloyal." If his sons want to have visitors at the home, Kandil has to go somewhere else, so he will not dishonor the gathering. He has become an invisible man. . . . That's why "Kandil" is as much of his name as he will vouchsafe for this book . . . and why his eyes kept scanning that restaurant—there might have been Arabs working in that kitchen.

His hands still have no feeling in them—and sometimes they don't operate properly—that makes it hard to work, even if he sneaks into Israel to find work. The Israelis won't give him a special permit anymore—much less a passport, so he could leave his village. (He can't go anywhere through Jordan—because the PA has put his name on the list of undesirables, as an informer.) Anyway, an Israeli passport wouldn't get him to Iraq—so he could see his young wife. He worries for her—but what can he do? . . . Could I help him get a permit from the Americans—so he and his old wife could get into Turkey, and then sneak into Kurdistan? . . .

I never did get to ask him about the Iraqis. It didn't seem germane. . . . But I did tuck in a question about his teeth: *Did they get screwed up—was he hit in the mouth?* . . . "Of course," Kandil said, "they beat me everywhere. Those animals kicked my mouth! But these teeth . . ." and he flashed a beautiful smile. "They are solid like stones. These teeth will be the last thing of me, that lives forever."

It took less than an hour to find her—though she didn't live in Shijaya anymore. Her friends in Hamas had moved her to another neighborhood in Gaza, because she was a target for the Israelis. Still, it turned out, "Mother of Martyrs" was name enough to track her down—she is famous among the Palestinians, too. Just within the past few weeks, we were told, she had "given another son to the struggle."

Her name is actually Mariam Farhat, though she is better known in the new neighborhood as Umm Nidal—after the name of her firstborn son, the one most recently "martyred." (In fact, *nidal* is the Arabic word for struggle . . . so she must have been aware when she named him, she would be known as the "Mother of Struggle" . . . and you could also say the kid came by it honestly.)

She had given birth to ten children, six sons. Two sons were now dead. Another was locked away in an Israeli jail. Yet another son, Wisam Farhat (he was missing some fingers from a grenade that went off before he could throw it), was in the front parlor of the apartment with us, respectfully fetching tea, and listening to his Mama talk about her sons. She was saying that she is proud of them all—especially her martyrs, because they died to make a nation of real Islam, and true justice. . . .

"The pain is there, and it goes on. I cry every day for losing my sons. But the goal that they died for is more important and valuable than my pain. Really, I did not lose them. I am just away from them for some time. But I am keeping them, for the next life, somewhere between the hands of God."

She was not a small woman, but she spoke with such urgency, and with such an evident effort to be calm, that it gave her an air both fragile and feverish. She wore a black headcloth that tightly covered her hair, her forehead and both sides of her face—it was pulled taut (rigid, it seemed) by a clip under her chin. She had full lips and round cheeks—she must have been, once, a pretty girl. But now the face peering out from its black shroud seemed so unnaturally without color—a shocking pale—save for deep shadowed furrows under the eyes . . . it was not a face one would want to inhabit.

"No one believes that a woman likes to lose her sons. But since our land is occupied, and they deal with us so violently, we have to defend ourselves. Otherwise, we will lose our existence, our feelings of nationality. . . . Really, I am so satisfied that they attained their martyrdom. . . ."

We had to stop talking from time to time, because the apartment house rises from the wall of a mosque. (What other real estate would Hamas own?) And every couple of hours in the afternoon, the *moazzin* calls the faithful to prayer—actually, an amplified sound track of a *moazzin* issues from loudspeakers on the minaret. From a distance, this call (*Allah hu akbar . . .*) is so gorgeously haunting, it's one of the treats of the Arab world. But right next door, and at minaret-level, it entered the room—*ALLAH HU AKBAR!*—like an air raid siren. The Farhats—Mariam, her son Wisam and husband, Fathi—simply went still, they didn't leave to pray, just waited for the call to end. They were not a whit disturbed. By the second time it happened, I knew if I lived in their apartment for one day, I would find that *moazzin* (no matter if he lived in Saudi Arabia) and kill him with my bare hands . . . but that was just my mood. (There is nothing like a sojourn in the Holy Land to make a man hate religion.)

I took the opportunity (our *moazzin* moments) to look around the parlor. There were two pictures—posters, really—with pride of place on the wall. Good Muslims do not display art that is a natural likeness. (There are no stained-glass saints looking down on the faithful in a mosque—no decorations, save for beautiful calligraphy and abstract forms.) But these posters—each a portrait memorializing one of the family martyrs—had their own religiosity. They were purposefully iconic. There, on the right, was Muhammad Farhat—nineteen when he died, and he didn't look grown-up enough to carry the big guns he was gleefully brandishing in both fists, held aloft at his sides. And on the left, the firstborn, Nidal, more serious, an adult—he was thirty-two years old—but still nearly dwarfed by the two guns he held. (I had never seen such guns—they weren't AK-47s, or M-16s, but something more serious—huge black things.) Each poster bore the name of the martyr . . . and also—in letters just as big, and illuminated, like the names, in gold—the brand label of the organization: Izzedine al Qassam, which is the military wing of Hamas. In fact, the organization got top billing (they print the posters, after all—and it looks more like a movement that way, not just a dead kid) . . . then, the poster read: *"With pride and fame, we announce the death of the Qassami martyr, Muhammad Fathi Farhat...."*

I had seen posters like this everywhere in Gaza, professionally mounted (billboard-size) on street-lamp poles that stud the median strips of the biggest city streets ... and smaller versions wrapped around school notebooks: they are luridly colorful and collectible, like baseball cards, so kids display them both to honor their heroes, and to announce their own affiliation with Hamas, or Islamic Jihad, or Fatah—whichever one they consider "their team." ... In the Farhat household, the posters were objects of veneration—reminders of honor and sadness. "Sometimes," said Fathi Farhat, "I sit here at night, alone, and I look at the pictures of my sons, and cry."

That was almost all he said through the afternoon. That, and he told (with some bitterness) how he was dismissed from the PA police force after his boy, Muhammad, became the family's first martyr. Maybe Muhammad's suicide mission somehow embarrassed Arafat ... or the PA feared the feral Israeli reaction ... or it had simply escaped their attention, till then, that the Farhat family was in bed with Hamas ... whatever the reason, the old man got the pink slip. It was a weekday afternoon when we made our visit, and there he was, at home, with his bare feet sticking out beneath the hem of his *galabeya* robe ... clearly, the career of raising martyrs hadn't been as good for him as it had for his wife.

"I don't want condolences, I want congratulations," she

announced to mourners who crowded into the family's old home in Shijaya after Muhammad's funeral. "It is a victory!"

When I asked her to describe Muhammad's mission, she told me how she knew a month in advance, watched over him like a baby and strengthened him, till the moment of his last good-bye . . . and on the night of the mission, she stood in the old home, waiting fearfully, listening to the TV until, at last, a news broadcast told her that he had succeeded—i.e., he was dead. What she had feared was he might be wounded, or captured, and deprived of his ticket to heaven.

I asked again: *What was the mission?*

"Ah . . . Muhammad was alone, and he got to the settlement Atzmona, and he killed a number of soldiers."

It wasn't quite that way. Muhammad did get to that settlement in southern Gaza, on a Thursday night in early March 2002. He cut the wire and snuck in, with an assault rifle and grenades. But he didn't attack the troops on guard there. He went to a school on the settlement grounds—he didn't kill any soldiers, at all. The school was for one hundred and forty students who had graduated high school (most were exactly his age, nineteen) who had chosen to delay going into the army, to study Judaism and leadership skills. There was a competition to get into that school. They were kids with a lot of potential . . . It was eleven-thirty at night. He went to one of the dormitory houses and threw a grenade in. The building caught fire. A boy named Arik Krugliak—a yeshiva kid who also used to volunteer with the ambulance corps—was burned to death. Then, Muhammad sprayed a hail of bullets into the burning dorm. Eran Picard, the child of two French doctors who had moved to Israel, got a bullet in the neck and later died at a hospital. Another child of French immigrants, Ariel Zana, died quicker, when Muhammad emptied a magazine into him—nineteen bullets. Then Muhammad moved on to another dorm room, but six kids were inside, and they blocked the door and kept him out. Asher Marcus, a boy from the Jerusalem neighborhood of Kiryat Moshe, was trapped outside that room, and Muhammad shot him dead. Forty kids were hiding under tables in the lecture hall, where they'd been listening to a disquisition on the Passover Haggadah—the three-thousand-year-old story of Moses leading the Jews out of Egypt. Muhammad shot out the lecture hall windows, then threw in two grenades. Tal Kurtzweil, a boy from B'nei Brak, who dreamed of being a pilot, took most of the force of one grenade. And though the other students ran to help him, he was dead in a minute. Then a soldier, who had sprinted from his home in the settlement, arrived at the school and shot Muhammad dead. . . . Six teen-age boys were killed. More than a score were wounded—one paralyzed, one lost a foot—and how many millions lost some hope? . . . And even that grim calculus does not include the reaction from Arik Sharon and his government, who commanded a killing machine much more formidable than Muhammad Farhat. Here is the lead of a *Ha'aretz* story written two days after the attack:

Some 42 Palestinians were killed over the weekend in the territories as a result of Israel Defense
Forces operations carried out after a late Thursday
night terror attack against the Atzmona settlement in
Gush Katif. Givati infantry troops operated in the
Gaza Strip, and Paratroopers took control of a large
area in Bethlehem and surrounding refugee camps.

In Tul Karm, a Golani brigade seized control of a
refugee camp; 17 Palestinians and one IDF soldier
died as a result of this operation, and some 1,300
camp residents turned themselves over to the IDF.
Hundreds of these men will remain in detention this
morning, IDF sources indicate.

IDF aircraft fired at least five missiles at targets
around the complex housing Arafat's headquarters in
Gaza City . . .

I didn't know how to tell Muhammad's mother—but I
couldn't see where the victory lay . . . or even how her son
had defended his people. I wussed out and asked, instead,
how her second martyr, Nidal, had died.

Eagerly, she switched to the topic of her firstborn. She
said she was so close to him that if she didn't see him for two
days, she felt she would go crazy with missing him. "But I
could not stop him from defending. I could only support."
. . . I asked again, what happened to him—what was his mission? And she told me he was not a soldierly type, but sober
and scholarly, a technical man. She told me he was married,

with four daughters and a son. She looked toward his poster, and said he was quiet and calm, and funny and honest. She smiled—the first smile I'd seen from her—and turned again to the posters, so my eyes would follow hers and see them anew. "Our martyrs—they're not criminals. They don't look like they belong with guns . . ."

I tried to speak as softly as she had spoken: "Did Nidal die with guns?"

The story came all at once—it took a minute or two. My interpreter, Safwat, couldn't ask her to pause so he could translate. He held up his hand so I would be silent—and then he told me, also, all in one gulp. . . . Nidal was a leader of the technical staff of Hamas—the bomb staff, you could call it. His mother called it, "thinking of new ways to struggle." They had been shooting homemade rockets (they called them Qassam rockets, after the name of their group) onto the soldiers and settlers in Gaza. But the Israelis took and cleared more land around their settlements and base camps—for "security zones" that were wider than the rockets' range. So Nidal dreamed up a new delivery method. They would get a little drone—a remote-controlled airplane—and they would fly the little plane over the security zone, to fire their rocket down onto the Jews. The problem was, in Gaza, there was no such hobby-plane. The plane had to come from Israel.

Nidal was clever and patient. He thought a mail order from Gaza for a toy plane might arouse suspicion. So he didn't write away for an airplane. He mailed a request (and payment) to a hobby store in Tel Aviv for a replacement set of wings. And after the wings came, he waited. Months passed before another member of his group mailed another request—this for a replacement fuselage, with motor. When the body of the plane finally arrived, that was the great day. Six members of the group gathered in an apartment to put the parts together. They had to test the radio control they'd fashioned. They needed to test for delivery range. At long last, they unwrapped their wings, and slotted them into the fuselage . . . which blew up. All six of them died.

I was bent to my notebook as I wrote down the story. Then I pretended to write more. I didn't know how to look at her. I didn't know what to say. This was the glorious martyrdom of her firstborn—*with pride and fame, we announce . . .* that the Shin Bet fucked him with a toy plane.

I thought later, I should have told her how it made me feel—though my feelings weren't the story, I thought a lot of others might share them. Most people deplore a waste. . . . I thought, maybe I should have said, there was no point telling me about his sweet personality. Dead kids don't have personality anymore. They don't have anything—no "feelings of nationality." But I didn't know how to say any of that. And I didn't tell her—I couldn't look at her and tell her—that in the end, I couldn't see the honor of it—dead kids, and a pile of corpses who used to be enemy kids.

What it made me feel was hopeless—that there wasn't going to be any Palestine while people thought God will reward them for making dead, or for getting dead, any which way. You can't build a country on the dead—nor on a pile of the enemy dead. . . . Nor on martyrdom, nor victimhood . . . nor on the obverse side of that coin—the fantasy of slaughter. . . . I should have told her the same thing I would have told Sharon: that it seems to me, you can't make a nation—not a strong or good one—based on whom you hate, or how many of them you kill.

But I didn't have the wit, or grit. I only did what reporters do: another question—*Just one more, ma'am.* . . . If Nidal got blown up, when did they get that picture: that one on the poster, with those guns? . . .

The Mother of Martyrs never heard that question. It would have shown how little I really knew about Palestine and fantasy—I would have lost honor . . . so Safwat, my interpreter, saved me. He stood, and began our good-byes. And only afterward, he explained to me: "Those are not real guns. They are carved from wood. All the photographers' studios have them."

III

What is a Jewish state?

In early April, 1949, the first Israeli Knesset confronted a great and fundamental issue. The one hundred and twenty members of that parliament had taken their seats only two months before. Now, they had to ratify the armistice agreements that ended the birth-war of 1948. With their votes, they would write their borders into international law. As it turned out, they would also vote to define their nation.

There were three armistice deals to consider. The northern border was not too problematic: for the most part, it would follow the line negotiated by and between the British and French, when those two nations took over this region from the Turks, after World War I. In the south, there was also little question where the border should run: it would (mostly) follow the old line that Britain had drawn as the mandatory power in Palestine. . . . But the eastern border—between the new State of Israel and the Kingdom of Jordan—was a mess, and a heartache.

That Green Line (so named for its color on their maps) zigzagged through the old Palestine, from village to village, sometimes farm-to-farm—and through the heart of Jerusalem—with no rationale, except where the last soldier had stopped shooting, when the U.N. finally made a cease-fire stick. So, every inch of difference between that Green Line and the old mandatory borders of Palestine represented a failure by the Jewish armed forces to defeat the Arab armies, and to beat the clock. Every voting member of the new Knesset was in some way a veteran of that desperate war, and the casualty lists had been enormous. So every inch of difference between that Green Line and the old borders was also ground that friends had fought and died for—how could they give up their claims to it now?

The prime minister, David Ben-Gurion, was not in the habit of pleading his own case before the Knesset. If he was going to play Moses, then his Aaron would be Moshe Sharrett, the foreign minister, who could talk the paint off the walls (in about seven languages, too). But on the great issue of the Green Line, the right-wing opposition party Herut filed a motion of no confidence—so the future of his government was on the line, and B-G, himself, had to defend it. He insisted that the new state had to show to the world a willing-ness to compromise. And the line on that armistice map was the best deal Israel could wangle, right now.

"No! No! No!" the Herutniks were chanting. They had come from a wing of the zionist movement that considered *Eretz Yisrael*—the Land of Israel—sacred and indivisible. Now, with fourteen members in the new legislature, they tried to shout Ben-Gurion down. "Lies! The armed forces of the Jewish people could take all of *Eretz Yisrael!*"

Ben-Gurion turned toward the hecklers and silenced them. "You're right," he said. "The Haganah [the new na-tional army] could conquer all the Land of Israel. But re-member: Deir Yassin is not our policy. . . ." That was the village where Jewish fighters swept in and massacred the Arab residents. (It was the Herutniks' own commando group, the Irgun, that did the killing.) . . . "So, we will occupy the whole of the Land of Israel, and there will be elections—and in our own Knesset we will be a minority."

The Herutniks weren't buying. "No! No! No!" they shouted. "There are millions of Jews all over the world who will come!"

Ben-Gurion said again, "Yes. But the new Knesset will prevent them to come." . . . And that was the end of the fight. B-G had drawn the issue in its starkest terms. They could choose all the land—a larger state—or a Jewish state. . . . By an overwhelming vote, the government survived. And the Green Line became law. No matter what shape the new maps showed—with whatever tortuous and indefensible borders—they voted to be "The Jewish State."

Now, what did they mean by *that?*

In Ben-Gurion's day, it didn't seem so complicated: A Jewish state had to be a place where Jewish people could come and live, not as guests or foreigners (who would be tolerated until the next pogrom), but as proprietors of their own land and destiny. And since their last few hundred years had made the Jewish people a tad antiauthoritarian (they'd had some bad experience with the Czar-Duce-Führer types) . . . the Jewish state would be democratic—which meant, of course, it had to be mostly Jews.

That all seemed neat and simple enough for most of the world to support the idea. That's why the U.N. voted Israel into being, and why the world looked the other way—at least, for the first few years—while the Jews chased a lot of Arabs out, and kept them out. (It's not like the world didn't know about that problem. But the world didn't care to do much about it—except to have the U.N. send over a bunch of tents.) . . . The idea, a nation of Jews—for the Jews, run by the Jews—seemed to make so much sense (it seemed so *needful,* after the holocaust) that even the Jews couldn't argue it to a standstill.

Not that they didn't argue, of course. They argued nonstop—not just about their borders, but whether the land inside those borders could be owned by private citizens. Or if the land was to be owned by the kibbutzim—the collective farms—should they be allowed to hire private labor? And what about the Arabs who didn't run away—should they be allowed to own anything? . . . They argued about their new constitution, or constitution-to-be (that one, they did haggle to a standstill—there's no constitution today). . . . They argued in Yiddish about their new-old language (in which ancient scroll could you find the word *tankim*—the Hebrew plural for tanks?) and they argued in Hebrew about Yiddish (that old language was an emblem of their slavery—it had to be stamped out!) . . . They argued about the nation's currency (What should that be called?) and how much of it they could spend on immigration, on streets or schools, on water for farming, or the overcrowded buses in Tel Aviv. There was a good whining dustup about the lamentable dearth of culture that was reflected in the new tax on classical records. And of course they argued with personal fury about who should do what, and even more, who should run what. (Why should *that schlemiel* hold such a responsible job?) . . . But they couldn't come to grips—never *nearly* argued out—what it meant to be a Jewish state.

There were a few deep thinkers who did try to raise that issue—Martin Buber, the famous philosopher, for one. He contended that the purpose of Jews on this planet (and in their state) must be *justice*—and their success would be judged first and always by their treatment of non-Jews—*justice for the Arabs of Palestine!* He started a political party to promote that. . . . Buber's writings were honored and studied all over the world—but as a pol in Israel, he was a bust. Who could think about justice for the Arabs, when it was Arabs trying to drive the Jews into the sea?

In those days, there wasn't—didn't seem to be—much confusion about who the Jews were, or what their purpose had to be. They were the tragic remnant of a cultured European people—the whole world saw them, all bones and woe, in the newsreels every week or two, after Hitler bought the farm in '45 . . . and then, there they were on the world's screens again, streaming off the boats in Haifa harbor, only to have guns pressed into their hands for their new struggle—a fight to the death with invading Arab armies. The infant zionist nation didn't have much affluence, or even comfort, on offer to its new citizenry. But it had what riches couldn't buy—a mission: the survival of the Jewish people.

But that mission brought up another topic to argue—religion. Not that the founders meant to take up the matter. It simply obtruded. Because Jewishness, after all, isn't just an ethnicity—a certain gene pool—nor could it be solely about how much of that gene pool was wiped out by some tyrant and his gas-chamber goons. Jewishness is also about adherence (or not) to a faith . . . and certain laws, and some traditions that pose as law . . . and chicanery that poses as tradition, too. So, if you rescue the Jewish people, the faith is a stowaway on the same boat. Once you decide you're a Jewish state, then you've got a new issue—Judaism—and that religion sticks like a tar baby, no matter how hard you try to slap it away. God knows, the zionists tried.

A lot of the founders were atheists (or damn near—you

might call them, perhaps, pugnacious secularists) who didn't want their modern utopia muddied up with any rabbinic mumbo jumbo. It's hard to remember now, when orthodox folk—religious settlers—claim they're the heritors and heroes of the zionist dream . . . but orthodox Judaism, the rabbis and yeshivas, were zionism's first enemy.

At the turn of the twentieth century, when the early pioneers got to Palestine, they found some Jews already in residence—mostly in Jerusalem—but they were ultra-religious dreamers, who dwelt in near–medieval squalor near the ruins of the ancient temple, so they could listen for the bells of the donkey on which the Messiah would ride into town. To zionist eyes, those bearded, beknickered and frock-coated Jews, with their curling sideburns and beaver-fur hats, were (at best) an embarrassment—they represented precisely what the New Jew was supposed to supplant. And (at worst) those Jews were a serious problem—because they didn't want a Jewish state. They wanted to live and pray amid the holy stones, and to get along with the Arabs, and the ruling Turks (or, thereafter, with the British) . . . and by their mere existence, and long history in that land, they seemed to contradict all the zionist urgency—the movement's fundamental claim that only in a nation-state of Jews, to be run by Jews, could the Jewish people survive.

Back in Europe, the face-off between the zionists and the orthodox faith was even more dramatic. In the *shtetls* and city ghettos, the rabbis were waging war, house-to-house (or, actually, son-by-son), *to stop emigration to Palestine*. It was a fight about competing visions of the future—and what Jews should do in the meantime. In the orthodox vision, Jews were supposed to live by the laws of Moses, study the Torah (and a few thousand pages of commentary about it), and pray to God to send the Messiah—their (only) salvation. The idea of a Jewish state, based not on study but on labor (with your hands!) . . . based not on God's law but on the principles of the Enlightenment—on Rousseau (May his name be stricken forever from the lips of Mankind!) . . . the idea of Jews toiling and fighting for a land of their own—so they could *write their own laws*—the rabbis regarded as a disgraceful heresy.

Of course, the enmity went both ways. Theodor Herzl, the inventor of modern zionism, wrote of the future homeland as a nation where the rabbis would be confined to their synagogues (as the soldiers would be confined to their barracks). All through the 1920s and '30s, the zionist agitators weren't calling for a Jewish state, but a "Hebrew state" (so their movement would never be confused with religion). And as to rabbinic law—the sanctity of the Sabbath, the separation of the sexes, or kosher food—their flagrancy was complete. In his splendid 1971 book, *The Israelis: Founders and Sons,* Amos Elon wrote about one group of zionist pioneers who marked the occasion of Yom Kippur (the day of atonement and fasting, the highest of high holidays) with a sojourn to the Western Wall, where they picnicked on ham sandwiches.

By the time of the nation's founding, those battles

seemed to be over—and it looked like the orthodox faith had lost. The reason, once again, was Hitler—he didn't care if Jews worked on Saturday, or studied near the synagogue's eastern wall. Either way, they were going to the death camps (where most of the rabbis were killed off, too). Three years after Hitler's demise, when the founders wrote their Declaration of Independence, there was no mention of the laws of Moses, but there was a claim that Israel would know how to defend itself. There was a vow to safeguard holy places, and a guarantee of equality for all citizens—"irrespective of religion." There was a promise to be faithful to the charter of the U.N. But the only reference (last paragraph!) to "faith in Almighty God" was rewritten by the Provisional Council of State to the acceptably vague compromise—"trust in the Rock of Israel."

Ben-Gurion, boss of that council, and first signatory of that Declaration, was a man who had little personal use for the rabbis and their rules. His own marriage, for example, was a civil ceremony in New York. Soon after, he would flout Jewish law again by abandoning his (pregnant) wife for his true love, Palestine, and the nation he meant to build there. When one of his cronies talked him into a synogogue, to give thanks on the eve of the first Knesset session, he remarked that it was the first time he'd been to *shul* in *Eretz Yisrael*. (At that point, he'd dwelt in that land for more than forty years.) ... So it came as something of a shock when his movement comrades—and all the other new citizens of the new state— found out that Ben-Gurion would cut a deal with the ultra-orthodox. In fact, by the time he signed that Declaration of Independence, B-G was already deep in dickering with the rabbis—and in the view of secular zionists, he'd already given away the store.

It happened in the year before independence—a U.N. commission was on its way to Palestine to research a possible partition and creation of a state for the Jews. The zionists feared that the ultra-religious would tell the U.N. *goyim* that there was no need for a Jewish state—that, in fact, such a concept was *against the faith—an affront to God* (which, inconveniently, was what the hyper-religious believed). So Ben-Gurion signed a letter to the Agudat Yisrael, the political arm of the ultras, in which he guaranteed that the new state would declare Saturday as a day of rest, that the government would serve only kosher food, and the new ministry of education would keep its hands off the Agudat's schools. And that was just the warm-up. He also turned over, lock-stock-and-barrel, all matters of family law—birth and adoption, death and burial, *marriage and divorce*—to the rabbis and religious courts.

As Ben-Gurion saw it, the deal worked fine. The Agudat rabbis met with the U.N., and though they didn't ask for a Jewish state, they didn't rail against it, either. . . . And the fact was, Ben-Gurion wanted the religious inside his tent. He feared that a schism between the Jewish state and the Jewish faith would split the new society he had envisioned. Anyway, there were orthodox Jews all over the world. He wanted them to feel this was their nation, too. (Some of them were rich—they could send money!) . . . And as a practical matter (he was a practical pol), he could use the ultra-religious votes in the new Knesset. To bring the Agudat into his coalition, he would not only guarantee autonomy for their schools, but government subsidies—serious loot. When the ultras demanded special units in the army (Their children had to eat kosher food!), B-G did them one better—the *whole army* would eat kosher food. He also bent (not to say twisted) a couple of basic principles: equal rights and duties for women; and *everyone* must go to the army. . . . Now, the Agudat boys in yeshiva (scholars of the Holy Word)—along with all the daughters of the ultra-religious—would no longer have to serve.

He gave them, in sum, everything he could give. The result? . . . The new Knesset spent more time discussing the Sabbath laws than any other issue. (Now that the state had declared Saturday a day of rest, what were they going to do to enforce it?) . . . Then, the ultra-religious wanted driving (and working, and cooking with fire, and any fooling around, too) banned by law on Saturdays. . . . Then, they wanted the army to stop for the Sabbath, and the state airline, and the radio. . . . And then, too, there was a problem with vandalism—manhole covers, and such, disappeared, because they had Hebrew writing on them—the Holy Tongue on a sewer vent! (Most ultra-religious spoke Yiddish; Hebrew they reserved for Godly matters). . . . And, by '49, there were riots in Jerusalem, when (because of daylight saving time) cinemas opened an hour before the Sabbath sundown. One movie fan got his arm broken, fighting off a devout Jew who was trying to strangle him. . . .

It turned out, there's a problem when you bring the rabbis into the tent. Immediately, they demand to know: *What are all these Enemies of God doing inside my tent?*

For years, whenever newspaper work brought me to Israel, I stayed at a certain hotel. It was an affiliate of an American chain—one of a dozen concrete high-rise hostelries that stud the beach road in Tel Aviv, like a Brobdingnagian set of bad teeth. Over time, I made friends at that hotel, and they began to clue me in on how they lived as Jews in a Jewish state.

There was a telephone operator named Aviva, who was a hefty redhead, probably in her sixties, who favored me with the play-by-play of her marital woes. Actually, her marriage was over. I can't remember, now, whether the husband had died or disappeared—but he'd been out of the picture for years. What I do remember is the long and costly drama of Aviva trying to get unmarried. She had to fly her (former) husband's brother into Tel Aviv—from Brazil. (The plane ticket cost a month of her wages. And that didn't count the money she needed to *schmear* the husband's brother for his time and trouble.) . . . Actually, what I remember best is how Aviva explained it: she said she had to fly in the brother-in-law, so he could "throw the shoe." . . . I had no idea what she meant. To me, that was an equestrian term. But this had nothing to do with a horseshoe. It was (it had to be) *his* shoe . . . because if her husband was nowhere to be found, then she became the "property" of the husband's brother, and the rabbis would not release her from the marriage until he (the brother-in-law) had thrown his shoe at her, and had announced, in a rabbinically satisfactory manner, that he had no interest in her marital favors and no intention of replacing his brother in her bed. (The cost to Aviva was just a bit of the price for Ben-Gurion's little deal.)

There was another switchboard operator—this one young, quite lovely and unmarried—who used to take me, at four in the morning, to south Tel Aviv, which was kind of a slum . . . and we'd breakfast at a Romanian joint, on splendid pork tenderloins. Of course, no one used the word *pork*—one asked for "white steak." I couldn't figure out why it tasted so delicious. Was that pork somehow "spiced" for me—by that girl, and the hour in that slum, and the tiny thrill of sin against the kosher laws? Or was it simply excellent meat? . . . When I asked the Romanian boss, he swore me to secrecy, then told me about a kibbutz in the south where they raised pigs—or, as he phrased it, with characteristic Israeli swagger, "They are Jews who make the best pork in the world."

I had to call that kibbutz. How could they get away with it? I knew there was a law (another deal with the religious) that made it illegal for Jews to raise pigs anywhere on the Land of Israel. It turned out, this kibbutz didn't raise its livestock *on* Israeli soil. The pigs lived on platforms—*over* the Land of Israel. I asked one official there: *How could a nice Jewish kibbutz end up in a business like that?* He told me, firmly: "It's not a business." . . . No. What the kibbutz did was *research*—a study of how pigs grow. (Advancing the science of agronomy was a mission of the kibbutz movement!) So, young pigs were brought to the kibbutz and studied, till they were full-grown. Of course, once they were weighty with meat, they were no longer interesting for study—so they were disposed of (at market price, to fund further studies)— and, for the sake of science, more young pigs were procured. Research went on continuously.

I went into research, myself—not growing pigs. But it seemed to me the business of Jewish law—and what Jews did to live their lives within (or despite) that law—was one great story of modern Israel. In those days, the Hebrew papers would be filled every Sunday with news of the latest violent Sabbath clash between the orthodox and motorists who tried to drive through Jerusalem. (The orthodox were the first people who tried to bend the will of the Jewish state by throwing stones.)

There were also more or less constant—often ugly— fights about "Who Is a Jew?" (and thus eligible for the bene- fits of immigration and citizenship, and to be treated with any decency in Israel). For instance, say there's a young man who is the child of a Jewish mother, but the mother was born an American Christian, and she converted to *marry* a Jew— but the conversion was overseen by a rabbi who was not or- thodox, but merely conservative, or (God forbid!) a rabbi of *reform* Judaism . . . but the kid grows up Jewish, and feels Jewish—in fact, he feels so strongly Jewish that he moves to Israel, and he gets in under the Law of Return (because,

after all, his dad was Jewish, and his dad's mother, and so on
and so forth—and anyway, he's just about the right age for
the army, so they take him in without question) . . . and then,
the kid gets out of the army, where he's met a nice girl, and
they want to get married . . . but the rabbi-mafia in Israel
won't give him a kosher-stamp as a Jew, because in their eyes,
he's not the child of a Jewish mother—because *her* conversion wasn't overseen by one of their own mob . . . so how can
he marry a nice Jewish girl in Israel—where there's no other
way to get married, *except* by that mob—and the rabbis now
demand to be *schmeared* to convert *him* . . . to which extor-
tion this boy will probably knuckle under (What else can he
do? Take it to the High Court? The rabbis don't recognize
the authority of the High Court!) . . . because, by now, the
pols in Israel have cut so many deals that the rabbis, by now,
control the business of "Who Is a Jew?" . . .

If it's not one poor schlub but the whole state that has to
knuckle under, then the path around the rabbis and their
rules can cost millions. To take just the simplest example—
say the excavators for a new road dig up some old ruins. (That
happens almost anywhere you dig here.) And in the ruins,
somewhere, there is evidence of people who died—say, a
fragment of human bone. Then, the whole road will be built
on piers. By Jewish law, a gravesite must be covered with
earth to prevent impurities escaping, because in the days of
the Temple (a mere two or three thousand years ago), there
were priests, and a priestly class—people named Cohen are
thought to descend from this class—and priests could not be

fouled by impurities from the dead. So, despite the fact that there are no priests, now the taxpayers must shell out to build the road on piers (like a bridge that may run for half-a-mile), so people named Cohen may drive on it.

There's a pattern that emerges from all of these cases. It seems that it's always easier to cut a deal with the rabbis than to fight it out. For secular people, these issues—even losing every fight about these issues—only add to life's inconvenience: there are places where they can't drive on Saturday, or they can't buy gasoline, or they have to pay more taxes because the *haredim*—the ultra-religious—are *schnorring* off the state for their whole lives . . . or the secular folk spend more days in the army, because there are so many *haredim* who won't serve at all. (When Ben-Gurion exempted the orthodox yeshiva students, there were about three or four hundred such boys. Now, there may be thirty or forty *thousand*—and they still don't do a day's service.) It's annoying—for a lot of citizens, it's infuriating. The Shinui party more than doubled its seats in the latest Knesset—mostly on the strength of its promise to stop orthodox "freeloading."

But no matter how broad the opposition to the ultra-religious and their rules, there is always more passion on the other side. For one thing, the *haredim* are sure they've got God on their side—the Torah tells them so. They are *saving souls* (no matter how unwilling the possessors of those souls may be)—so they have the good-Godly righteousness of America's seat-belt busybodies, or the antismoking Nazis—everybody must live by their fears. (*Haredim* literally means "the fear-struck.") . . . Anyway, who could argue with these rabbis? They argue for a living. What is Jewish scholarship but a nonstop, nitpicky, all-sides-considered-and-dismissed lifelong *wrangle*? It's more than a living—this is their life. To choose to dispute with them, you'd have to be a head case. It's like entering a sweepstakes for lunch with Alan Dershowitz. (Second prize, two lunches.) The fact is, for the *haredim*, these issues aren't matters of preference; it's not about convenience, or fairness, or democracy. If they lose a fight about the Sabbath laws, they think—they *know*—God will Smite Them Down. . . . In his classy debut book, *1949: The First Israelis*, the historian and journalist Tom Segev quotes the head of the Agudat Yisrael, Rabbi I. M. Levin, plaintively explaining in one of those early Knesset fights: "Can you not understand that for us the Sabbath stands for the very existence of the Jewish people, and its violation means the end of the state and the destruction of the nation? . . . For us it is a matter of life and death."

There's another pattern that emerges here—you could call it a habit of mind—that may be as Jewish as the Torah itself. That is the willingness to live amid strictures and exigencies that grow more twisted, more rigid and onerous, with each little deal or concession—or every exercise of force by one's antagonist—and still, no one does anything to change it (not fundamentally) . . . and it gets to the point where no one from the outside can look *for one minute* at this contorted mess, without exclaiming: *Why don't you do something about it?* . . . It is the habit of living with impossibilities. You could view it as adaptive behavior—the product of two thousand years or so, when things were trending basically worse. You could even say, without this habit of mind, there might be no Jews today. (Or, perhaps, there would have been many more: without this willingness to live from bad to worse, there wouldn't have been six million Jews left in Europe to be slaughtered by the Nazis.)

It's a habit of mind summed up in a phrase that you hear in Israel from time to time—an old Yiddish saying that made it into Hebrew—*"Either the lord of the manor will die, or his dog."* What it means is, *something will happen* to change the status quo—why deal with it now? It's easier to live for the meantime with this difficulty or that impossibility—we'll just cut a corner here or there, and get around it. Here's a small example: on my last visit to Tel Aviv, I moved into an apartment house—four stories, eight flats—not a bad building, in a good neighborhood. I was surprised to see a vacant, trash-strewn apartment on the first floor front; and I was dismayed to find out that the path to the main door, past that eyesore, was broken, with no drainage—so, in any rain, one waded to the building through a small lake. It turned out there was a dispute between the owner of the apartment and the building association—this had been the situation for years. With the American assumption that this could be fixed, I asked my neighbor what was to be done. Of course, he told me, with an eloquent shrug: "The lord of the manor will die, or his dog—something will happen."

The problem is, this habit of mind is not applied solely to

little examples. Moshe Dayan's classic answer to all inquiries about the occupied territories—"I'm waiting for a phone call"—was just another way to say the same thing. In fact, you run into this attitude on almost all great Israeli issues— wherever resolution would require Jews fighting with Jews. Say some settlers on the West Bank are taking potshots at the neighboring Arab village, so they can start a fight, and the army will come in to take more land as a "security zone." With an hour's focused labor you could find out what's happening—and, if you didn't mind a fight with Jews, you could stop it, too. But nobody (no one in recent govern- ments, anyway) wants to make a fight with the settlers. It's always easier to send in the army again, or to keep send- ing money—and water, electricity, machinery, teachers . . . whatever it is they're demanding today. Of course, you agree that Jews should settle where they like in the whole Land of Israel. . . . Then, alas, you might have a problem with the Americans—because they say they want you to stop building up the settlements. And you can't have a fight with the Amer- icans—they could cease to send money!—so you say, well, you're *trying* to stop those crazy settlers. Of course, you agree entirely with your American friends—the aim is peace! . . . The problem is, the two groups with whom you agree don't agree—you could call it a Road Map to disaster. But sometimes there's nothing to do but buy time—with a few pleasant lies, wherever needful . . . and either the landlord will die, or his dog. It's a nice Jewish way to get along.

I asked Batya Gur about this phrase of folk-wisdom.

She's Israel's preeminent crime novelist—an artist in He-brew—but she has enough Polish *yiddishkeit* left in her to know where some of that Hebrew came from. Sure enough, she asked straightaway, "You know the story, don't you?" . . . (Sure enough, I didn't.)

"Well, there was a great landowner in the Pale," she said. By "the Pale" she meant that area of Russia—some of it now Poland—where Jews were allowed to abide in the czar's day. "One day, this landlord calls in his Jew. . . ." (The phrase "his Jew" was also considered. In those days, peasants belonged to the landlord, who had all power over their lives.) "And he says, 'I want you to teach my dog to talk Yiddish. And if you don't, I'll kill you.' " . . .

"So the Jew says, 'Well, it's an interesting problem—and I'll have to consider . . . ,' and he goes home, where he tells his family. They immediately go into mourning. No one can teach a dog to speak—much less Yiddish . . . he's dead. The wife is tearing her clothes.

"The next day he goes to the landlord, and tells him: 'I've thought about it, sire—and I'll have your dog speaking Yid-dish in five years.'

" 'Agreed,' says the landlord, and the Jew goes home again. His wife is ecstatic. He's alive! She's already lifting the black shroud from over the door—when she asks: 'Well, what did you tell him?'

" 'I said I'd make the dog speak Yiddish in five years.' She puts the shroud back. 'How could you promise that? Are you crazy? You've made me a widow!'

" 'So you'll kill me with worry?' he says. 'It's five years! . . . Either the landlord will die, or his dog—something will happen.' "

On matters of dispute with the rabbis and the faith, there's no other attitude available. It's always easier to get along, somehow—and buy a little more time. Here's one more story I learned, long ago, in that hotel. I've always remembered it because it taught me how far things could go—in fact, how far they had gone in thirty years since Ben-Gurion's deal with the rabbis—while everybody waited for the lord of the manor, or his dog.

In that hotel, as in most of the other big incisors on the beach, a good bit of business was conducted on the Sabbath—with a splendid and elaborate buffet. Of course, by law (by a deal with the rabbis), all those big hotels had to be kosher. But the food could be prepared on Friday, before sundown, and probably a bunch of non-Jews were employed to set it out on Saturday, and to light the little Sterno cans under chafing dishes, and such—all that could be done within the letter of the kosher laws. . . . And so, by midday Saturday, the great dining hall of the hotel would be grandly glutted with good things to eat—and packed with customers. Everybody came, tourists and locals—even religious (who wouldn't sin by cooking at home)—and they'd present themselves, hungry, to a hostess who would ask, at the door: "Meat, or dairy?" . . . Because, of course, it's one of the kosher laws that one must not mix meat with milk. You can't have a nice pastrami with cheese—*can't be done*—that much was clear.

See, the way they did it was, you would answer the hostess at the door, and depending on your answer, she'd hand you a big empty plate from the set for meat—or a dairy plate, just as big and empty. And then, you'd be directed to one side of the hall, or the other, where you could load that plate with all kinds of legal delights—and at the tables on that side, you would find the legal (meat or dairy) silverware, and glassware, and such . . . it all worked like a charm. But then, one day—on one such profitable Sabbath—a customer protested, and crisis ensued.

As I was told the tale, it was actually a tourist, but a religious one. (To be precise, as I was told, it was "one ess-chole from Cleve-lond.") And he protested to the management, because—as he claimed—the steam from the chafing dish of Swedish meatballs was drifting over the hall, all the way to the dairy tables . . . where it befouled—it made unkosher— his blintzes! . . . *The hotel was in sin!*

Oy! . . . Well, of course, the rabbi had to be consulted— that is, the rabbi whom the hotel was required to pay off—on staff, as it were—to make sure the milk plates didn't get piled on the meat plates, and things like that. And this rabbi was, of course, torn by dual loyalties—grateful to his employer but faithful to the laws of Moses, and to the rabbi-mafia that *caused* his employment . . . and anyway, if he'd been much of a scholar, he wouldn't have been a hotel rabbi—and the upshot was, he didn't know what to do. By this time, it was also Sunday—you can't phone up a rabbi on Saturday—and the buffet was long gone. How should he know if the steam was drifting? . . . So, he decided to call in the Chief Rabbi of Tel Aviv.

Now, that was *a rabbi*—municipally appointed precisely as a mark of his prestige, and great learning—and so he knew, the wisdom of great rabbis in the golden age of scholarship would narrow this question. After all, even if it were conceded—let us concede it—*the steam was drifting . . .* still, the prohibition against mixing milk with meat ("Thou shalt not boil the kid in its mother's milk") pertained to meat or dairy products *that a Jew might eat.* Therefore, this problem—this threatening protest from the "ess-chole from Cleve-lond"—was only concerned with food . . . and so this question must devolve to one further and crucial inquiry: *Is the Steam Food?* . . . The Chief Rabbi also was enough of a pol to know that he wasn't going to shut down the Sabbath buffet at every big hotel in Tel Aviv with only *his* neck on the line—so he called in the Council of Torah Sages.

Now, these were the Rabbis of Rabbis—a dozen of them, as I recall, and *nationally* appointed—in recognition of their vastly formidable knowledge and unassailable reputations, and great flowing beards that bespoke decades of scholarship . . . and (as the Chief Rabbi of Tel Aviv was doubtless glad to hear) *they agreed* that the question devolved to: *Is the steam food?* . . . However, this question led (as do all questions, among great sages of Jewish law) to another question, which had to be researched—and that was: *What is food?* To be precise, the Sages had to determine—what is the *proper test* of What is Food? . . . and that (like all questions of Jewish law, with Sages) required further research and intense discussion.

By this time, it was midweek, and the hotel staff was going quietly crazy. Were they shopping for their *shabbas* do? Or were they out of business? . . . The man who really had his neck on the line was a bright young guy from Brooklyn—let's call him Itzhak—who was the Manager of Food and Beverage ("food 'n' bev," as he used to say) . . . who said a lot of unkind things about rabbis, in general—and particularly that week, as he imagined his budget hanging upsidedown for ritual slaughter. This Sabbath buffet was his cash cow. . . . But (Praised be His Name!) good news was soon forthcoming, because the Council of Torah Sages had come to agreement.

The question was, indeed: *Is the steam food?* . . . And in the wisdom of the ages, there was, indeed, a proper test for What is Food? . . . It was thus:

"If a dog will not eat it, it is not food."

Now, it should be noted (as it was noted by the rabbis) that the converse does not apply. For there are many things that a dog will eat that are not proper food. But if a dog will *not* eat it, it is *not* food.

And so, late that same worrisome week, the staff was commanded to set up the buffet. And on the buffet table, under rabbinical supervision, they lit the Sterno under a full chafing dish of Swedish meatballs. But for this chafing dish there was also a tent of cellophane erected, so the steam from the Swedish meatballs could be trapped, with rabbinical supervision—in fact, the Chief Rabbi of Tel Aviv was in attendance—and the steam from the meatballs would gather in the tent, from the top of which a tube protruded . . . and the tube wound down from the top of the tent, past the edge of the buffet table, almost to the floor, where its last couple of feet were wrapped with wet, cold dish towels . . . so the steam would be condensed, and it would drip (as it did drip) into a bowl on the floor.

"Brrring in the dog!" the Chief Rabbi commanded—and the doors to the kitchen opened to admit a frisky young mutt. In excitement, he nosed around the corners of the room, the chair legs, table legs—they probably all smelled of food to him—but at last he cantered to the meat buffet table, and there was the bowl on the floor. Sure enough, he approached. He gave the bowl a sniff—then turned and pursued his sniffing elsewhere . . .

The dog did not eat it! It was NOT FOOD. . . . They were *not unkosher.* And they were *back in business!* . . . There were profuse thanks for the rabbis—and, of course, invitations to that Saturday's buffet—while they shook hands, all around, and the rabbis went off to guard the laws of Moses elsewhere. And, of course, they didn't stop to check the chafing dish—not the meatballs part, but the bottom of the chafing dish, where the liquid sits, to warm the food above with steam—which was a good thing. Because, if they had, Itzhak Food 'n' Bev's neck would have been cut, for sure. He had put Pine-Sol in the bottom of that chafing dish.

The problem is, while the Israeli majority waits for the land-lord or the dog, things keep happening—lesser changes are always being made by accretion. Another street closes in Jerusalem. (Big deal—what's one street more or less on a Saturday?) . . . Then, the religious take over a municipal swimming pool. (Well, we have to understand their sensitivi-ties—men and women must not swim together.) . . . Then, they demand their own bus system: men and women must sit separately on their buses. ("Their buses" are much like "their tent"—it's any bus on which they find themselves.) . . . Then, the government's director-general for antiquities makes a deal that any archeology dig must stop, while the *haredim* swarm over the place, to make sure no gravesites will be dis-turbed. (The director-general says that peace deal with the orthodox is his "ultimate achievement" on the job.) . . . What has happened by accretion is, the Jewish state has been forced to conform to Jewish law.

What also has happened is precisely the schism Ben-Gurion feared (if he *didn't* make the deal)—there are now two societies of Jews in Israel. One is strictly for orthodox folk—and the other allows varying views on the faith, but it doesn't want anything to do with the ultras. I had a visit in north Tel Aviv with Uri Avnery, a famously left-wing pub-lisher and former member of Knesset who is now the guiding spirit of Gush Shalom (the Peace Bloc—the same group that got under the skin of the air force commander Dan Halutz). "You know," Uri said, "when I see one of those Jews in the black coat, with the hat and *peyus*, I look at him as I would look at a tribesman in New Guinea—they have no more connection to me than that." And in this rare instance, Avnery finds himself in the majority. Opinion surveys consistently find that secular Israelis consider the *haredim* a threat to Israel—a menace graver than the Arabs.

Of course, the enmity goes both ways. The leaders of Israel's secular society are regularly and hatefully denounced by the rabbis—as murderous foes of Jews and Judaism. That sort of rhetoric spurred the assassination of Prime Minister Rabin, in 1995—after which event the rabbis professed themselves astonished, dismayed, and blameless. (Just 'cause they called him an Enemy of God didn't mean they wanted anyone to *hurt* him!) . . . With prayer and study, that spasm of contrition passed, and the ultras went back to painting swastikas on the reform Jewish seminary, or fire-bombing synagogues that were not sufficiently orthodox—and denouncing pols, too. *"God has sorely tried us,"* announced Rabbi Ovadia Yosef, the spiritual leader of the Shas party (and a former Chief Rabbi) in a speech broadcast to his followers around the nation and the world. *"He brought upon us this Yossi Sarid, this Satan—may his name be erased!"* [Mr. Sarid was the leftish minister of education, at that time—just before the Purim holiday in the spring of the year 2000.] ". . . *And how can we continue to restrain ourselves, how much more can we take? How can we continue to suffer from this wicked person? God will uproot him!* . . . *Haman is cursed?"* [Haman is the killer of Jews in the Purim story.] *"Yossi Sarid is cursed! . . . God will confound his*

plans, and strike his thoughts. He will repay him as he de-
serves. Just as He showed us with Haman's death—the re-
venge wrought upon Haman will be wrought upon him. And
when you say, 'Cursed is Haman!' after reading of the Book of
Esther—say, too, 'Cursed is Yossi Sarid!' "

As for old Uri Avnery—they don't even bother to call
down curses on him. For years, they've simply called him
"The Canaanite." And everybody—even a bad Jew—knows
what must be done to Canaanites. They must be *driven out*
of the land, as God commanded in the Torah, in the Book of
Numbers, Chapter 33.

In fact, that's the very same chapter that religious settlers—and all the right-wing orthodox—cite as their personal imperative and political program. For it commands
them—it commands the Jews—to settle the land and drive
out the old inhabitants. It's the same chapter cited by one of
Arik Sharon's cabinet ministers when he traveled to Washington to rally opposition to George Bush's new Road Map to
Peace. (Of course, Sharon told Bush he was *for* the Road
Map—but what the hell, it's a *long* map—and the landlord
will die, or the dog. . . .)

Now the LORD spoke to Moses in the plains of Moab
by the Jordan, across from Jericho, saying, "Speak to
the children of Israel, and say to them: 'When you
have crossed the Jordan into the land of Canaan, then
you shall drive out all the inhabitants of the land from
before you, destroy all their engraved stones, destroy

all their molded images, and demolish all their high places; you shall dispossess the inhabitants of the land and dwell in it, for I have given you the land to possess.' "

Now, these are not complicated verses—and there's no two ways to look at them. This is God's commandment. This is Jewish law. And in the eyes of the faithful, there is no choice—for them, or for the Jewish state. Because in that same chapter, God also says to Moses:

But if you do not drive out the inhabitants of the land from before you, then it shall be that those whom you let remain shall be irritants in your eyes and thorns in your sides, and they shall harass you in the land where you dwell. Moreover, it shall be that I will do to you as I thought to do to them.

So, it's either-or—"them or us," as the Herut party slogan says. And how can we call it a Jewish state, if it plays fast and loose with Jewish law? . . .

But if the mission of the Jewish state has changed from the original—a state where Jews may live in safety, and by their own beliefs—to a state that conforms to, and enforces, Jewish law . . . then I'm going to need some help, here, with a question I just can't get around.

So, Rabbi, forgive me—I must have missed this in Sunday school. Could we review? . . . If the Jewish state is about

Jewish law, then how is that different—in any moral sense—
from an Islamic republic?

His surname means silken-gold—or golden-silk (I could
never keep that straight)—either way, it bespeaks his standing in his society, and on the planet. He is one of God's aristo-
crats. Yehuda Meshi-Zahav is an orthodox Jew in Jerusalem.
In fact, by his reckoning, he is an eleventh-generation
Jerusalemite. His forebears were some of those who came
(from the Pale: Russia, Poland, take your pick) not as zionists—they came before the zionists—simply as Jews.

And Meshi grew up in the old neighborhood, in the old
ways—as a Jew, not an Israeli—even though, at the time of
his birth, the state was well established (almost of bar mitzvah age). Still, in Mea Shearim, and the other orthodox
neighborhoods of Jerusalem, while he was a boy, the life was
the old (or timeless) life of the Torah. A righteous man would
have nothing to do with the Godless little Denmark or Swe-
den that Labour zionism seemed to be creating in this place
that should have been (and was in God's eyes) holy.

In fact, Meshi came of age as an enemy of the state. Zionism was The Evil—along with zionist cops, nonreligious
women (with their bare arms!), men with their heads uncovered before God—and people who called themselves Jews,
and yet they drove through Jerusalem (through his neighborhood!) *on Shabbat!* They were all avatars of The Evil. . . .
Those were the early days of throwing stones to enforce the
Sabbath's sanctity—at least in their own few streets—but the

haredim were disorganized. Communication was basically by poster, which the disciples of some rabbi would plaster onto the old stone walls—calling on the faithful to denounce this, or combat that—so some men would get it in their heads to go out and throw stones. It was all so feckless—just a random act of frustration by outcasts who didn't matter— or so it seemed to the powers of the surrounding zionist society . . . until Meshi took over. From the time he was twelve or thirteen years old, his nickname in the neighborhood was "The Operations Officer." The righteous and their rabbis would call him in to lead their demonstrations, and he made their God-addled scholars into *a threat*—a phalanx of black frock coats and beaver-fur hats that was . . . a miserable menace. By the time he was old enough to have his crimes recorded, the cops had opened thirty-four files (prosecutions) against him.

Which makes it more remarkable what has happened now, and where he stands: In his mid-forties, Meshi-Zahav is a hero of the zionist nation. He is the creator and the boss of Zaka, which is a nonprofit cadre of orthodox volunteers who show up at the scene of terror bombings (or big auto accidents—any carnage) to collect and care for the bodies, or parts of bodies—in fact, every shard or smear of bone, brain, blood—in conformity with the laws of the Torah.

It's a terrible job—those bomb scenes are, as the Brits might say, bloody ugly—but it's also, in these latter days (since the high-tech and peace bubbles burst more or less at the same time), one of Israel's few growth industries. And

Meshi has built an empire: He fields a force of hundreds—almost a thousand volunteers, all over the country. He has fund-raising offices overseas. (He's known around the world—he was called to assist in New York after the Nine-Eleven attack, and after the nightclub bombing in Bali, Indonesia.) He operates the most modern (and quickest) beeper-news network in Israel. He has amassed an armada of jeeps and ambulances—and motorcycles for his new flying squad. . . . And he has crushed all competitors (of which there used to be a couple). . . . Meshi is the Microsoft of body parts.

But it's not only as an entrepreneur that he is celebrated. As the public is reminded from time to time, the work Zaka does is a *mitzvah*—a good deed which is commanded by the scriptures. (In fact, such reminders bombard the public. Whenever Israeli TV slips into CNN mode, flipping live, back and forth, from the hospitals, to police headquarters, and back to Fred Furrowbrow at the scene of the latest outrage, there's one thing Fred can always intone while the camera seeks out the grisliest pictures: *"And of course, you see the men from Zaka here, doing their holy work."*) . . . Withal, there's another (bigger) reason why Meshi is a hero—with a sheaf of commendations from politicos of every stripe, up to and including all the last few prime ministers: Meshi is the man who brought the *haredim* into the mainstream of modern Israel. That is, he gave them a part to play in the main event—the conflict.

We met for an interview, over lunch. It took a good two

months to arrange. My chief researcher, who had to do the arranging, was a modern, very bare-armed woman named Pony Brzezinski—and though she knew everybody in the secular elite, or knew somebody who knew them, she didn't know Meshi or any of his crowd. (In a way, that was exactly what I meant to research.) . . . Anyway, she finally got him, which was a tribute to her perseverence. And it was a tribute to Meshi—or to how far he'd come—that he would sit down to break bread, and try to make himself understood, with a nonreligious female and a ham-on-rye Jew from the States.

(Of course, the bread we broke together was kosher—pita bread, in great steaming stacks—along with heaping platefuls of overcooked meat, and coarse-chopped salads, and hummus, and pickles in profusion. Meshi picked the restaurant, a kosher barbecue joint that caters to the sort of *haredim* who actually work, and work up an appetite. He entered to glad greetings from the owner and waiters, cooks and customers. It turned out this was one of his haunts, where he'll bring the whole Zaka crew after a bad bombing—when, for hours, they've been sweeping bits of bomb-charred flesh off the pavement, and such—and he thinks they could use some decompression . . . so he brings them all, shoves together twenty tables, and feeds the boys to bursting—and more often than not, he will also make the very Zaka joke: "This burned flesh smells worse than the last!")

I asked him about how far he'd come, and he said it was a change of heart that went back to the stone-throwing days.

Every Saturday, he'd get arrested. They'd put him in the patrol car, and he'd talk with the cops. And little by little, he divined that the last thing they wanted was to be on the streets, fighting him and his crowd—what they wanted was to go home and have the peace of *Shabbat* with their families. After a while, he got in the habit of staying after demonstrations, even if he *wasn't* arrested, to talk with the cops—his friends. And maybe from those talks, he also came to understand that the bare-armed woman driving by in her car—the Evil One—might have been a nurse who had to work the early shift, and now all she wanted was to get home to *her* family. "I discovered, this Evil, it's even nice," he said. "The hate was from not knowing the other side. I don't regret the demonstrations, I regret the hate. . . ." And to Pony—not for translation—he added: "We hated more than you. Because we didn't know anything."

By the time he'd grown into a young man, he'd got so large about this, he was giving tours of Mea Shearim to groups of secular Israelis. He'd take these Jews through his Jewish neighborhood, and they'd gawk like any know-nothing tourists. (One lady said, "I feel like I'm going to the Amish!") . . . And then, too, Meshi stopped throwing stones. For one thing, every Saturday, the cops closed the streets around the orthodox enclaves. Anyway, Meshi saw that demonstrations were not a career. He knew a bit about the wider world, now—what it cared about—and that topic was terror.

He was in his thirties when the bombings started to

wrack Jerusalem. One of the first and worst was a bus that blew up, in the Friday morning rush hour, and just outside of a school. It was a terrible scene—kids crying amid the dead on the pavement, and bits of bodies everywhere; fire trucks, cop cars and ambulances rending the air with sirens, and jousting for position in a jumble that probably cost lives. (This was 1995, and Israelis weren't organized to cope with such terror.) . . . One woman was brought to a hospital with the bottom of her leg blown off. And doctors phoned back to the scene, to police and firefighters, the city and the army, trying to find that leg, while they could still sew it on—*they could save her leg, if they could find it now!* But no one could find anything in that mess, and that woman lives today as an amputee. . . . Late that afternoon, as a sad Sabbath sundown neared, a *haredi* man, with his black hat and frock coat, walked into a police station. He was pulling behind him one of those shopping carts that Israelis favor—it's a stiff vinyl carton (almost always plaid) on a frame of aluminum, with wheels on the bottom. Anyway, this religious presented himself at the front desk, and to the cop on duty he presented a human leg. Of course, the cop knew right away whose it was. "Where'd you get this?"

"I was walking by that bomb this morning," the *haredi* guy said, "and I found it. But I had to hurry, to buy my *shabbas* cakes. So I put it in my shopping bag, and I carried it all day, till I could return it."

Of course, the cops were outraged. But what could they do? These *haredim* were hopeless, helpless—*like children—*

of this world, they knew nothing! And who could they complain to? Who would help? The rabbis? They were worse than the regular idiots—they knew so much, they knew even less! . . . But there was one religious guy the cops could talk to. They complained to Meshi-Zahav. And he saw their point clearly—not that *haredim* were idiots, no—but they were clueless in a modern emergency. (Yeshiva training didn't cover that sort of thing.) And if they meant to live here, they *ought* to know something. They could even be *helpful*. . . . So, Meshi organized a course to train twenty-five ultra-orthodox men on what to do when something blows up. And those twenty-five became his first volunteers. That was the start of Zaka.

Very soon, there were posters on the old stone walls—*denouncing Meshi*. He was complicitous with the Godless zionists, and their abomination of a state, which was delaying the Messiah and salvation. And the denunciations picked up steam when he announced that Zaka's second act—phase two—would be a course on what to do, how to help, *for ultra-orthodox women*. At that point the rabbis came to scold him, face-to-face—his own rabbi, as a matter of fact. The idea that wives and daughters would be out of the house—*learning!*—was anathema. (Collection of remains for burial is, after all, a commandment of the Torah, and ultra-orthodox women do not study Torah.) Plus, they would be talking to people outside their families—which is a sin. And they might have men teachers, or have to help men who were not of their kin—which was mixing the sexes—a blasphemy! Meshi promised that the class would be only for women. And he wouldn't take women out on the streets to work alongside his male volunteers—that wasn't good enough. Finally, as he recalls the scene, he told the rabbis: "Look, don't fuck with me. I'm from the same house where you grew up." Then he put out his ad, seeking volunteers—and *two thousand* signed up, just from the neighborhood of Mea Shearim. Meshi went back to the rabbis: "So," he said, brandishing his two thousand names. "Do I give the course, or not?" . . . The rabbis caved in, and Zaka was a power.

Meshi is still denounced, from time to time, but his standing with the *haredi* commonfolk remains unchallenged. He gave them a sense of belonging in Israel that they never had before. And he is still employed as a spokesman for the umbrella group of ultra-orthodox who question the legality of a Jewish state—a position that he articulates with fervor. I asked him about my thesis that standards in Israel had changed—that everything changed, since '67, in the long occupation of the Palestinian lands. And by the time Pony finished translating the question, Meshi was already shaking his head.

"The problem isn't '67," he said. "It was 1948. That is when we turned away from the law of the Torah, and tried to replace it with the laws of a state. The people of Israel got the Torah in the Sinai without one centimeter of land. The world knew about the Jewish people without us having one centimeter of land. So, being Jewish, you don't need a state. You can be a Jew in Germany, America, Morocco—the meaning is simply that you're keeping the rules you got from the Torah. That's the only meaning of it.

"Three thousand years ago, we got those laws—and now, instead, we are depending on one hundred and twenty Knesset members. Some of them are following Torah, some of them are not. Some of them are Russians, and we don't even know if they're Jews—so what can you expect?

"If things don't change here, I don't need the land. I can be a Jew anywhere. We had a contract with G-d, years ago, that this land belongs to Jews. Then, we started to break the rules. That's why the Palestinian is taking over now."

Throughout a long lunch, I kept writing down descriptions of Meshi-Zahav—such a notable-*looking* man . . . and I recorded the particulars of his white shirt (he had stripped off his coat), with its pocketful of messages he had to return, and the fringes of the holy garment dangling out from the shirt's hem . . . and the ginger hair, tinged with first-gray in his curling earlocks, which brushed the shoulders of the shirt . . . and mostly, his face, which was big and pale and bony, with a prominent chin, but not pointed—flat and forward, with wisps of ginger-gray beard that began there—goatlike, or *camelish*, a stubborn chin. . . . But the particulars don't add up to how he looked—or what I kept trying to describe in those notes—the earthly force of him. If I had to give it a name, now—what I failed to write down—I would call it the *vigor of his Jewishness*. In fact, I saw it at work. For across the table, I saw Pony lift her shawl from the chair next to her and wrap it around herself. She said she was cold. But it must have been eighty degrees in that restaurant. She wrapped up her shoulders—and then ("I don't know why I'm so cold!")—she brought the shawl up over her head, until just her face was peeking out. Little by little, she'd conformed to what she knew of his rules—what she thought he expected—as she translated.

". . . We'll stick to this land as long as we keep the contract," Meshi was saying. "If we don't, we will lose it."

Then Pony had a question of her own. She asked him: "So, if I know this land is mine—am I Jewish?"

And he answered in the most Jewish way—with an even sharper question. In fact, it was the question with which the *haredim* have challenged Israel for more than fifty years. Meshi said: "Can you run away from being Jewish?"

I told him that for a non-zionist, he was doing well in the Jewish state—and he agreed. He said the head of the prime minister's office called him up, in recent days, and asked him to keep the P.M. informed about what blew up, and where, and casualty reports, and such. Zaka knows what's going on faster than Arik Sharon does. . . . I said, by my count, Meshi was also more popular than Sharon—maybe he should think about replacing the old man. Meshi shook his head again, but with a smile: "Him they can get rid of in two years. Me they have for life."

Lunch ended abruptly when a couple of gleaming jeeps pulled up outside the barbecue joint. The cars were stuffed with *haredi* men—impossibly stuffed, like a clown car in the circus—but the shotgun seat in the lead car was empty and waiting for Meshi. I didn't meet him again. But I followed his progress—which wasn't hard—he's in the news all the time.

A few months after our interview, he was named as one of fourteen honored souls who would light the torches—the beacons on Mount Herzl—to usher in zionism's highest of high holidays, Israel's Independence Day. Predictably, his participation drew fire from true believers on all sides. His own grandfather denounced him, more or less as a zionist pinko . . . and the real zionist pinkos denounced him as a religious fanatic, an unreconstructed enemy of the state. But, as usual, Meshi gave as good as he got—and won the day with the public.

He said, he would gladly light the beacon—and affirm (as the ritual requires) that he did so "for the honor of the State of Israel." In fact, he considered his participation as a *kiddush Hashem*—a sanctification of God's name—and, thus, his duty as a Jew. "We have to learn to live together, and not simply side by side." He said that his experience with Zaka had taught him one big thing: the enemies of the Jewish people do not make distinctions between religious and secular—so why should Jews?

The way I saw it, in a couple of sentences, Meshi took the argument back more than fifty years, to the days when Hitler made the Jews act together. And he won the public to his side because he put his finger on the one thing that can keep Jews from making war on each other, now. They have to hang together—as long as they have the conflict.

I take it back about the two societies of Jews in Israel. I was way wrong—there are many more. In fact, there are two just among the *haredim*—two distinct traditions, with different histories, each with its own mores and mavens—you could call it two tribes.

The first—or first to be considered, because their power is long-standing—are the Ashkenazi orthodox . . . who are white guys (or kind of gingy colored), who came from Europe—and their rabbis and their music and traditions of worship came from Europe—along with a mistrust of zionism and the searing life lesson of the holocaust. They were the powers of the Aguda—the other side of the coin from the zionist founders (who were, as Meshi says, from the same house).

The second group is made up of the orthodox faithful from Asia and North Africa—Jews from Muslim and Arab countries—who came to Israel after the founding of the state, through the Fifties and even the Sixties. They are called the Sephardim, because their tradition of learning and worship came by way of Spain (where the Jews had a good thing going until the Inquisition—1492), and the word *Sephardim* literally means "the Spanish." Anyway, this Sephardic bunch never got along great with the Aguda rabbis—with any of the European founding generation—because those founders insisted on treating the new immigrants like "colored folk," who were somehow dirty or deprived, and ignorant of everything except their own traditions, which the Europeans didn't consider worth learning. (You could call it racism—within the race—like African-American men who won't go out with some girls, because their skin is too dark.)

The inconvenient thing (at least, from the Ashkenazi point of view) was there were *so many* of these Sephardim. They were brought in by the hundreds of thousands, because Israel needed to build a Jewish majority—and then, too, they made more kids than European Jews. By the 1970s, they were a majority of Jews in Israel, or near enough to where the powers of the government and its census bureau (all Europeans, of course) didn't want to ask anymore. (They suddenly adopted the ideal that it *shouldn't matter* where people came from.) . . . But Menachem Begin figured it out. He knew that Sephardic votes would put him (at last!) into power, and complete his life's hegira from nutcase and outcast—Ben-Gurion himself compared Begin to Hitler—to B-G's own chair, as prime minister.

Begin was as Polish as Pope John Paul. But if you saw him at an election rally, you would swear he grew up on couscous in Morocco. Sephardim loved him—they did put him over the top in 1977—and Begin took care of them, too. The Sephardic orthodox started feeding off the treasury (for their schools, yeshivas and social programs) just as eagerly as, or with even better appetite than, the Aguda. They also formed their own political party, to rival the Aguda and, more or less as the stinger, to extract the nectar from the flower of the state—which was called Shas. In fact, with charismatic leadership (Ovadia Yosef—that rabbi who was orotundly denouncing a secular, a few pages back) . . . and with thorough disregard for fairness or democracy (both in short supply, in their tradition) . . . Shas has outstripped the Aguda—and the tribe of Shas has grown stout with good eating.

There is even a third sub-nation of the religious—at least, their leadership is religious. That is the tribe of the settlers. To be accurate, there are all kinds of settlers—some committed to "redeeming the land" (which is a lovely way to say, putting Jews on it) . . . and some committed mostly to cheap housing. (Various governments have offered various blandishments to move Jews into the territories—while they told various U.S. presidents that they were "scaling back" on the settlements.) There are even a few settlers who moved beyond the Green Line, because "out there" they can stay stoned—it's good land for growing dope—and listen to Pink Floyd all night. . . . But you'd have to call the *movement* religious—not just because its guardians and promoters wear skullcaps, but because the whole enterprise of grabbing hilltops from the Arabs, to ring each with barbed wire to protect a new ghetto inside, while you call this the Land of Israel (or Greater Israel, or Ancient Israel) . . . when there are no Israelis for miles outside your barbed wire, and you can't even drive to your job (in real Israel), or shop for a pair of socks, without an army escort . . . is, prima facie, an exercise of religion—i.e., an act of faith, not susceptible to reason. The tribe of settlers also shares with the ultra-orthodox tribes—both Ashkenazi and Sephardi—the religious tic of quoting the Torah to make everybody else shut-up-and-just-send money.

Anyway, it is inarguably true that the most interesting settlers are religious. For them, where they live and why is not a matter of mortgage rates or an easy commute, but a window on their beliefs. And when you get close enough to sort them out, you can see those beliefs come in all kinds, too.

I had a charming and confusing afternoon in a settlement on a hilltop in the Judean wilderness—a place called Tekoa—with the spiritual leader, Rabbi Menachem Fruman. I knew he came out of the Rabbi Kook yeshiva, which was the incubator of Gush Emunim (the Bloc of the Faithful)—they were the real Tanks-and-Torah hard-liners when I first learned about the West Bank. And I also knew that Fruman now ran a yeshiva in Tekoa, where students split time between Jewish scholarship and army duties—I thought that must offer some handle on where he stood. But everything about the man was a surprise—starting with his appearance. If you can use this word about a fellow dressed up in the garb of eighteenth-century Poland, Fruman was stylish. He was lanky, at languid ease in his movements, with long silver tresses that fell upon the shoulders of his black coat—and he'd flick those tresses into place with a coy movement of his fingers, like a high school blonde who leads with her hair. I didn't expect to use this word, either—but the man was pretty.

Still, he wasn't as pretty as his talk, which began with a story of his father, who one day, long ago, looked out at these Judean desert hills, and asked: *"Menachem, do you see them?"* And Fruman said, "See what?" . . . *"There!"* his father said. *"Abraham and Isaac are going there! You see them? . . ."* For this was the route, from Hebron toward

Jerusalem, where Abraham took his firstborn to sacrifice him by God's commandment—although, alas, Fruman couldn't see the patriarchs, as his father did. "I was the vinegar," he said. "I didn't have the same sweetness of the vision. But my father said to me: '*Menachem—for two thousand years I wasn't here.*' " . . . And from there, it was an easy segue to Fruman's own history with these hills, which began at age twenty-two, when his yeshiva training was interrupted by the Six Day War. (In Rabbi Kook's yeshiva, they were scholars *and soldiers*—in fact, a lot of paratroopers.) "You know, the word *yeshiva*, it comes from the Hebrew 'to sit.' When we came back from the war, it was hard to sit." So, one by one, the boys departed to found settlements—and in the movement to "redeem the land" they are now patriarchs.

When Fruman spoke of this land, it was all about love. (The reason he left the yeshiva: "I heard the call of love.") He and his wife had published a book of verse—all love poems to the land. He said that love is gladness, yes—but troubles, worries, quarrels are love, as well—the strife in this land is about love, too. He said, the Arabs call it "*dar es-salaam*," the land of peace—and he approved, because this is the land of God—and in Islam, "The Peace" is one of many names for God. He moved on to another Arabic word, *el haq*—which can mean justice, or truth, or another name for God. And again, he approved—because for him, also, God and truth are the same thing. Fruman said he has studied Islam for twenty years, and he will not, cannot, claim that as a Jew, he has that One Great Thing: "I don't have God or The Truth, and they don't have God or The Truth. But God is between us." He said his life's work is making a meeting over the differences.

I asked, a couple of times (with a shocking lack of mystical appreciation), what was supposed to happen to the Arabs, if the Jews took over all the "land of peace"—for instance, the folks in the Palestinian village on the next hill, a town that's also named Tekoa. Fruman said—with a smile and a comedic shrug—"If they want to keep the name, okay!" Then, to reinforce his message, he counseled me to look around as I departed the settlement and pray that I would also see what his father saw—Abraham and Isaac. "I don't know if you will," he added. "But I do know where to look for God. He is right out there, somewhere between their Tekoa and ours." . . . As to the inquiry (all inquiries), Fruman said: "That's a discussion that could take two days." We didn't have two days, so he told me what he meant to tell—which was how he went to talk and pray with Sheikh Ahmad Yassin, the spiritual leader of Hamas . . . and how often he went to visit with his friend Yassir Arafat. In fact, last time Fruman saw his pal, they were interrupted by Mahmoud Abbas (the soon-to-be, and soon-to-be-ex, prime minister), who said to Arafat: "I was glad to see your friend Menachem is here." And Arafat quickly corrected him: "He is not my friend—he is my brother!" . . . Fruman liked that. He found time to tell that twice. There was also time for one question to me: Did I know of a group called the Unification Church? He had an invitation to address them in New York. By chance, had I heard of a Reverend Moon? . . .

I had a couple of visits in the northern West Bank, the hills of Samaria, with a matriarch of the movement—and mayor of a settlement called Kedumim—Daniella Weiss. I didn't have any problem there with mystical content. With me in tow, a couple of paces behind, she launched a quick tour (everything she does is quick) of her settlement's perimeter. She pointed out, there was no barbed wire—she doesn't believe in it, doesn't like the mentality it creates inside. And with a general's grasp of terrain and tactics, she showed how Kedumim commands the valleys below, and a major route to and from the Arab city of Nablus. These are facts. Facts serve her. She keeps them at the ready—for instance, the facts of the Israeli budget—which (she states as fact) shortchanges settlers. Or the facts of the Torah—she studies them every day. In her house, she observes the rabbinical advice that there should be no meal without discussion of the Torah. But this is not to celebrate its majesty or mystery. It is to learn what to do. Because when she is confronted with a problem (and only a brave problem would confront Ms. Weiss), she wants to do what Abraham, Isaac and Jacob (or Sarah, Rachel and Leah) would have done . . . what they did do—because it's all there, in black and white— her guide to conduct, today and every day.

For instance, as she notes, it was Sarah who sent Abraham's second wife Hagar, and her son, Ishmael, out to the desert (and out of the world of the Torah altogether). This Daniella takes not only as a guide to conduct, but as evidence that women can make—must and do make—the most fundamental decisions. . . . Or, in the story of Exodus (the trek out of Egypt, not the ship that sailed from Hollywood), when the men of Israel lost their faith in God's covenant, it was the women who gave the Jews the strength of will to make it to the promised land. So, what she gives to Kedumim and to the settler movement is precisely faith and will—both she has in long supply. You could take one look at her, in the municipality office—a small woman, but erect in her chair, with both arms up on the desktop, her eyes alert under the cap that hides her hair—and you'd see in an instant that she is in her place. That big desk, the whole office and its building (which is only a house trailer, after all)—in fact, all the offices, and the entire machinery of the state of Israel, along with its prime ministers, its governments, the army—they are all more moveable and malleable than Daniella Weiss.

This is the sort of fact in which she takes pleasure—and pardonable pride. After all, it's not her will for which she claims credit, but God's—which was the force that yanked her, thirty years ago, from a comfortable home in the Tel Aviv suburbs, out to the hilltops of Samaria. The proximate cause was the Yom Kippur War, which she regarded "as a direct conversation between God and the people of Israel." It was a warning, she surmised, and a commandment to redeem the land and possess it, as she says, "with all your body, with all your soul and with all your might." And though her husband was well employed in the diamond trade, and her friends thought she'd gone crazy, a life of immersion suited her. (I know it's the wrong metaphor here, but in America we'd say she goes whole hog.) "I can't say why," she says. "But I want to go into a thing as deeply as you can. For me, activism is not telling others what to do. I have to do it myself. . . . It's too high, what I say. . . ." (I think she meant, too grand.) "But I cannot take a day off. Because I think the nation misses me. I must work for the State of Israel."

She can't sit back and let others—even those in high office—steer a course for the Jewish state. She knows them—and knows for a fact, they do not have the faith. She had her first long talk with Arik Sharon twenty-five years ago. That was about the time when he was the army commander responsible for pulling Jewish settlers out of the Sinai so Israel could do the deal with Sadat. And at that time, she told Sharon—tried to tell him—that he must study Torah every day, and learn to let it guide him every day. Why should Israel remove Jews from the land? For the sake of the world's good opinion? . . . What about the example of Abraham—the first Jew, and father of all? As Daniella says: "He was off to one side in the world, and *everybody was against him!*" . . .

She also knows that Sharon heard her well—but he didn't have the will to remake his life. For they spoke again, about one year ago, when an Arab gunman snuck into

Kedumim's sister settlement, Elon Moreh, and shot to death Daniella's son-in-law. Prime Minister Sharon called to offer condolence.

"It was kind of a confession," she says of that call. "He said: 'I remember when we had our talk all those years ago—what you told me. I didn't do it. And now, I can't work that way. I'm very far from it now.' "

She doesn't consider Sharon worse than others she has dealt with. They're all politicians. They live in safety, in a cordon of security—and inside the Green Line. As to faith, they're all in the same leaky boat. That only confirms for her what she thought thirty years ago: it's up to her—no one else will understand. . . . "I live it every day," she says. "They don't."

For me, that was another confirmation that the settlers deserve a place on the list of the new tribes of Israel. Because that's one requirement for a tribe unto itself: the feeling that the others—other Israelis—cannot possibly understand. That, and victimization—which is the logical next step. And it helps, too, if you can make a case that the current well-being and future of Israel depend mostly on its treatment of *your group*. You only have to convince yourself. Because that's also a tenet of this New Tribal Theory—each tribe is mostly preaching to itself.

To borrow a name from physics, you could call this a Grand Disunification Theory. I can't claim any credit for it. Two men—great talkers, who wouldn't talk to each other—both talked to me about the New Tribes of Israel, all in one week. The first was a fellow named Elyakim Ha'etzni, who is a right-wing gadfly, a columnist and talk-show host—kind of a Rush Limbaugh figure in the politics of Zion. And he was delighted with the new tribal state of affairs. He talked about it like an Act of God—or, as he's equally likely to conclude, further evidence of the genius of the Jewish people.

I didn't ask him about it. With Ha'etzni, you don't have to ask. We sat down in a fusty old Jerusalem café, and he was off and running. His first topic was the miracle and genius of the new Russian immigration. "Many things in Israel come now to a better balance," he said. "Do you know there's a new TV channel in Russian this week? Not a cable channel—a broadcast channel! They have their own newspapers, their magazines. The airlines between Moscow and Kiev and Tel Aviv are full all the time. People can have two passports now—Israeli and Russian. This is very good! What a wonderful thing—from Russia, a million Jews came! Okay, people say they aren't Jews. But do you know there are five hundred families from Russia living now in Kiryat Arba? . . ."

Kiryat Arba is Ha'etzni's home—a settlement on a hilltop overlooking the Palestinian city of Hebron, and a real epicenter of the Tanks-'n'-Torah crowd. To him, that's as Jewish as you can get. I managed to tuck in a question about what I saw as a split in the society, between religious and secular Jews—I used the word *sectarian*.

"Sectarian? No, it's tribal. The society has divided into tribes. First there's the Ramat Hasharon tribe. . . ."

He gave it the name of a rich suburb north of Tel Aviv. What he meant was the crowd of Europeans, the old Labour party aristocracy. They used to run everything. Now (at least, in politics) they're out of the swim. That's what he meant by "a better balance"—and why he was pleased to list so many other tribes.

"Then, you have the tribe of the Russians. . . . And you know the tribe of the Old Left—which is always crying for the Palestinians. . . . And the tribe of the Settlers—which is doing exactly the reverse. . . . And the old Right Wing goes with the settlers. . . . Then, you have the tribe of Haredim, the ultimate religious."

He took the ultra-orthodox all in one breath—but in his tribal view, their traditions didn't matter. "All the *haredim* were drawn into the magnetic field of the zionist state. So, also, the life of the whole country became more religious. Do you know half-a-million visited the tomb of Sarah in Hebron? . . . Last year, on [the holiday of] Sukkot, buses left at four o'clock in the morning, from all over Israel, to carry people to the dawn prayers in Hebron. The *haredim* are more and more involved. You can't find anymore where the Bible Land of Israel ends and the Zionist Land of Israel begins. They met in 1967, over the Old City of Jerusalem. They meet now in Hebron and Kiryat Arba. Do you know, the number of religious students—at the height of European Jewry, around the end of the nineteenth century—the number of people studying Torah in the yeshivas was *less than we have in Israel today!* This is wonderful! . . ." And what delights him most is the swelling power of the tribes on the right. "What you see is three together—the Russians, the settlers/right wing, and the *haredim*—those three tribes combined to sink the Left."

A few days later, I was in a Tel Aviv office tower, slick with brushed stainless steel—built for high-tech—but high-tech's in a slump, these days . . . so, it's also the office of Eitan Haber. He's a former newspaperman, who went into politics at the behest of Yitzhak Rabin—for whom he wrote speeches, and served as right-hand-man—while Rabin was prime minister, and trying to make peace. Now, Haber works as a consultant to other pols or companies who need his skill—as a crafter of concepts, he's worth paying for. . . . I had come to ask about the changes in the society. But nothing I mentioned as a change—the consensus that peace is impossible, the hard-edged capitalism, ex-generals running all the big institutions . . . none of that struck him as fundamental.

"Look. The real problem is a disintegration and a tribalization of the society. . . ." He let me write that down, and then proceeded, with a reporter's practiced cadence—as if he were dictating a story to the city desk.

"First, you have about one million Ashkenazi *sabras*—born in Israel from European families—or the Ramat Gan aristocracy." (He was using the name of another fancy suburb. That might have been his neighborhood. It was his tribe—though he didn't spare them.) ". . . They're the intellectuals, heads of high-tech companies, the heads of the army—and they're looking down with hubris on the entire rest of the population.

"Number two, the Russians, also about one million. They are living in their ghetto. They have their theaters, their papers, their own TV, their groceries. They don't need us. They are in their little Moscow, like a Chinatown. We knew a lot of them were not Jews—so we didn't welcome them with open arms and warm hearts. Only five or six years after they came, we found out they had brought us so much IQ. They are the new intelligentsia.

"Number three, Israeli Arabs—also about a million, also in their ghetto. They also have their papers, their own TV, their own politics. They live in Nazareth, or in their villages, isolated since the first *Intifada*. No Jews are coming to those villages, anymore.

"Number four, the ultra-orthodox—less than a million. They also have their own papers, forty or fifty stations on the radio—no TV because they don't watch TV. They don't want to look at us. Nobody has any contact with them.

"Five, the settlers, a quarter-million. Not necessarily orthodox, but I call them *parve* religious—neither milk nor meat. Unfortunately—and I can say unfortunately—they look on us as a different country. They say: '*WE are fighting the terror. WE are endangering our babies. And you hate us—you are cursing us, on your way to the French Riviera.*' They feel they are the pioneers, like we all used to be.

"Sixth—and the most dangerous (also, most numerous)—the Sephardim who came from Arab countries.

They're the cooks, the drivers, the workers. It's the most dangerous for the life of Israel because they have gone completely tribal. Their whole politics is about getting a share of the pie for the Sephardim—this is exemplified by Shas. . . ."

When I finished, at length, writing down the list, I asked Haber why it was so dangerous. And of course, the answer was all about tribe—but mostly *his tribe*.

"I say this society is like a flamingo. I mean, it is standing on very, very thin legs. All the burden is on our shoulders. The taxes, the economy, the leadership of the army—all rest on us. How much burden can we take? Yes, there are lots of Moroccans fighting, going to the army. But who are the pilots? The Ashkenazim. We have to pay the taxes. They don't pay—they don't work. The unemployed are the ultra-orthodox, or the Arabs—or the Russians (that's our fault— they want to work) . . . but we pay for all of them. The *parve* religious—they are now number one in the army, moving up—why? Because my tribe is not so anxious to fight for them on the hills of Judea and Samaria. And that is the biggest threat to Israel—although nobody knows it. . . ."

Only then—and cruelly, without warning—I told him I'd heard a similar analysis, a few days before, from Elyakim Ha'etzni. . . . Poor Haber! I know I ruined his day. . . . But I have to thank him, now—along with Ha'etzni—because I think they're both right. You can see in your first two weeks in the country that the ultra-religious don't talk to the seculars, the seculars don't talk to the settlers, the Russians don't talk to anyone but Russians, and so on. Whether you're pleased about it like Ha'etzni, or aggrieved like Haber, it's one of the big things that happened to Israel. It was always fractious—now it's breaking apart. But I diverge from them both as to why it happened, and what it means.

Some of this tribalization did come to Israel from outside—from other Western societies. The zionist state has always been kind of trendy in its social engineering. Zionism itself was just a Jewish version of European nineteenth-century nationalism—as Labour zionism was a fun-house-mirror reflection of the socialist revolution in Eastern Europe. (At the risk of offending, you could even say the founders had a fling with those two in combination—say, National Socialism? . . . In the old zionist posters, the New Jew looked suspiciously outdoorsy and athletic, with tousled fair hair, an aquiline nose, blue eyes filled with passion for the Fatherland—except for the lederhosen, creepily like unto The New German.) . . . These days, trends mostly come from America—so, in the last couple of decades, multiculturalism has been in vogue. There's a rash of hyphens: American-Israelis, Russian-Israelis, Iraqi-Israelis, even Palestinian-Israelis—that last one drives the Jews nuts . . . but whether you favor that trend or not, it doesn't make for unity.

Still, there's a deeper (and local) reason for the tribal trend, and the way it has been allowed to play out. Maybe I see it in sharper relief because I went back to Israel after so many years—I missed all the little steps in between. But it seems apparent (in fact, shockingly overt) that the function and rationale for these tribes is to get all they can for their own folk—and to hell with the others—everybody's takin' care of Number One. Shas often takes the blame for this ethic—it was a party organized with the stated goal of getting more of the pie—but they were simply more open about it. All the tribes listed by those two great talkers have their snouts so deep in the treasury trough that the public finances are perpetually in crisis. No one can keep track of the give-aways—or how they're engineered: for instance, the yeshivas in the settlements, which suck their sustenance from the defense budget. (Because, you know, they're strengthening the, um, *fiber of the nation.*) . . . And once you get yours, the idea is to take care of your own. The problem with the orthodox used to be that they'd take public money to attack the state, or to force the state (and the rest of the Jews who happened to live in it) to follow their rules. Now the problem is the reverse: they take the public money and spend it to insulate themselves from the nation—their own neighborhoods, their buildings, their schools, their day care, (pirate) radio stations, book publishing, buses—not to mention their own sinecures of power and patronage within the government, that no one else may touch. . . . And, of course, they won't listen to—they fear, mistrust and vie against—anybody from outside the group.

I got mine—for me and my people—because we had the power to get it, and keep it. . . .

What is that, if it's not the ethic of the occupation? Once again, it started with the Arabs. But as always, it came back across the Green Line to the Jews.

I'm not asking you to imagine some viral contagion of ethical failure—or mysterious spores of aggression drifting, like steam from the Swedish meatballs, over the Green Line toward Tel Aviv . . . what I'm talking about, anybody can see. When I blame the occupation for breaking apart this society, I'm talking about policies that the government of Israel announced. Take, for example—as both Haber and Ha'etzni did—the tribe of the Russians. Deliberate policy created that tribe.

See, Israel had a problem—and not a little *pisher*, but a big-league crisis. (When Israelis talked about it—when they dared—they tended to call it the "time bomb.") . . . In 1967, the army conquered all the land of Greater Israel—*Eretz Yisrael,* or Bible Israel, call it what you will—and for the next quarter-century or so, they hung on to it. The problem was (as the problem always was), it was filled with Arab people, in this case millions of them. And the proximate problem—the "time bomb" they whispered about—was the moment that Jews could see rushing toward them, when the Arabs would be the majority in that land. Some people said the moment would arrive in ten years. Some people said it was already here. But no one could deny it would happen—it was happening. . . . You could say they had forgotten what the Knesset knew in 1949. They could have a larger state, or a Jewish state. Now, they were trying to have both.

When you got down to it, there were only three choices—none looked easy or appetizing. They could give up the territories—kiss the land and its Arabs good-bye—but of course, that meant a fight with other Jews, the settlers, and no one wanted that. . . . They could hang on to the land, and try to kill or expel some Arab millions—which was a tad Nazi-ish, and a *hasbarah* nightmare—still, it was something to think about. . . . Or they could hang on to both the land and its people, and control by force, with a system of Apartheid—i.e., with a majority that had no political rights. . . . This last was the choice, by default.

But in this case, the landlord did die, and his dog, too—a miracle happened—the Soviet Union collapsed. And there—in what would now be Russia and Ukraine . . . suddenly unfettered by Commie chains (they could leave whenever they wanted!) . . . and suffering in the ruins of the (former) state economy—like manna the good God (praised be His Name!) dropped from heaven on the Hebrews . . . *there were more Jews!*

To make a long story short, Israel went shopping and bought a million of them—brought 'em home on the plane. . . . This wasn't just stated policy, but a triumph to be trumpeted! A million new Jews! Suddenly, the time bomb wasn't ticking so loudly.

Of course this required a few small adjustments. It cost a fortune, for one thing—they were wooed to the sacred homeland with loot and plenty of it—but what's a few billion, or tens of billions, between friends? . . . Then, too, a lot of them weren't exactly Jewish—but what the hell—if they would mention how their grandfather said one day, that his

mother used to be (you know, before the Commies, and all).
. . . And there was the inconvenient fact that you couldn't try
to *make* them too Jewish, or even too Israeli—for instance,
by slapping them into months of classes on Hebrew and
"Jewish life," like Israel did for immigrants in the past—if
you tried that with these folks, they wouldn't come. (One
thing Russians knew, after nearly eighty years of Communist
rule, was how to get your own from "the system"—they
worked the Jewish Agency and the Jewish state like a pump.)

So, all of a sudden, Israel had a new system of "absorption." All the camps and classes, all the zionist pep talks and
field trips on Israeli history—well, that was history. The old
system was replaced with "open absorption," or "market absorption"—i.e., a chunk of money, and what you did with it
was your affair. You want to buy a car? You want to buy an
apartment? You want to buy your apartment in Moscow, and
rent in Israel? *Yofi*—suit yourself. . . . Hebrew? Not a problem. You can say *Shalom?* Okay—have fun! . . . No wonder
Russians only talk to Russians—they're the only people they
can talk to. Meantime, they'll learn a bit of Hebrew in the
army. . . .

What happened was, the conflict required more Jews.
And if they turned out to be a tribe unto themselves—well,
that's life in the Middle East. After all those years of fighting
about *Who Is a Jew?*—everybody knows, these folks ain't.
The latest study for the government Minister of Diaspora Affairs—on immigrants from the former Soviet Union, during
the year 2000—concluded that two-thirds were not Jewish.

Anyway, who needed a study? My market in Tel Aviv was half Russian stalls and stores, with hams hanging over the counter, and signs (some in Russian only) decorated with dancing pigs. And not even the rabbis were throwing stones.

What happened was, once the orthodox bought into the conflict—the religion of the state—then *Who Is a Jew?* didn't matter so much . . . the question was, who was good for the Jews—or good for what the Jews meant to do with their Jewish state. And the Russians were good for the conflict: they quickly earned a reputation as the most brutal bad-ass checkpoint soldiers available within the IDF. (Where they come from, authority *is* brutal—and now, they have—they are the authority.) . . . Or you could sum up the matter in another way: it didn't matter if the Russians were Jews—because the mission of Israel had changed again—from the rescue of the Jewish people, to the rescue of the Jewish state's occupation.

Blonde, with wide blue eyes, and a little smudge of a nose—she looked about as Jewish as Marilyn Monroe. (Of course, with inducement, Marilyn had gone Jewish, too. In fact, I just saw—her menorah was up for auction.) . . . Dr. Anna Kazachkova came to Israel in 1999, from Komsomolsk-on-Amur, in far-eastern Russia. In her old land, in her old life, she was a pediatric surgeon—and mother of two: a girl, Anya, and a boy, Alex—but in the years since her emigration, she hadn't practiced her profession. In Israel, everything changed.

Actually, the changes in her life started well before—
back in Russia, when her husband, also a doctor, died of hep-
atitis that he caught in his hospital. Then, she was a single
mom in a place that she didn't feel was her own (her family
had been assigned to the Far East by the Communist authorities)—you could say she was ripe for a move.

Why Israel? . . . For one thing, because she could go—
they would help her. And then, too, there was a fortune
teller—an astrologer who read her chart—and he told her:
"You should be in Israel." (He was probably on the payroll of
the Sokhnut—the Jewish Agency—because he also offered
to introduce her to the agency representatives. But that
thought never occurred to Dr. Anna. In those days, suspicion
wasn't her long suit.) And, after all, she could say she was
Jewish—or her mother's family might have been—back
when, before the Bolsheviks.

But the big reason was Anya, her firstborn. Komsomolsk
was terribly cold, and Anya wasn't a hearty child—or it may
have been Dr. Anna who didn't have the heart for Russian
winters, and her daughter's childhood ills. As a mother, she
was overprotective (all the more after Anya's father died) . . .
and she laughed a little, now, when she recalled her days as a
doctor—every disease she saw in the hospital struck her with
a new fear: *Anya might get that!* . . . Anya was fourteen—a
little blonde, very like her mom (who proudly showed photos
at our café table)—when the Sokhnut pushed the paperwork
through and gave Dr. Anna airline tickets—along with a nice
sum of money and a "refresher course" on Jewish traditions

(every one of which was new to her) . . . and the Kazachkova family flew off to a new life in Tel Aviv.

It wasn't easy. It was strange, a bit lonely—and so many hoops to jump through before she could work as a doctor. . . . But she could see, it was good for Anya—who came to flower in this new, warm clime. She became a city girl, an Israeli girl—not wild or loud—her mother wouldn't permit that, and it wasn't really in her nature. But Anya's photos show a tanned and hale fifteen-year-old—nothing frail about her appearance—a girl with enough confidence to dress up as a cat for the Purim masquerade . . . or to flash a coquettish grin, in short shorts and a shirt that never got to the shorts (it stopped somewhere north of the navel). "That's when," as her mother says, "she dressed up like an Israeli." . . . Still, it came as a shock, when one of the teachers told her that all the boys in school were in love with Anya. "I never thought she was that social," Dr. Anna said. "I didn't know—till after . . ."

That's one grief that tugs at her, now—she'll never know. Ten days before Anya turned sixteen, she and her best friend, Mariana, went to a birthday party for another classmate, Yulia—Friday night, June 1, 2001. It was Anya's first big party with boys. Then, all the kids went to a disco (that was a first for Anya, as well)—a place on the beach called the Dolphinarium—which was blown up, that night, by a suicide bomber. Yulia, the birthday girl, and Mariana, and Anya, too—all died in that explosion.

So many Russian kids died that night—sixteen of the twenty-one victims were teenagers—the whole country mourned. People talk about it now as the moment when they changed their minds about the immigrant Russians—they were Israelis, after all. Because it didn't matter if they could talk Hebrew, if they had come for the money, or they flew back and forth to Moscow or Kiev. They were proper citizens of the Jewish state, because they had paid the price.

For Dr. Anna, that was also the time (that moment when she saw her daughter in the morgue) when she became an Israeli forever. "Because this is my only place. Anya is here." . . . The first Jewish funeral she ever saw was Anya's. She didn't know she had to sit *shiva* (hosting guests at home for seven days, in respect for the dead—a rabbi told her what to do). But none of that strikes her as odd or foreign, anymore. Anya's death also made her a Jew.

Now she tugged at a delicate gold chain around her neck and fished from her sweater a Star of David—she wears it every day. Her son, Alex, was recently a bar mitzvah boy—which wasn't the hard part. Before that, he had to be circumcised. Now, every Friday, she said, she lights the Sabbath candles. . . . And another thing changed: for the first time in her life, she is always watching the news. She's always thinking of the parents of the latest victims . . . or were there any new explosions? . . . Is the army going to hit them? . . .

Back in Russia, she never paid attention to anything like that. She dimly knew there was a war with the Chechens—but she didn't know why. As to Israel's conflict, she knew what the Jewish Agency told her—which was even less. "The

Sokhnut colored everything in pink." Only now, she was learning—trying to learn.

She said the bomber who killed Anya "must have been an Arab who lived in Israel—how else could he have gotten to the very center of the country?" (Perhaps she thought of Israel as a country like Russia—with vast territory around the "very center.") . . . She spent a day in the courtroom at the trial of the Palestinian leader Marwan Barghouti. Israel was accusing him as a terrorist kingpin, a mastermind of suicide bombings. I asked Dr. Anna what should happen to Barghouti. . . . "Well, he's a member of Knesset," she said. "So, he can't be sentenced to death." Barghouti is not an Israeli—much less a member of the Knesset.

But in the end, it doesn't matter what she knows or doesn't know. She is a proper Israeli, now, because she shares the essential mind-set—there is no choice. She doesn't study, anymore, for her tests to resume her work as a doctor. She's too depressed. Anyway, she's calling Alex twenty times a day on his cell phone to make sure he's all right—she can't escape the feeling that she was, somehow, a bad mom—and she won't let him take a bus, so she drives him anywhere he needs to go. The car is new—she got it with no taxes. And she's buying a new apartment—another special deal. She gets a lot of help, not just as a Russian, but as a victim mother, a category unto itself. And there are special grants from British Jews and American Jews, for victims . . . and ceremonies organized by the municipality of Tel Aviv—and the municipality of Herzliyya took the victim families out on a yacht to throw flowers on the water . . . there's the organization of victim families, and the organization of Dolphinarium dead, and the organization for Russian immigrants. She said she feels like everybody does for her—but right now she can't do much for herself. And she wouldn't, couldn't, ever leave: "After I brought my daughter to be killed here? And I have her grave here? Never." . . . She wants peace—or an end to the terror, "for everybody in Israel—*shalom.*" But that can't happen. "The Muslims want to kill not only Jews, but Christians and everybody else," she said, "and make Islam all over the world. It's stupid. . . ." Then, she shrugged in a most Israeli way—as if there were nothing more to explain. "Arafat people," she said.

It was Yossi's luck to grow up in that time when it seemed that Israelis could do what they wanted—the whole country was about choice. When he was a kid, things were solid, moving forward. In the 1950s, it seemed like everybody knew what the country was for—how a life should be lived— except for fights, you know, with the religious. But that was only in the papers—it wasn't his life. There was his Dad, on Yom Kippur, switching lights on and off, flipping on the radio . . . it was an earnest, secular, Labour-voting household—the Aharon family, immigrants from Iraq.

And he came of age at that moment when choices seemed to grow limitless—the world of his people was expanding—with the Six Day War, the wide new lands it conquered, and the feeling that they could do *anything*. . . . He was a young man through the 1970s (even into the 1980s) and he smiles now as he remembers all the things he tried out in that disco decade. . . . And even through the late '80s, with the first *Intifada*—when the news of the nation got so serious—that wasn't his life. He never had (he never needed) a political idea of any sort. Yossi made it to a happy-go-lucky middle age, with an art store in West Jerusalem, and with friends, music, good times. He made a little money—enough, anyway. He had his health—a lot of nervy, eager energy in his stocky frame, all his teeth (and all good) to enliven his smile, even a helmet of thick black hair without one strand of gray—and a lovely, soft-spoken girlfriend, Tami, whom he married, soon after he turned forty. It was time to settle down. . . . Looking back, you could call it a window in time. But from the comfort of your home—when you feel at home—you don't notice the window, but the sunshine on the wider world outside.

It was 1992 when Yossi and Tami Aharon started looking for a place to make a family and a future. The first land Yossi found was a hell of a deal—but with Israeli complications. It was Arab land, or formerly Arab land, near Jerusalem—just outside, near Abu Dis, off the road that leads to Bethlehem. It wasn't annexed to Israel after the '67 War—but the way Yossi was told, the Israel Lands Authority had bought it, and they offered sweet deals to show that Jews could live there. He was all signed up to get two *dunams*, about a half-acre. Some trust that was affiliated with the settler movement

Gush Emunim (they also wanted Jews on that land) put a trailer on his plot, so Yossi could live there, while he built. . . . Then, Rabin got elected as prime minister—and every permit that Yossi required was stopped, dead in its tracks. Rabin was looking toward Oslo, to a peace deal—and all settlement on Arab land was frozen.

Yossi and Tami had to move in with his parents. They had their first child—things were tight in that house—and his father wasn't well. But they made do. They waited more than a year. No one could give them an answer on what would happen with their land, their deal. The house trailer they were supposed to use got pulled off the land—it ended up in Tekoa, the settlement to the south, where Rabbi Fruman holds court.

By happenstance, Yossi had customers from Tekoa. They came to his art store for brushes, paints, canvas . . . they seemed okay, their checks were good. They used to tell him—before he had any connection to the place—what a wonderful home they had there, how he ought to come visit—they said he ought to move out there, too. Now, when he told them his trailer ended up there, they pressed the invitation. He should bring his family, and stay for *Shabbat*. . . . So Yossi, Tami and their newborn son went out one Friday afternoon, and his customers got together to host a festive Sabbath supper and to talk up life in Tekoa—that was nice. . . . And they slept in one of the trailers parked near the edge of the settlement—no TV or anything, not on the Sabbath— so they turned in early, and Yossi woke at first light, he went outside . . . and that was gorgeous. He could see open land from there to forever—an unbroken line of sculpted hills and rosy sky, to the red sun rising over the Dead Sea—a view of splendid vastness you wouldn't see from anywhere near Jerusalem. And as the sun climbed, there were children who came out to play, and they saw him and called to him: *"Shabbat shalom!"*—to a stranger!—without an ounce of wariness or mistrust. And Yossi thought, you'd never see that in town—never! This was the sort of place a kid *should* grow up . . . maybe his kid.

The Tekoa folks told him they could give him land for his house—for almost nothing—and with an option for more land, as much as he wanted. He could have a little farm! It didn't matter if he was religious or not. They had secular people, too. (They called it a "mixed settlement.") And no government problems—Tekoa was on the government maps, as a place where Jews were supposed to settle. In fact, with the government's help, they could get him modular prefab structures—he could put three or four together for a house of eighty or ninety square meters—plenty of house. And the whole thing, land and prefabs together, would cost maybe ten thousand shekels—like two or three thousand dollars (when anything like that, anywhere near Jerusalem, was bound to cost two or three hundred thousand!). . . . It was a deal that they had on offer for the Russians—but they could get him in . . . which was the dream of every Israeli: suddenly, Yossi was on the inside—he had *protekzia!* How could he turn away?

It was 1994 when he bought his land. The way they worked it out, he only had to buy a half of one *dunam*, but he would have an option for five *dunams*—more than an acre—and anyway, there was no one around his land. They gave him a trailer, to stay out there, when he'd come to visit. He started making plans to build, right away. Not that he meant to build quick and dirty—anything but. With the money he'd saved on the dream deal for the land, Yossi had in mind a dream house, too. He would take them up on the prefab concrete boxes, but after that . . . well, it turned into kind of an art project.

He wanted to cover the concrete walls with stone—but not the prefab façade stone that he could buy in sections—that wouldn't look right. He wanted stone walls like he saw on the oldest houses in those hills—stones that were part of that ancient land, with each stone fitted to its neighbors. The only ones who still did that work were the Arabs, so he brought in masons from the nearby villages. They eyed each stone, then chipped and chiseled, till it would sit in the wall like God set it there. The work on one stone could take an hour. But it was beautiful to watch each one take shape.

Anyway, Yossi came to like the company of those craftsmen. They looked at things like he did—as a chance to make beauty, where before there was none. They could talk together—they talked all day—and Yossi learned to laugh with them about the way Jews built: with houses that came out of factories, so they looked like factories, too. And when he'd come out to stay in the trailer near his house, it was really just him and the Arabs—not many other folks came around.

Partly that was because he wasn't in the center of the settlement. Few settlers would happen by on their normal errands. But he knew, it was more than that. To tell the truth, even before his first wall was complete (granted, each wall might take a year), Yossi knew he wasn't making friends in Tekoa, like he meant to—like he felt he should. He could understand why the orthodox settlers shied away. There was nothing religious about him. They must have looked at him (at best) as a bad Jew. But he was disturbed to find out, most of the secular settlers were Russians. And they didn't even talk Hebrew. He couldn't exchange two words with them—even with all the goodwill in the world.

He did his best to fit in, or at least to join in, whenever he saw a chance. At the store, or in a meeting, he'd hear about some problem, and he'd jump to help. He heard the school wanted a pen to keep animals, for the children to look at and learn from—sort of a petting zoo. Yossi took time off from his house to build it. They had a problem with the electric gate. He fixed that . . . It worked, more or less. Folks started to talk to him. But it didn't solve the problem—that only got worse. Settlers who meant to make friends invited him to come with them at night—they were going out to shoot up the hot-water tanks on Arab houses. Or they were going to some village to catch chickens in the yards, and slaughter them. Yossi wasn't comfortable with any of that—and they could feel it. . . . So, more and more, the Jews left him alone. It was Yossi and the Arabs, talking together, chipping stone together, at that edge of the world.

In 1996, Tami had a second pregnancy—a tough one— and they were running back and forth to doctors in Jerusalem. In the middle of her term, she was ordered not to move at all. She and Yossi stayed in Jerusalem for several months. By the eighth month, Tami and the baby were out of danger, so they came back to Tekoa—but things had changed. There was a new settlers' council in office, and Yossi's estrangement had turned into policy. . . . His trailer had been moved—even farther from the settlement's center—out to an area that the settlers called Tekoa Gimel (or by the terms of the Hebrew alphabet, Tekoa C). That was settlement land, but on a separate hilltop, well away from his house, and outside Tekoa's fence. The council members said it was simply an administrative matter—all Tekoa's trailers had been moved out there. But Yossi was the only one who lived in a trailer—except for a few soldiers, guards who also had to camp on that hill. There was no water out there, nor provision for sewage, no electric power, no driveway—there was barely a road.

From the point of view of the mainstream settlers, you could see how the move made a hard-knuckled sort of sense. If Yossi wanted to hang out with his Arab friends—okay—let him do so outside the fence. . . . The odd thing was, the move started to make sense to Yossi, too. He was changing in ways he never would have predicted. For one thing, he found inside himself—maybe for the first time in his life—a sure understanding of what he liked, and what he wanted to do. He still didn't have any political sense—anything you could call an ideology—but he did get a sense of mission . . . which is maybe what those desert hills breed, or what a man needs to live there. What he liked was making something out of nothing—not getting something from someone (certainly, not taking it from someone) and possessing it as his own— but creating something new, from his own imagination and work. . . . It may seem highfalutin' or impossibly old-fashioned to say so, but in a sense, he'd found the old religion—not the ancient religion, but the one he'd grown up with—the ethic of the nation's inventors, the Labour zionist settlers who still ran the world while he was young.

So, this bare hilltop where his trailer had landed became his canvas. He graded his own road. He bought pipe and brought water from the main settlement, he bought conduit and cable to bring electricity. He dug a septic system. Where he needed help, he hired it—his Arab friends—and their sons and cousins. Between this new work and his house (where work continued, albeit more slowly), he was spending a fortune . . . but he had an idea common to dreamers— that when they (the settlers) saw what he had done, they would thank him, maybe even reimburse him, or *reward him*. . . . After all, this was what their movement *was about*—he was settling another hilltop for them.

And in the meantime, he wasn't waiting for anyone, or anything—he would have his farm right now. The Palestinian villagers taught him how to turn the land, and tend it. They brought him animals, and helped him build his pens. Their womenfolk taught Tami how to care for sheep and goats, how to shear wool and how to cook a feast with lamb and rice, chickpeas and saffron. . . . They'd feast together at every opportunity—Jewish holidays and Muslim ones, too—like Yossi, Tami and their kids had landed, by act of God, in a big local family. And they extended that family: Yossi planted grass—a lawn for his little farm—and then he put up a plastic swimming pool . . . so, the soldiers used to come to cool off, and have a beer. It turned into kind of a DMZ clubhouse— Yossi and Tami, and their kids, and their Arab friends, and *their* kids, and the soldiers—they sat around every night with food, wine, talk. . . .

The drive from Jerusalem to Tekoa only took a half-hour or forty minutes. But it always took Yossi two or three hours. His friends in the villages would be offended if he didn't stop for coffee, or a meal. Everybody in those villages knew him. In a town called Zatara, Yossi and the mayor got so friendly that Yossi volunteered to teach a class in Hebrew for local kids—to help them find work, if relations with Israel ever improved. (The mayor said: "Could you help me teach them Arabic, first?") . . . By this time, the government of Israel had changed again—and under the new prime minister, Bibi Netanyahu, life in the West Bank was growing steadily more bitter. But even when the army slapped down curfews and closures, Yossi continued his village visits. Now, he'd bring food, medicine or supplies that his friends couldn't get. The

way they figured—Yossi and his friends—it didn't matter so
much what was happening, now. Well, it mattered: If your
kid had a wracking cough and you couldn't get antibiotics,
nothing else mattered. . . . But it didn't change the big
thing—peace was coming, sooner or later (even Netanyahu
said that). And meanwhile, they were showing how it *could
be*—if Jews and Arabs were neighbors and friends.

Yossi and Tami came to believe this so strongly that they
brought it up at the settlers' council. Tami said it was her
dream to start a kindergarten for Jews and Arabs, together—
or maybe a whole school—so theirs would be the last generation of people who didn't know their neighbors, and feared
or fought them. . . . And by the time Israel's government
changed anew—this time it was Ehud Barak who got
elected, on a platform of peace—Yossi had enough of a personal political program to stand up before the settlers' council, again. This time, he suggested that they ought to start
thinking of the future—how they would give up Tekoa, if
they had to. Peace was coming, he said, and they ought to
hand Tekoa back to the Arabs with dignity—to recognize the
precious place it was—and so they wouldn't look like *shnor-
rers*. He knew that would raise some hackles. But he wasn't
trying to talk down to them—or lecturing from the outside.
This was something he had to think about, too—his own
house was all but complete.

It was a measure of what an outsider he was—of the cold-
war non-contact between him and the settlers—that he
didn't understand how they looked at his house, at the

Aharon family—and mostly, at him. He should have known. . . . He should have gauged where he stood in that community when he saw the reaction of the settlers to his farm. "Why are you doing that? . . . You shouldn't be doing that!" . . . He should have known when kids at the school asked his kids: "Are your parents Jewish or Arabs?" . . . Surely, he should have figured it out the first time someone snuck up to his trailer and broke the glass in his bathroom window, or when his tanks of bottled gas disappeared. But he believed what he preferred to believe—maybe it was just some kids, acting out. . . .

To tell the truth, he could only see what his stubbornness allowed him to see. That's part of the package, with a sense of mission—that stubborn streak is the difference between a mission and a job. And Yossi had put his life into this place, now. Surely, they must see that—and honor it. He'd given up his business in Jerusalem—sold it for his personal settlement fund. Now, he was on the land every day. To use another phrase that's almost too old-fashioned to say, he was redeeming it, because it redeemed him. Or here's another sappy old truth the zionists had figured out by the time he was born— you could call it the reason the Jews could not be driven into the sea: When a man has put his life, his family and his own sweat onto the land, it's almost impossible to drive him off. Nothing mystical about it—it's just he'd rather die than give up. . . . You could even call it the same reason that Palestinian villagers can't be driven away, now—or another fact that the Jews forgot, now that Ben-Gurion is just a face on a bank-note—it's why the occupation *can't* win.

Anyway, Yossi was Israeli enough to hang on till his house was done. Even when it came clear that he would never be accepted in Tekoa, he thought, perhaps, the settlement nabobs would buy the house and resell it to someone they could accept. Or if the Oslo thing ever worked out—some-day—the government might buy his house as part of the price for peace. The exterior of the house was all finished. Even the garden wall (also chiseled stone) was almost per-fect—no mortar required, and it would be there forever. And most of the inside was done, as well—interior walls and trim, plumbing, electric—now, he and Tami were working on the fun stuff. . . . One Sabbath morning, they were sitting on a ledge of stone across the road—maybe twenty yards away from the house—dreaming up where they would plant trees to give shade. And they watched a group of religious settlers walk by, on their way home from the synagogue—young peo-ple, mostly, with prayer books under their arms. And they stopped in front of the garden wall, and began to kick the stones—then, they were pulling stones out of the wall with their hands—one-handed to keep hold of their books. Yossi put a hand on Tami's arm for silence—he wanted to hear: "We've got to get rid of them," the settler kids said. "This house is unclean. It's got to go." Tami couldn't stand it. She jumped up and screamed at them: "Aren't you ashamed to be destroying on the Sabbath? With the holy word in your hand? *Don't you have any shame?"* . . . They scuttled off without a word of response.

That's when the cold war heated up—in the springtime of 1998. Posters went up in the center of the settlement, accusing the Aharon family of stealing water, stealing electricity and fostering terrorism in Tekoa. (Fostering terrorism meant bringing in Arabs.) . . . Then, while Yossi was at work on his house, someone went to his trailer and killed the ducks and geese. . . . Then, Yossi was at the trailer, when his dog dragged himself home, spurting blood from a wound in his neck. It turned out that Animal Control—the state veterinarian service—had been visiting Tekoa, to keep the pets up to date on inoculations. But the settlers said that Yossi's pet was a wild dog—the vet's assistant shot him. Yossi found that out later. For the moment, his dog was bleeding to death, his kids were wailing in tears in the yard—and there was nothing he could do but run to the trailer where the soldiers slept, to borrow a gun, and kill the poor dog.

On the eve of the following Sabbath, June 12, 1998, a car sped up the drive that Yossi had graded, and skidded to a halt in front of his trailer. A member of Tekoa's security committee got out, and presented a document. He was gone by the time Yossi read what it was—an eviction notice. He was no longer welcome in Tekoa. . . . All the settlers signed a paper when they first came to the settlement—it gave the Tekoa council the right to judge, over time, whether they should be accepted as a part of the community. Of course, this "probation period" was only supposed to last one year—and Yossi had been in Tekoa for four—but he didn't care about that. He was too happy—he was thrilled with that eviction notice.

By that time, he knew he had to get out—the only question was how, and how much he would lose. Everything he had in the world, he'd sunk into that house. Now, he thought, they had given him his exit strategy. With that paper in his hand, he could show—he could prove in court—that they didn't want him. They were forcing him to leave. From there, it should be a simple matter to require them to pay for his house—and the work he did for the farm, at his trailer. . . . He was already planning: he would have his work valued by a professional appraiser. (Maybe he should get two or three appraisals.) Then, he could simply send them a bill. And if they didn't like it—too bad! He'd get a lawyer, make them see reason. . . . He ran to tell Tami the news. It was a great day!

Late that night, they were still basking in a happy glow— it was like the doors of their jail had swung open. Suddenly, they had a future again. It was just Yossi and Tami, talking quietly in the trailer—the kids were asleep, and there were no visitors in the Sabbath silence. They were startled by a knock at their door. It was the head of the security committee with an announcement—one sentence: "Your house is in flames."

The security man didn't take Yossi to the house—or offer any help. Yossi took off running for the house. Tami called the police, and stayed with the kids. She would be alone in the trailer all night. No one would come to offer consolation—or just to sit with her. When he got to the house, Yossi saw in an instant—it was a disaster, catastrophe. The flames were so high—like a fireball had engulfed the house—it must have been burning for a long time, at least a half-hour. No one had tried to put it out—no one had called the fire department. There were fifty people standing around, watching. Three kids were playing with a garden hose, pointing it over the fence, so a little stream of water muddied the garden. That was the help. . . . When a fire truck came (it was Tami's call that fetched them), the engine was too small to fight that fire. So everyone just stood around—and Yossi with them—watching the house burn down to bare rock.

The Tekoa security staff would later tell police that of course, they saw the glow of the fire—they thought it must be car lights. Yossi told police that the security men must have known precisely when and how the fire was set—but the cops only asked: "How can you prove it?" Of course, they said they would investigate—but they also warned him, he was a suspect. The other settlers told the cops, Yossi set that fire—some insurance scam—he owed the Arabs money. (The Arab workers denied that. They owed Yossi money.) . . . Mostly, it was a curtain of know-nothing silence that descended around the scene. In the daylight of the morning after, Yossi went to the house, but there was nothing left—no roof, nothing inside the blackened concrete—the prefabs had buckled out of square, so the stone walls outside had given way, and some rocks had burst apart with the heat—there weren't even five stones together anymore. . . . He picked through the stones, trying to find something—what, he wasn't sure. Evidence of his work? That he'd been there? . . . That afternoon, he was back again, but there was nothing more—and nothing to do. He kicked around for an hour amid the ash and rocks—his fortune. He was a pauper now. (There was no insurance.) By the second day, he didn't want to go see it—to hang around with the smell of ruin in his nose? What for? . . .

He hung around the trailer—him and Tami and the kids. He didn't send his elder boy, Ma'or, to kindergarten. (But even the teacher didn't call for four days.) . . . The soldiers came by to say they were sorry. And his Arab friends came with food. But Yossi had nothing to tell them. All they had done together was gone—and that was that. He said he was waiting for the cops to call—but they didn't call (and he knew they wouldn't). Anyway, they couldn't bring back his house. No one could give back all the years of that house. . . . What he wanted was something for him to do. The house had been his polestar. When he got up every morning, there it was, with its jobs, its needs, its emergencies. He never had to think what to do—there was too much he had to do. And now—with every bit of him on red alert (his mind was racing, his heart was racing, his life was under attack!) . . . there was nothing to do.

He'd wake up in a lather—he had an idea!—how to hit back. One day, he drove—he sped—into Jerusalem. He had to see his friends at Meretz! That's a left-wing political party—zionist, but against the occupation—Yossi had found

them (or they'd found him) during his long political awaken-
ing. He had friends there, who were members of Knesset.
They could call the cops and insist they get to the bottom of
this thing! . . . And another idea: they could give him
posters—those big Peace Now placards that said END THE
OCCUPATION. He would wrap up his whole burned house
with them—like a stick in Tekoa's eye! . . . But by the time
he'd been in Jerusalem an hour, all his brainstorms were
mired in complications. His friends said an MK's call to the
cops would make the case a political matter—not what he
wanted, in their opinion. The hope was this matter would be
treated as a crime. . . . And the posters, yes—they could get
him the posters—in fact, they did send a whole truckload.
But Yossi didn't put them up. The only ones who'd see them
were the settlers. And that would just confirm for them that
he was a left-wing troublemaker—i.e., he deserved to be
burned out.

He didn't hear word one from his neighbors in Tekoa.
Not that he sought them out. Oh, there was one letter, hand-
written by an American settler. She was very upset about
what had happened—and she offered to *testify for him*—you
know, about the terrible way they had hurt his dog. . . . Five
days after the fire, he was favored with a visit from the settlers' council—not the local council, but the settler movement in Judea and Samaria (that is, the West Bank, in
Bible-speak). They told him they were alarmed and dismayed by this event—so, they had come to ask: "What can
we do for you?" . . . Yossi and Tami said: "We want our house

back." That wasn't what the settlers had in mind. But perhaps, there were other things—*a lot of help could be given* (money wasn't mentioned, but its smell was in the air). And they also offered advice on "how to handle this problem. . . . We can handle this ourselves. There's no need to talk outside about this."

They were too late. That horse was already out of the barn. The day after the fire, a Channel One crew was on-scene in Tekoa. And Yossi talked. He told the cameras the settlers burned him out—he told them why. The crew must have shot four or five videotapes. They couldn't get enough—and Yossi couldn't stop talking. But for some reason, the interview never made it on air. Channel One ran a simple announcement—this fire had happened—with silent footage of the blackened walls, and no comment on it, one way or the other. (The only TV interview that did run was on Al Jazeera—the Arabic news channel from the Gulf. Yossi showed off his Arabic. Tami tried her hand, too—and told of her dream that one day Jewish and Arab kids would go to school together. Al Jazeera ran the story over and over.) Meanwhile, Yossi's friends in Jerusalem had also called the papers. So, by the following Friday, there were weekend magazine features. The papers played the story down the middle: he said—they said. Rabbi Fruman was interviewed, of course. (He's kind of famous.) He suggested that Yossi's house was torched by Peace Now agitators—you know, to make the settlement look bad. . . . But one way or another, Yossi got enough ink to make someone do *some-*

thing for the family. They couldn't just be left out there in the ashes.

A friend from Meretz wangled an invitation from Kibbutz Ruhama, in the Negev—Yossi, Tami and the kids were welcome to stay there. And they did spend a month—people couldn't have been nicer. But after a while, Yossi couldn't sit still. There was nothing happening about his life—or the house that used to be his life. The Ministry of Housing pushed through an emergency grant to rent the Aharon family an apartment in Jerusalem. That was nice, as far as it went. It gave him a base of operations. Yossi spent all day making files with the letters that he wrote to the government, and the government wrote back to him, and his lawyer-letters, and the settlement's letters, and letters from the cops or the prosecutor's office. (There was only one letter from the prosecutor—informing Yossi that nothing could be proved about the fire, and no charges would be filed in his case.) . . . But how long could he sit there, piling up papers, in a place that wasn't his? He didn't want to be a ward of the state. He had a house—which was taken from him. He wanted a house of his own in return. What were they doing about that?

To cut a long story short, Yossi, Tami and the kids ended up living in a tent in the garden of the Knesset—as a more or less permanent cry of accusation—just outside the office of Prime Minister Barak. The tent was bedizened with placards and banners that told Yossi's story—or he hoped they made it clear. One big sign read, I'M HERE BECAUSE I LOVE YOU. That was Yossi's shorthand assertion that he wasn't an enemy of Israel and its enterprise: He was a good Israeli—a Jew, a zionist—*a settler!* . . . That wasn't how the settler movement saw it. The settlers also had a tent in that garden—another permanent cry of protest, this one against Barak's plan for peace. The settlers' tent was a grand affair where rotating shifts of the faithful were brought in—along with rabbis, dignitaries, foreign contributors—and truckloads of supplies and fresh food. They wouldn't give Yossi one cookie. They'd pass his tent on the way to their pavilion and opine, by way of greeting: "You deserved to get your house burned down. It's a pity you weren't in it."

The politicians weren't so hostile. They all said hello—all knew him by name. (It's Israel—everybody knows everybody.) One right-wing stalwart, a cabinet minister, Tsahi Hanegbi, was an old school chum. But the best he could offer was a friendly scolding: "If you'd stayed with us, Yossi, this wouldn't have happened." Avigdor Lieberman, founder of his own right-wing faction, made his home in a settlement not far from Tekoa. Yossi asked him: "Don't you want to know what's going on next door?" Lieberman brushed him off: "I don't get involved with things like that." Yossi even had a talk with Rehavam Ze'evi, who was such a famous right-winger (later famously assassinated by Palestinians) that he wanted to push all the Arabs out of the West Bank—send them to Jordan, let them call *that* their country. Yossi tried to tell him, it was his *responsibility* to help a Jew who'd been made homeless. "Look," Ze'evi said. "I'm your brother—okay. But I'm not your friend. Go talk to your friends."

The sad part was, his "friends" on the left wing weren't any more helpful, when it got to the bottom line. The folks from Meretz wrote letters for him—more paper to keep in his files. The supposed defender of secular Israelis Tommy Lapid simply said: "I heard about it. But I don't get involved in private matters." After months in that tent, Yossi even had a visit from the prime minister, Ehud Barak. He gave Tami a big hug, and assured Yossi: "The whole matter will come to my desk, and I'll take care of it. Leave it to me." But more months went by—and nothing was taken care of. When Yossi went to the P.M.'s office to ask what was happening, Barak's assistant told him, he had made himself *too famous*. "Look— if your problem didn't involve the press, we could close it"— and he clapped—"just like that. But with all this attention, every settler will want a new house." Yossi even appealed to Shas—why not? He was one of theirs. His family was Iraqi. They told him—sure, we can help! "All you do is say the Arabs burned you out. There's a special fund! You'll have a check in your hand in two weeks!"

The Aharon family might still be in that tent . . . if it wasn't for Yossi's health giving out—over time, strain took its toll. First, it was his vision—he went blind in one eye. (A slipped cornea, doctors discerned.) Then it was his circulation—his heart never would stop racing. By 2002, his blood pressure was so bad, he had to undergo open-heart surgery. So, he's living on disability, now—scraping by. He can't work—he's barely making rent on an apartment in Jerusalem. Arab friends still bring food, when they can get through the checkpoints. When I made my first visit to the apartment, Tami showed me a chicken that had arrived from a village near Tekoa that morning.

Where Yossi really lives is nowhere—he's an embarrassment. The Sharon government doesn't want to hear from him. (An Arab contractor offered to rebuild Yossi's house for free—the government would not issue permits.) His court case against Tekoa bogged down. (He still had his eviction notice. But the Tekoa council changed its story—that was all a misunderstanding, their lawyers claimed. That was just because Yossi's house was complete—they were only evicting him from his trailer.) And in a counterattack, Tekoa lodged charges against Yossi—for stealing electricity, stealing water, and "bringing enemy people into a Military Zone."

Truly, that last bit is the heart of the matter—he had the wrong friends. And even Yossi came to recognize, this was more than simple prejudice. Because, by his friendships he was, in fact, a challenge to his settlement and to the state. He had traduced the state's latter-day mission—which is the conflict. Or you could call him a heretic against the state's new faith, which is the way he tends to say it. That's what he wrote—in huge Hebrew script, on the biggest banner over his tent: I WASN'T THEIR KIND OF JEW.

IV

Why is there no peace?

I'm about to say something terrible here, just because someone has to. Of course, I know, everybody's going to hate it, and hate me. (Don't laugh—I may show up at your house to hide.) But any Jew who's not an Israeli, and not on psychotropic drugs, could solve this Peace-for-Israel thing in about ten minutes of focused thought. Compared to, say, Cyprus, or Northern Ireland, it's a piece of *babka*.

First, let's clear the table, as it were—no room for cake or coffee in this clutter of myths. And in fairness, let's start with our own corner—because the folks in the Holy Land will get nowhere near a deal without the U.S. to help it happen. In my little town, when I tell people that I'm writing a book about the Arabs and Israelis, about half of these good Americans (the half that doesn't want to hear any more) will shrug, and say something like: "Well, they been fightin' each other for hundreds of years." Generally, I take the remark as intended (as an invitation to shut up). But the fact is wrong, and leads to unhelpful attitudes. It's a nice American way to say: *That's not our business, we can't sort that out.* But we are the only ones who can sort it out—and since the holy-in-the-head warriors have made bombs of our airplanes, it behooves us to try. The fact is, Arabs and Jews lived in peace, or at least in habitual calm, for hundreds of years under the Turks—whom they equally and severally feared and resented. Anti-Semitism (or properly, anti-Jewish feeling) was an import from Europe—like zionism—and it was not coincidence that they took root at the same time.

It is also a fact—a hopeful one, it seems to me—that systematic violence by Palestinians against the Jews on this land did not start with the arrival of the first Jews, nor even the first zionists in Palestine. It did not start with the creation of the Jewish state, nor even in '67, with Israel's triumph and takeover of all the land of Palestine. A program of wholesale violence against Israeli Jews as Jews, especially against civilians, started much more recently, and only after the Jewish state stepped up its program of settlements, expropriations, assassinations . . . the shootings and suicide bombs started after Israel turned over policy on Palestine, and the Arabs who dwelt in it, to Jews who justified their seizure of the land, their occupation and the violence required to maintain it, simply and solely by their Jewishness—a promise to them by their God.

I consider that hopeful because it means to me: there does not have to be a war against Jews because they are Jews in the land of Palestine. One of the myths that clutters this table is the insistence—mostly by know-nothing American zionists—that the roots of this conflict are religious. Palestinians (it is claimed) attack Israel because they hate Jews. And so—in this closed and convenient circle of "logic"—the ultra-Muslim resistance groups (Hamas is the MVP in this league) sprang to the fore in the terror-war against Israel, because Islam teaches hate for the infidel Jews. It's a perfect paranoid circle of "proof" that is satisfying to the zionist hawks, because it confirms their deepest belief: *The whole world is against us, so it doesn't matter what we do.* It not only "explains"—i.e., explains away—anything Israel might do in combat. It also helps make the case to Americans that (blind) support for Israel is a blow against religious zealotry and terror. And it's dangerous to argue with. Because if you try to refute it, or question what Israel does, then you can and will be accused of hating Jews, too. But it is—start to finish—a lie.

In the first place, Islam does not teach hate for Jews, but accords its deepest respect (deepest among non-Muslims) to "people of the book"—that is, to the Bible-believers, Christians and Jews. Why do Muslims consider Jerusalem one of their holy places? It is not because they are spoilsports and mean to take it from the Jews and Christians. It is because, according to *their* holy book, Muhammad ascended to heaven—there to receive Allah's imprimatur—*from Jerusalem*. But why from Jerusalem? Why not take, you know, the nonstop from Mecca? . . . Because he detoured for a chat with his honored fellow prophets, Moses and Jesus. . . . To be sure, there are Jew-haters among the Palestinians. There are millions of Palestinians, tens of millions of Muslims, and plenty of bigots among them. But they did not learn their bigotry from Islam.

And speaking of down-deep Islam, it is also true that zionists who try to scare the world with the prospect of an Islamic republic in Palestine must do so without support from the facts. It is often lamented by believers in Palestine that its people are the most indifferent Muslims. They pray seldom. They drink wine. Their women go about (to jobs and schools!) with their heads uncovered. Palestinians are not Koran-thumpers. The supposed specter of an Iranian-style theocracy is, to most of them, laughable. And this was reflected from the start in the movement that expressed their dream of nationhood. The PLO was not Islamic, but nationalist and leftist (just as irreligious as, say, zionism)—it looked for ideology not to Mecca but Moscow.

I had a talk with Danny Rubinstein, the senior *Ha'aretz* reporter on Palestinian affairs, precisely on the topic of the new Islamic tint in the latest wave of violence. He told me about his visits to Hebron. That is the most conservative and rock-ribbed Palestinian town—no radio station, no TV in the homes, not even a movie theater. But there is a bookstore, and Danny always stops in. "In the old days," he said, "I'd stand there and I'd watch Palestinian kids coming in for books by Marx and Engels, Lenin or Stalin. Now, they all want Islamic books. But it's the same kids, and the same fight. It's still all about the land—what's changed is only the perception of who is leading the fight."

So what happened? How did it come to be perceived that the Islamic groups were leading the national struggle? It happened only since Arafat agreed to do a deal with the Israelis. That brought him to Palestine, where he kept his chair with a mixture of patronage and thuggery. But in the ten years since he arrived, he has brought the Palestinian people nothing but deeper misery. Jewish settlements have more than doubled, more land is lost every week. The occupation was not eased but bitterly tightened. The PA's policy of negotiations has brought, well, to use a technical term, *bupkiss*— and Arafat was seen as enmeshed in the web of his Israeli masters. The Islamic groups, who rejected the deal, gleefully crowed: *We told you so!* And they did another smart thing: Unlike Arafat and his cronies, the Islamists used what money they had for programs (schools, clinics, day care) that helped the population. They are seen as the "clean" alternative. . . . Still, it begs the question—how did they get any money in the first place? How could such a horror get started? Well, Hamas, just for example, was started and financed for years with the help of the Israelis, who thought such a group would serve as counterweight and a thorn-in-the-side to Yassir Arafat.

One more myth to unclutter: the conviction of most Israelis, and almost all American zionists, that Israel offered Arafat the moon—everything he wanted, or should have wanted—in the Bill Clinton round of Camp David negotiations. The way Israelis say it shows the national genius for "explaining." By their account, Prime Minister Ehud Barak offered Arafat *ninety-seven percent of the land!* And that idiot, Arafat, turned it down! (*"We tried to give him a country—just like that!"*) . . . The only question Israelis leave open is whether Arafat then had to scramble to get out in front of his own people's rage, and purport to lead the terror-war that followed—or if, instead, while he was smiling and pretending to talk of peace, he was already planning his dirty campaign to murder Jews. Israelis never can decide whether to brand Arafat as a hapless and irrelevant moron, or as evil-genius incarnate. But either way (in their view), the *putz* is killing children despite incredible Israeli generosity.

It's the kind of figure that's exact enough to stick in your head—for a lousy three percent! That's the discount merchants used to give, if you just paid your bill on time—the sort of chump change credit-card companies give back in cash! Who goes to war over three percent? That's caveman stuff—antimodern. It's ungrateful! And it misses the point with stupidity so thorough it must seem willful—it's like arguing with Ivory Soap! (*Yeah, but what's the other fifty-six one-hundredths of one percent?*) . . . It's a beautiful piece of *hasbarah.*

But what was the three percent—and what did it mean? Actually, by the bitter end of the peace talks, the Israelis were proposing to keep about six percent of the West Bank—three blocs of their settlements (all the big ones), and the new highways that lead to them. In exchange, they would cede to the Palestinians desert land in Israel that was, in area, equivalent to three percent. But the map that resulted from Israel keeping just six percent would have yielded a "Nation of Palestine" that was actually three small ghettos, each walled off from the others by Israeli fortifications, or roads patrolled by the Israeli army, or fences with checkpoints. In other words, a citizen of Palestine still couldn't go around his own country—say, from Nablus to Hebron (not to mention the wholly separate ghetto of Gaza)—without the acquiescence of Israelis. In addition, Israel proposed to keep five army bases in the Jordan valley (on the east side of "Palestine"), and to maintain full control of the airspace above "Palestine," and the water aquifers below "Palestine," and the seacoast and all the borders of "Palestine."

"Less than a Bantustan, for your information," was Arafat's (rather huffy) summation, in a subsequent interview. The way I'd say it, the Israelis proposed to continue their occupation, with a prettier name—"Palestine." Then, they were surprised and affronted when Arafat packed up his ratty little bag of marbles and went home.

The failure of those peace talks—and the war of terror

that followed the failure—has been much hashed over in Israel and elsewhere, by hawks and doves, each to prove his own point. The right wing in Israel treated Arafat's "rejection," and the start of the second *Intifada,* as proof that no peace was possible (negotiation itself was a mistake)—and it *never will be* possible, while Arafat bestrides Palestinian politics. ("We have no partner!") . . . The left-wing analysts faced a tougher task—explaining the failure, and the terror attacks that followed, while asserting that peace talks (and peace) were proper policy. The admirable historian Tom Segev met this question head-on, in one of his interviews: "When Barak tried to force the Palestinians to declare that the conflict was over, while simultaneously not being willing to make major concessions, this was guaranteed to fail. Arafat cannot look into the eyes of three million Palestinian refugees and declare: 'The conflict is over, and you remain as refugees.' It's not that Arafat is not a partner for peace—it is that he has been treated in a mistaken way."

But I'm not sure it was a mistake—not in the sense of an inadvertence. I'm not sure it's right even to call the talks a failure. Because, in the end, Israel got what she wanted—in fact, what she proposed—a continued occupation. (And with none of the trouble of changing names on the map.) . . . The IDF went back to its checkpoints, and even stormed back into the cantons that had been ceded by Rabin's deals to Palestinian control. . . . Even that *shlub* Yassir Arafat went back to Ramallah, transformed once again from a dupe to a hero. . . . Everybody went back to business as usual—and I

do mean business. For that's the terrible thing I have to say—
no one else will.

Why is there no peace?

Who wants one?

Let's drop the gloves. It was a phony "peace process" from
the jump—from the basic idea that underlay Israeli attitudes
and actions: *"So, okay. We'll give them a country. But a country of our devising—this is as much as we'll give."* . . . Who
are they to give nationhood?

The Palestinians *are* a nation—and they're *in* their
country.

This is, of course, a matter of international law—endorsed not once but over and over by the United Nations—
and not just by the General Assembly, with its implacable
anti-Israel majority of tin-pot third-world nations (that gaggle Bush the Elder once called "the little-wiener countries")
. . . but also by the Security Council, with U.S. acquiescence—that is, by the kind of vote that counts—precisely the
same sort of vote that is Israel's international legitimacy.

But beyond that—or underlying that—this is also a fact:
It is a fact so laughably obvious that *anyone can see it* . . . as-
suming that they can, even just for a moment, see the Jew
and Arab, each as a human with an equal right to a place on
the planet. In other words, the only nation that can't see this
is Israel.

When Israelis talk about this idea—understanding the
equality of Arab and Jew—they say, "We have to talk to them

at the height of the eyes." In other words, at eye level—with neither party having to look up or down at the other. The problem is, there are few Israelis who use the phrase—they are the exception. As for the rule—the vast majority—you could take, for example, Prime Minister Barak, who blamed his failure on (what he saw as) the Palestinians' incapacity for truth: "They are products of a culture in which to tell a lie . . . creates no dissonance," Barak said to the historian Benny Morris. "They don't suffer from the problem of telling lies that exists in Judeo-Christian culture. Truth is seen as an irrelevant category. . . . There is no such thing as 'the truth.' "

Of course, arrogance is Barak's middle name. But in his attitude toward Palestinians, he is in the Israeli mainstream—and in a long tradition of Israeli leaders implying that Palestinians are devoid of values, or not exactly human. Menachem Begin called them "beasts walking on two legs." (Arafat was "the beast with hair on his face.") Begin's chief of staff, Raful Eitan, thus recommended more Jewish settlements: "When we have settled the land, all the Arabs will be able to do about it will be scurry around like drugged cockroaches in a bottle." Begin's successor, Yitzhak Shamir, compared the Palestinians to a plague of locusts. (But, as he vowed to settlers in a 1988 speech, they would be "crushed like grasshoppers . . . heads smashed against the boulders and walls.") Barak's entry in this sweepstakes was, "crocodiles—the more you feed them, the more they want." The tradition continues because it's good for business—it can help a pol with Israeli voters. You can hear the same attitude, any day of the week—almost any time you ask a Jew why so many Arabs, down to toddlers and babies, are dying in the conflict: *"They push their own children in front, to give us a bad name. Human life means nothing to them."* If the Palestinians were not less than human (at least, less human than Jews), then how would the occupation make any sense?

And only with this attitude in mind do Israeli "peace proposals" make sense. No Israeli government has ever tried to make peace on the formula that everybody knows is a winner: *Give back the land.*

I don't mean, give back the land except for the settlements, or the roads or the military bases. I mean, give back the land—the West Bank and Gaza. East Jerusalem (and the Dome of the Rock) for the Arabs, West Jerusalem (and the Western Wall—let that be the triumph) for the Jews. After that, they could work out the details—neighborhoods exchanged, water rights, maybe a fence. Would it be a mess? Plenty of mess . . . but worse than what they have now?

No mainstream Israeli politician could propose this because . . . well, it's way too even-steven! Israel gives up plenty! And the Palestinians—what do they give up? . . . Well, it's helpful to consider what they have given up. They have recognized Israel and conceded to it seventy-eight percent of the land that was their country. They have dropped their "three no's"—no peace, no recognition, no negotiation. And they would give up their claims to their old homes in Israel. (The Israelis could help out with a stout-hearted acknowledgment of responsibility for the refugees. On that, withal, they could even put some money where their mouth is—*"See those fancy settlements we're leaving? And that gleaming new city of Ariel? Bingo! New homes for the former refugees!*) . . .

Anyway, back in the real world, no Israeli leader can quite pony up to the fact that the Palestinians are a nation, a people with rights equal to those of Israelis. True, they've come some distance since Golda Meir ("There are no Palestinians")—but it's been three steps forward, two-and-a-half back. In the first Camp David go-round (under Jimmy Carter's aegis), the Nobel Peace–laureate Menachem Begin agreed to "autonomy" for Palestinians . . . but not before he held up the deal at the eleventh hour to change the documents (which were in English)—where they spoke of "the legitimate rights of the Palestinian People." Begin uncapitalized "people."

In the mid-1990s Yitzhak Rabin did recognize the Palestinian People—he was killed for that. But as to their rights . . . well, that's the main reason he wanted the deal—to relieve the IDF of the responsibility for suppressing them. "I prefer the Palestinians to cope with the problem of enforcing order in the Gaza Strip," he told the popular daily *Yediot Ahronot*, one week before he signed the Declaration of Principles. "The Palestinians will be better at it than we were because they will allow no appeals to the High Court and will prevent the Israeli Association of Civil Rights from criticizing the conditions there by denying it access to the area. They will rule by their own methods, freeing—and this is most important—the Israeli army soldiers from having to do what they will do."

Well, it's a dirty job—kennel keeper—but it did get Arafat out of Tunisia. It made him and his best pals rich— Kings of Ramallah! . . . Until the Israelis got so pissed off— Arafat didn't keep the dogs penned up! . . . And they blasted everything he had, or thought he had, to useless rubble. Now, they say, they don't know what to do with him. . . .

Then again, the Israeli withdrawal—from all the West Bank and Gaza within five years—that never happened, either. So, everyone's happy.

Come to think of it, that's been the story with every new peace plan—it just didn't work out, the withdrawal part, and then—well, these terrible things kept happening! It's the same reason Arik Sharon is now *for* George Bush's Road Map to Peace . . . except for some few reservations, and, you know, adjustments, and corrections and some emendations, and some matters which will have to be discussed bilaterally . . . for a few weeks, or years, until some new outrage withers any proximate pressure, or wipes out any thought of peace— *This is war! How can we talk to them now?* . . . until Arik goes back to his farm (the biggest private farm in Israel, which American taxpayers helped to obtain for him), and his friend George moves up to Commissioner of Baseball—and . . . what were we talking about? Oh, yes, the Road Map. Well, that's got a couple more years to run yet, doesn't it?

Which brings me back to my own corner of the table. Since I've been watching this murderous circus act (twenty-five years, I regret to say), the Americans have always had a peace plan they're pushing, and special envoys, and fly-in visits by the Spook-in-Chief, and roundtable confabs, and reports to allies on the latest private discussions, and . . . they've never done squat to make it happen—not since Jimmy Carter left . . . or for a few months when Bill Clinton wanted the world to forget the name Monica Lewinsky. Mostly this was a matter that remained not-quite-bubbling, back-burnered . . . and the Israelis (correctly) saw inaction as consent—they did as they pleased. Every once in a while, there would issue from Washington some murmurous disapproval of a killing spree, or a land grab. But you could never call it a red light—or even a solid yellow (more like the "Don't Walk" signs were starting to flash). Just a few months back, President Bush had to disapprove *sternly* . . . because his pal Arik would not stop building Israel's Great Wall— using U.S. dollars, of course—and it was too painfully obvious that the Fence Map was about to obliterate the Road Map. It was embarrassing! So Bush cut Israel's loan guarantees. He got headlines. The White House got a ton of tough mail from zionists, and reams of e-hate. But the Wall is still a-building (double-speed, as Sharon saw fit to announce) . . . because it turned out the guarantees Bush cut would cost Sharon's budget three million dollars. When Israel's got its face in the trough for three-point-five, or four, or five *billion—every year* . . . we cut three million? They spill that much.

I wonder why those nasty Arabs don't seem to like us.

And on that topic, I have some (equally unsolicited) advice for the Palestinians—specifically for the leadership, Chairman Arafat and his boys—not that they'll care. But they should. That's where the advice would start: *Your cause has so few friends in America, it might be good to hear them out—even make a few changes.* . . .

First, the easy stuff: try not to be so consistently hapless. For instance, next time there's a major-league negotiation (hint: if it looks like the U.S. Prez wants to announce it on the White House lawn as his personal triumph, that's Big League) . . . try showing up with a big-time team. Bring at least one or two maps of your own. Maybe next time, you could bring one actual lawyer—and someone to talk English on TV. And if you do end up with someone brilliant on the team, like Hanan Ashrawi, or Dr. Haidar Abdel Shafi, don't rig it so they're the ones who go home, while your pudgy old cronies with the half-shaded glasses stay on CNN every day. It's your children's future, not a tryout for *The Sopranos.*

Don't try to diddle the Prez—he only looks dumb. Or if you do mean to lie to him, pay attention to the details. For instance, when the Israelis caught that ship crammed with weapons steaming toward Palestine? . . . Mr. Chairman, if you mean to tell G. W. Bush, man to man, that you had nothing to do with that ship, then don't let the Israelis storm into your compound and find papers that showed your own treasurer *rented the goddamn ship!* (Paper burns, you know.) . . . And for that matter, don't diddle with us. Don't condemn the latest suicide bombing, and then have your Ministry of Education (next day!) send a fax around to every school with a biography of the bomber, so that students may study the new hero's life. Maybe you could also stop sending money to buy off the bomber's family.

And since we're on the subject—now, we're into the big stuff—suicide bombing is a lousy tactic. I don't mean just morally lousy—though it is—vicious and indiscriminate, designed to kill the innocent. What I mean is, it's done a lousy job for the cause of the Palestinian people and their goal of getting a nation.

For one thing, Mr. Chairman, it brought you Arik Sharon (and reelected him). And no matter how good he's been for your career—I realize, you may need him, just as much as he needs you—he hasn't been exactly salubrious for your people. The dead and the also-dead now number in the thousands, and the live ones can't make a living. Any suicide bomb will serve him as pretext for any action he desires to take. (It doesn't matter if the bomber is from Hebron and, "in retribution," Sharon sends his aircraft or troops to kill in Gaza—he knows the rest of the world isn't picky about the geography.) And despite his somber speeches (every couple of months, whether he needs to or not) about "painful concessions" he may someday make for peace—if a miracle happens, and you do get a nation while Sharon is in charge, it will arrive in pieces so small, you'll never get the Mercedes out of first gear.

But it's not just Sharon the bombings brought on—

there's more, and worse. Three years of suicide bombs have sent a message to the whole world. Because the rest of us, non-Muslims, don't see that bombing as the act of a brave youngster who is on his way to heaven and his virgins. We see a kid who is sent off with dynamite stuffed in his shirt—sent off by his handlers in the Palestinian movement—because they hold his life (not to mention, he holds his own life) to be of *no value* . . . except insofar as it's thrown away to kill Jews (any Jews nearby, doesn't matter who). . . . In other words, we get exactly the libel the Israelis have been trying to plant on the Palestinian people for the last fifty years. So—as they used to say in New York—wisen up.

Here's an idea! You could jail the people who arrange the bombings. Save space by *not* jailing people who criticize you! Neat, huh? . . . And if you know of a kid who seems to think that God will reward him if he dies killing Jews—well, get him some help. You could start a mental clinic! Dr. Eyad El-Sarraj would be an excellent director. (Remember him? You had him jailed—and tortured, too.) . . . Money? Not a problem! You could use some of the loot the Israelis used to deposit for you—in your secret account in Tel Aviv.

See, from the jump, it's been a phony war, too—or, at least, not what we think of when we use the word. A succession of Israeli premiers—Netanyahu, Barak, Sharon (everybody since Rabin was killed, and his successor, Shimon Peres, failed to hold on to power)—has blamed Arafat for the terror in Israel, the suicide bombs, the growing pile of dead Jews.

Every one has (at some point) vowed to teach Arafat a lesson, and has (at some point) "declared war" on the terrorists, or on the Palestinian Authority, or on Arafat personally. A lot of Palestinians died for these pronouncements, a lot more lost land. But terrorists have never been in short supply. The PA is still there. Arafat is still in charge. Most recently, Arik Sharon had his cabinet locked away for days, supposedly deciding whether the IDF should continue to imprison Arafat in his ruined *Muqata,* or capture him and expel him from Palestine, or simply kill him. When the cabinet emerged, it was solemnly leaked that expulsion was the government's choice . . . of course, he hasn't been expelled. Arafat is the keystone of the status quo—i.e., what Israel wants.

Every government of Israel, under each of those prime ministers, was financing the PA, on which it "made war"— and paying off Arafat, too. Arafat's "secret account" at a Tel Aviv branch of Bank Leumi—now "discovered" and supposedly shut down—was never secret to the Israelis. It was a banking convenience for them, to permit, as we might say, direct deposit. They were well aware, money in that account was off the books of the Palestinian Authority—it was the Chairman's money, to buy loyalty for him, to be doled out to friends, or meted out as honor-*baksheesh* to the families of "martyrs." Did that bother the warrior Jews? Not so's you'd notice. Not till they (and their American buddies) began— for their own reasons—to rail against PA corruption. At that point, Caroline Glick, columnist for the *Jerusalem Post,* asked the U.S. special envoy, Dennis Ross, why the U.S. had never made much of Arafat's corruption before. "Well," Ross said. "It wasn't as if the Israelis were particularly concerned about the problem."

The Israelis have known, for a long time, exactly how Arafat works—paying off in dribs and drabs, here and there, for the honor of a family, or to recognize clan leadership . . . sending gifts (ten, twenty, fifty thousand) to his favored lieutenants to help out with the new villa, or on the occasion of the daughter's wedding, or to help with a "stipend" for the son at the Sorbonne . . . covering the tracks of cronies who stole millions (once they knew that *he knew*, their loyalty would be assured forever) . . . lubricating his path, like a snail, with a trail of slime. By '93, when they did the deal that brought him back to Palestine, the Israelis had been studying Arafat for twenty-five years. They knew *everything*—down to and including his *kidney and liver functions*. (The Mossad rigged his toilet and got a urine sample at an Oslo hotel.) They brought him back precisely because (as they thought) he was the sort with whom they could do business. Their rage at him now is because (as they see it) he wouldn't stick to the deal.

What was the deal? . . . Well, first the part that pissed off the Israelis—Arafat was supposed to be their top cop. As Rabin so frankly stated, the Israelis expected Arafat to squash the resistance of his own people with all the same PLO brutality that had made him Israel's most hated enemy. . . . But Arafat failed—and then he reneged. When it came clear that the resistance continued (and picked up steam) without him, he had no choice but to act, once again, as its leader.

Why would he ever agree in the first place to act against his own life's history, and the sole rationale of his organization? Why would he suddenly serve as the muscle to protect the occupiers of Palestine? . . . Was he really confused—he thought they gave him a country? There was no recognition of a "Nation of Palestine" in the Declaration of Principles he signed. . . . But there was the recognition that mattered to him—*him*. Arafat's main effort at the Oslo peace talks—his sole precondition and preoccupation—was to change every reference to "the Palestinian negotiators" or "the Palestinian people," so it referred, instead, to "the PLO."

For the rest, Israel got everything she wanted—anything she could dream up. She got complete control of "security," of course . . . control of the borders, the water, the air . . . the continuation in force of Israeli military regulations—i.e., the legal framework of the occupation . . . a huge new land grab—thirty-five thousand acres (now, suddenly, "all legal") for new settlers' "bypass roads"—which would remain under IDF control . . . another grand new land grab, with agreement to consider the Israeli settlements in "blocs"—which meant all the land between them was suddenly "legal," too . . . the division of the rest of the West Bank into smaller areas (two hundred twenty-seven separate "enclaves," by Amnesty International's count)—with access in and out controlled by Israelis . . . the division of Gaza into three tiny ghettos (access—same deal) . . . Israeli control of people and products exiting the West Bank and Gaza Strip—the Palestinians cannot export without Israeli approval (in practice, they cannot export) . . . Israeli control of all imports into the West Bank and the Gaza Strip—in practice, the Palestinians have to import from or through Israel. To be precise, a "customs union" gave Israel control of tariffs, standards and quotas on imports and exports. In other words, the territories (and the Arabs in them) became the perfect and legal embodiment of a captive market. Israel collects all taxes and fees—which she then remits to the PA—so Israel is also Arafat's paymaster.

In sum, what Israel got from the Oslo deal was a codification, continuation and legalization (by solemn treaty) of its occupation in the West Bank and Gaza—at least for a few more years. (Of course, Israel was also supposed to withdraw its armed forces during those years. But that didn't work out. What the hell—they kept the parts they liked.) No wonder Barak proffered more of the same at Camp David, for a "final status agreement." No wonder Barak was so shocked and dismayed when Arafat wouldn't swallow. He'd seemed so compliant when Rabin rammed it down his throat . . .

You know, it's just possible, Arafat, too, ain't as dumb as he looks. Maybe he wasn't fast asleep through Oslo. Maybe his single preoccupation was all he needed—it made the Oslo deals the last he'd ever have to sign. After all, for ten years, that has kept him in Palestine, and alive. It has made the Israelis send millions every month, to pay his freight, too—no matter who declares war on him. There's never going to be a real war on him. Because the way it worked out, after all, the Israelis don't have any deal to legitimize their occupation, they don't have any deal, at all . . . except with the PLO—with him.

Get serious! A real war against the PA—anything that we would describe as war—would result in Arafat's death, and the rest of the PA thugs also-dead, or on the run . . . on day one—*before lunchtime.*

It doesn't happen because there are powerful interests that prefer, instead, the status quo—not the chaos that would certainly result from such a war. It will likely disappoint some Americans when I say, I don't mean powerful U.S. interests, restraining Sharon for the sake of peace. (These days, U.S. pressure is not exactly harsh—anyway, that never stopped Sharon before.) No, the interests that protect the PA are purely local. . . . Maybe it's true—as the *hasbarah* claims— that Arafat and his cronies failed as Israel's partners for peace. It surely is true, if we're talking of peace as Israel proposed it. But that doesn't mean they were not—are not— partners.

Let's take the case of a Palestinian who is partner to no one, save perhaps his wife: he is a head of household, who has provided for his family, as honor requires, by his labor— it doesn't matter what labor: say, he ran a shop in Gaza. He's done well enough to have a house, and now, in the fullness of time, his son must wed. Except the son doesn't have a job—

what job? So the father must construct an addition to the house. Honor requires no less. And the construction will require, let's say, some gravel. And the gravel must come from Israel—that's quite a business in Israel. Except this Israeli gravel will cost our hard-pressed shopkeeper twice what it costs in Israel. Because there's only one place to buy the Israeli gravel—a legal monopoly run by and for the princes of the PA. And, of course, the new rooms will require some lumber—obtainable only from a similar monopoly (original provenance—a supplier in Israel) . . . and cement (same story) . . . and the steel bars to reinforce the cement . . . and tiles . . . and bathroom fixtures . . . and the hot-water heater . . . and . . . and . . . and. It's all the same story—or as the Palestinians say, "same-same." Our shopkeeper will pay maybe double the price for every item he'll need. Or, to put it another way, his every occasion of normal need will be twisted to provide commerce for Israel, and pure profit (it adds up to billions each year) for the Tunisians. Of course, this doesn't stop with construction materials—you could follow the story of this fleecing down to the cooking oil, flour and meat that his wife used, making lunch for him today . . . and beyond, to the cigarette that our worried home owner now smokes as he drives to the double-price lumberyard. That's an Israeli smoke—Time is the brand name—available only through a PA monopoly . . . just like the gasoline that keeps his car moving.

While we're on the subject—the gasoline is instructive. Because every month, Palestinians buy more than ten million gallons of Israeli fuel. . . . It doesn't matter that they could buy gasoline from Jordan or Egypt at half, or even one-third, the price. (Israeli gas can run five bucks a gallon.) The deal is, the fuel must come from Israel. In fact, it comes from one Israeli company—Dor Energy—which took over this fabulously lucrative business immediately after Arafat took power in Palestine. (*Someone* had connections.) . . . Then, the price is further jacked up by the PA monopoly, which keeps all the gas station owners in line.

It doesn't matter what level of "closure" has been announced, or who has "declared war" on whom. The petroleum tankers must get through—and they do. In fact, at a main crossing between Israel and Gaza, there's a nice army-guarded petroleum depot, where Israeli trucks back up and pump their fuel load into a tube, which snakes over a wall that hides Palestinian tankers on the Gaza side. No one has to see or shake hands with anybody from the "enemy camp." But the fuel goes through—business is business. And—what do you know!—though that crossing occasionally takes a rocket or two, or a mortar attack from the Gaza side (just a month or two back, there was a suicide bomber) . . . the petrol depot has *never been hit,* or even interrupted in its operations—go figure! Another amazement: the Palestinian tankers never have a problem delivering in safety. . . . It turns out, one stakeholder in the PA oil monopoly is Muhammad Dahlan, the Gazan chief of Preventative Security—the PA's enormous secret police force. In fact, the oil business pays for Dahlan's secret police force, which, in turn, made him such a power that he became Arafat's fair-haired boy, chief of security for all Palestine.

On the West Bank side, the story is a bit different—more amazing. I have driven my Israeli rent-a-car throughout the territory, on highways and country roads, often lost, sometimes just wandering—past settlements, in and out of Arab villages—to the IDF's stern consternation. ("Don't you know they shoot at Israeli cars?") But I don't feel threatened—because I can often snuggle up behind an Israeli oil truck—a nice, safe place. . . . Now, my terrorist training is a little spotty, but it seems to me, if you mean to blow up Israelis, what better target than an oil truck? A grand big boom. . . . How about nailing one when it's stopped at a checkpoint—with all those soldiers nearby? That never happens. . . . How about when it pulls up to deliver fuel at the bright gas stations—Israeli gas stations, with Hebrew signs—that operate on the verge of the highway outside of all the big settlements? Never happens. . . . It's true that gunmen sometimes shoot at vehicles, expecially on the settlers' bypass highways—they'll shoot up a mother and three kids in a little sedan—but the big fat target of a tanker sails through. (The only oil truck I know of that was ever hit was an independent—a Jewish father-and-son team, who were selling oil to an Arab village just past the Green Line—undercutting the cartel—*they* got blown up.) . . .

What it means to me is—if one thing can be protected, then anything *could* be protected. I don't listen anymore to the PA's hand-wringing about the impossible job of controlling the Islamist hard-liners. . . . Impossible? What about the oil trucks? . . . I don't listen anymore to Israeli "analysis" that attempts to slice and dice the Palestinian movement. (*"Well, the Tanzim was for the cease-fire, but the Islamic Jihad and Hamas had to show that they weren't knuckling under to the Fatah"* . . . baloney!) They'll slice, dice and hypermystify, until it's clear that only "the security experts"—the IDF and the Shin Bet—can be listened to on the subject of the terror-war. . . . But what about the oil trucks? They can't be hit because there's muscle behind them. And the muscle is money.

Money keeps the PA in business, and the business of the PA is money. There's nothing nice or nationalistic about the methods. Take, for example, the poor Arab *schlemiel* who owned thirty acres of desert land near Jericho. Arafat's cronies decided that would be a good place for their sleazy new casino, the Oasis. The big PA stakeholder in the new casino was Arafat's "top economic adviser"—that is, his bagman, who handled the money—Muhammad Rashid. He was in for thirty percent of the action. . . . But this Palestinian, a guy named Hamdouni, didn't want to give up his land. (Isn't that the Palestinian story? Well, here's a real Palestinian ending.) Arafat's thugs threw Hamdouni in jail, and tortured him for seventeen days, until he signed over his land to the PA.

At that time, the land around Jericho was a PA enclave—the Israeli army had pulled out of that zone. In fact, if I remember right, it was the only zone of full Palestinian administration. But with the Israelis still in control of overall "security," and all IDF regulations still in force (Israeli "withdrawals"—you know, for the last thirty-five years or so—have been more or less illusory. Have I mentioned that?) . . . it should come as no surprise, there were also Jews with an interest in the founding of that casino. One was an Austrian businessman named Martin Schlaff—he bought in for forty-five percent. Mr. Schlaff was a pal of Sharon's—a visitor at the P.M.'s farm—and did a lot of business in Israel. He would have liked to do more. He'd been trying for years to set up a casino inside Israel. (And *here's* a coincidence: the prime minister's office is, at this moment, working on a big proposal to legalize gambling in Israel.) . . . Another investor was Schlaff's Austrian bank, an outfit called BAWAG—Bank fur Arbeit und Wirtschaft—which bought in for ten percent. (Why not? It was a beautiful deal—a franchise to run the casino till 2028—and tax-free for the first ten years. In fact, it was a monopoly for Palestine. No one else could run a casino on PA land.)

Now, bear with me—I hate all these foreign names, too. But I want to mention some more remarkable coincidences. It stands to reason that BAWAG would need a lawyer in the Holy Land—someone smart to look after its interests—a well-connected lawyer would be better. So BAWAG retained, as counsel, the director general of the prime minister's office under Yitzhak Rabin, a fellow named Shimon Sheves, who—I am sure—served them well, until his unfortunate indictment for soliciting a bribe . . . at which point Mr. Sheves needed a lawyer. So, Mr. Sheves hired his friend and fellow attorney, Dov Weisglass, who by coincidence, was

also the number-one factotum in the prime minister's office—chief of bureau for Arik Sharon. (I'm certain that Mr.
Weisglass served his client well—he got the High Court to
overturn Mr. Sheves's conviction.) . . . Another coincidence:
Mr. Weisglass was also the lawyer for the Kasino-king, Herr
Martin Schlaff. (How 'bout that?) . . . So, it was surely pure
coincidence that when the casino ran into trouble—the start
of the second *Intifada* in the year 2000 forced it to shut
down, and the slime-flow of millions ceased to moisten the
partners' pockets . . . and Arik Sharon was also stretched
thin for money, at that moment, near the close of his campaign to become prime minister—a meeting was hastily convened in Vienna, with at least three known principals: Mr.
Sharon's son Omri; the lawyer-to-the-stars, Mr. Weisglass;
and the PA bagman-in-chief, Mr. Rashid. (The elder Sharon
still insists, there was no bargain discussed at that meeting—
money in exchange for a promise to reopen the casino. In
fact, the casino was *never even mentioned!* No, that was only
a back channel for statecraft: Arik Sharon was hard at work,
making peace.)

Just one more—as we say in Iraq, the Mother of All Coincidence. You may remember Sharon's *reelection* as prime
minister, in 2002, was interrupted by a nasty whiff of scandal.
It turned out those old money problems from the first campaign had forced him to take a million or two from his old pal,
the South African Cyril Kern . . . except, it seems, now (as
police believe), the money did not come from South Africa.
(In fact, Mr. Kern may not have had such a great sum of

money to loan.) The millions that landed in Sharon's pocket came from an account in Mr. Kern's name, in Austria—at the BAWAG bank. When the stink ensued in 2002, another transfer of millions arrived in the pocket of Sharon's son Gilad, which he used to pay off the original stinky "loan from Mr. Kern" . . . and the money for Gilad Sharon was transferred from (of course) BAWAG . . . raising the prospect that the same interests who slimed Sharon's pocket in the first place, sent a second, equal and sufficient slime—more or less as air freshener.

Well, we'll let the police sort that out in due time—or not—it doesn't change the main point: The PA's slimy business intersects with Israeli business at the highest levels of Israeli political life. Things are not as they seem.

This is another of those sudden truths you see everywhere, in little ways, once you step back a pace or two, and the pattern shows. On a raw winter day, I stood at a checkpoint in an Arab village outside Jerusalem. It was a period of great tension: there were attacks inside Israel every week, and "incidents" in the territories—one or two dead, or four or ten—seemed liked every day. The Sharon government was boasting of "strong measures" it imposed on the Arabs, and assuring Israelis that curfews and closure were forestalling most attacks before they could happen. (Some assurance—it could be worse?) . . . I went out to that village not to watch for an incident, but to watch the watchers—two ladies from Machsom Watch—an organization of decent souls who show up unannounced at checkpoints (*Machsom* is the Hebrew for checkpoint) . . . and with clipboards at the ready (to note any bad behavior), monitor the actions of Israeli troops.

My Machsom ladies were darlings—childhood friends from New Jersey, who'd moved with their families to Israel, decades back, for the good and sufficient reason that they loved it. Now, in their seventies, they still cared enough to put their own time and bodies on the line, in an effort to prevent the Jewish state from shedding its last decencies. Not that they thought they succeeded. . . . I asked our driver and mission-leader, Rose Weinberg, whether they had seen anything terrible at the checkpoints. "What do you mean 'terrible?' " she said. "It's all terrible. Everybody is suffering." Her colleague, Rina Harrison, said she now questioned, for the first time, whether she should have made this her home. "I didn't mean to move to South Africa."

The checkpoint was a bunch of dirty plastic barricades that blocked off the main village road that used to lead to Jerusalem. Except, at some point in the past, someone had adjudged that *not barricade enough*—so the main street was bulldozed into a high mound of dirt and stones, which, now, in winter rains, was mud and stones. So the people of the village couldn't get to the checkpoint on the main street—they had to go around the mound, into the mosque, then out to a smaller perpendicular street through a little side door. But, clearly, someone in authority had objected, so a smaller mound of mud and stones was pushed up to block the mosque side door. And this smaller mound had then been bridged with a path of planks—actually, two or three rickety boards . . . so the residents now went into the mosque, and then stooped to climb on the teetering boards through the side door, so they could then descend on the slippery mud to present themselves at the checkpoint. The elderly had the toughest time. But they seemed to bear up in grim silence. The ones I watched—you couldn't not watch—were the young women in their city shoes, little pumps with medium heels, so carefully matched to their dress, and purse. You could see the story in one glance—they were coming home from office jobs. They cared enough to dress carefully, perfectly, in respect for those jobs and for themselves. But respect is the number-one target in this "war"—and the first casualty.

There were hundreds of people going through the checkpoint—and some not going through—young men, mostly, who were invited to sit on the mud while their papers were vetted. The man in charge was a Border Police lieutenant—smart and serious—he was working hard. And he kept his platoon of policemen on the jump—barking at bus drivers who'd parked too close to disgorge their loads of workers . . . shouting in Hebrew for this one to move on, and this one to stop . . . poking with the muzzles of their guns into boxes and sacks that were laid on the mud for their inspection . . . then, everything stopped. The lieutenant was yelling orders. Four or five policemen ran, with their rifles, in their flak vests, down the side street, and then, past the second or third house, they turned right, down a lane, into the fields. They were after a kid the lieutenant had spotted, walking through the field to get around the checkpoint. But why that kid? As my eyes followed the soldiers, I saw, for the first time, there were dozens of men and boys walking through the fields. While the lieutenant was still yelling, I saw another Palestinian man—he looked to be in his thirties. He came out the side door of the mosque, carrying a carton. It looked like a produce box—but who could tell?—the box was closed. And as the policemen brought the errant boy back to the checkpoint, the man with the box walked calmly down the lane, and through the fields, himself. If nothing stopped him, he could be in Jerusalem within the hour—with his box. Closure is an approximate science. It depends how much of a show you mean to put on.

In the same period of high tension, I traveled to the Karni crossing between Israel and Gaza. Here, too, closure was not what it seemed. On the Israeli side, there was a line of trucks grinding toward the gates, with belches of black diesel smoke—a line that easily ran for a mile. There were eighteen-wheel flatbed trucks and trailer trucks, and old rickety trucks with wooden slats on the sides. I wrote down what I could see of the cargo—sacks of rice stacked high on a flatbed, sacks of sugar just as high, boxes of onions, manure, hay, wall panels and roof panels, tin roof sheeting, fence posts, steel barrels, thousands of steel rods, sheets of glass, mountains of ceramic tile, dump trucks full of gravel—lots of dump trucks . . . and straight trucks crammed to the top of their slat sides with used stuff—old water heaters that the

Palestinians could refurbish, used washing machines, refrigerators, house doors, aluminum jalousie shades. . . . One of the truckers, who was out on the pavement giving his legs a stretch, said this wasn't too busy a day. Sometimes, he had to sleep in his truck before he could off-load into a border warehouse, or onto a Palestinian truck.

"Good business," I said.

"Business, business," he said through a grin. "Everything we tear down, they have to rebuild." He rubbed his thumb appreciatively against the pads of his fingers—the international sign for money changing hands. "You'll recognize the trucking contractors," he said. "They always come around in some snazzy car."

Of course, on the Palestinian side, there was a vast herd of trucks, too. Truckers there often have to stay for days. There are "permits" to obtain, after all, and officials who have to be paid to issue permits. And higher officials who have to be paid to opine that the permits are correct. And on that side, too, there are a few snazzy cars—which belong to those higher-ups, the officer corps that "controls"—i.e., milks—the Gaza side of the crossing. They are officers of Muhammad Dahlan's Preventative Security.

I bring up his name again because you'll probably hear it more and more. The Israelis have mentioned him as a possible successor to Arafat. Dahlan is also said to be a great favorite of America's CIA, which works closely with PA security bigs—needless to say, in the interest of peace. Recently, he further endeared himself to the Americans, when they (and the Israelis) were marginalizing Arafat with revelations about corruption. Dahlan chose that moment to make his own clarion call for "reform." He's a polite fox, who chews and swallows, and buries all the chicken bones, before pointing out the hole in the henhouse wall.

Years ago, when I first saw the Gaza Strip, the big name, the big family, was the Shawwa clan. Rashid el-Shawwa was called in the papers, the "Mayor of Gaza." But in fact, he owned Gaza—and the people in it—as a feudal landlord. What he didn't own, his friends owned, by his sufferance. And more or less coincident with my first visits, Mr. Shawwa was building a splendid house. I think it was supposed to be for his son. Anyway, it was the latest and greatest, and huge, of course—a palace. When I went back to Gaza to research this book, I heard that grand house had been sold. The buyer? Muhammad Dahlan. By happenstance, I had a friend from the Shawwa clan—I lost no time in needling him: "Isn't it nice," I said, "that Mr. Dahlan saved enough from his police salary to buy your grandfather's house?"

Mysteriously, and with a sly smile, my friend began to pat his hand down his breastbone, to his belly. "The salary," he said, "pays for the tie."

For the next several minutes he listed sources of Dahlan's wealth. The oil monopoly was number one—thirty percent off the top, just for starters. That's before the shakedowns of gas station owners (who also need "permits"). Cigarettes—he's in on that, too. (And stores that sell cigarettes need lots of "permits.") Frozen food—that's his. Cooking oil, too, some people say. Anyway, the oil and frozen food has to come into Gaza on trucks—so, the border crossing is a license to print money. There's the cold-storage warehouse—lots of fees to be collected there—more fees if the "permits" to unload from the warehouse are, somehow, delayed. Oh! And the forklifts that do the unloading—those are Dahlan's, too.

He told a story of his friend who ran a paper-goods factory—tissue paper, napkins—not a big operation. But the guy used to do all right. Of course, his machinery had to come from Israel. And one time, a machine broke, he needed a part. He called to Israel—the part would cost eighty bucks, more or less. On the appointed day, he sent his driver in the truck to the border. But the driver had to wait, one day, two days. (Parking fees, each day.) Then there was the "import fee" that had to be paid before the part could be located. The truck driver called—he'd run out of money. So, the owner went to the border, and paid the fee—more than the part cost. After most of a day, a higher official informed him, the part had been found—but it would have to be "tested for safety." That test would cost five hundred dollars. He paid that, too. What else could he do? . . . It took most of a week at the border. But he got his part—for about ten times the price.

"How can he stay in business?" I asked. "That's only one little part. What about all the paper pulp, the raw materials?"

"Oh, that's not a problem," my friend replied. "All the raw materials are shipped through the settlements."

"The Jewish settlements?"

"Of course. They get shipments directly from Israel—with the army to guard. They mark it up a little. That's how they stay in business. But it's cheaper for us. There's no Dahlan in the middle."

The dead, and the also-dead? Well, that is as it seems—they died—and their families' grief and rage are real enough. But you could call it the cost of doing business. Actually, it's more than that. Because every strike and counterstrike in the terror-war helps to cement the hold of the principals on the business.

Take, for example, Yassir Arafat. It has often been observed that his popularity in opinion polls teeters near nowhere—invisibility—until his rescue by Israeli action against him. But it's bigger than that—and simpler. The conflict is Arafat's life, and his metier. If the Palestinians had a country, and the job of their leader was to build that country—strengthening its institutions and enhancing the welfare of its citizens . . . well, then, my candidate, and the candidate of most Palestinians, would be A.B.A.—Anybody But Arafat. . . . Without the conflict, he's out of a job.

You could say the same about old General Sharon. Without the conflict (and the fear it engenders), is there any way that Arik Sharon gets anywhere near the prime minister's chair? Not close enough to sniff the leather. . . . He's been fighting this conflict with everything that falls to hand—guns, tanks, settlements, budgets, the lives of his compatriots—

since 1948. . . . That made his career. It is his career. Without the conflict, there is no Sharon.

In defense of Arafat—at least he buys his loyalty with hard currency. Sharon obtains his with the cheesy scrip of fear. It's easy to manufacture—easier still to put in circulation. His countrymen are so ready to fear, so given to fear, so comfy with fear . . . it's almost too easy, it's child's play.

You can see this pattern just by marking the strikes and counterstrikes (and the occasional cease-fire, or possible cease-fire) on a simple calendar. You can trace the pattern back to the early days of Sharon's rule. In the summer of his first year, 2001, Hamas had observed a cease-fire on Israeli civilians for a couple of months, until July 31, when the Israelis assassinated two Hamas commanders in Nablus. Nine days later, a Hamas suicide bomber blew up a Jerusalem pizzeria. . . . After the 9/11 attacks on the U.S.A., the Palestinian factions tried to show goodwill with an agreement against attacks inside Israel—until November 23, when Israel put a hit on the senior Hamasnik, Mahmoud Abu Hanoud. Nine days and ten days later, Hamas suicide bombs killed Jews in Jerusalem and Haifa. . . . A month and a half after that, January 14, 2002 (again, during a cease-fire that had been announced in December), Sharon ordered the assassination of an Arafat lieutenant, Raed Karmi. That produced the first suicide bomb by Arafat's own party (they were slow to begin—it took two weeks) on January 27.

Remember that one-ton bomb the Israeli Air Force dropped on a Gaza apartment house, to kill the Hamas big,

Salah Shehadeh—along with sixteen-or-so also-dead? . . . I left out one part. That air attack scuttled another cease-fire deal between Arafat and Hamas. And it fetched up another suicide bomb (Hamas is reliable) nine days later.

By the end of that year, Sharon was working harder for peace. He wasn't hitting one at a time. On December 26, 2002, Israeli forces assassinated leaders from Hamas, Islamic Jihad and Arafat's own bomber corps—all in one day. Of course, there were mitigating circumstances: all those factions were meeting in Cairo with another dastardly plan for a truce. And Sharon could not stand for that—he was running for reelection. (Not to worry: Arafat's own boys put Sharon over the top with a suicide bomb that killed twenty-two Israelis. They took New Year's Day off, so it was ten days later.)

Sharon's campaign was a study in fear. If his poll numbers dropped, something terrible happened—dead Jews all over the TV. If the Palestinians failed to help out with a bombing, a statement would issue from the army, or some civil defense big, pumping up the fear of Iraqi chemical attacks. (Every Jew in the country was obliged to get a gas mask. They crowded into "emergency" offices and storefronts, staffed by the army—where they wangled, cajoled and argued for more gas masks, or newer masks, or special masks for tiny kids and grandparents.) The news industry also helped out—it is, after all, a commerce: fear sells papers, and TV time. It didn't matter that two years of Sharon had produced more suicide bombs and dead Jews than the previous seven years combined. Sharon stood for strength—that was good enough. (That fabulous jingle also helped out: it was a mark of God's favor, or at least His Sense of Humor, that Sharon rhymes with *bitakhon*—Hebrew for "security.")

Sharon's majority coexisted with an equally solid majority—a steady two-thirds of Israelis—who tell pollsters that they want peace, they're willing to give up land for peace, and the settlements on that land, as well. (That contradiction led the old Commie gadfly Uri Avnery to remark that Israel must be the only country with two hundred percent of its own population.) Fear is the factor that makes sense of those double majorities. Fear turns heads—or turns them off. And fear may always be with Israel. For without fear—without dead Jews, attacks on Jews, grief or hate for Jews—without threats to Jews, zionism itself has no rationale.

Even Arik can't do it alone. But as the old Jew says in all the old jokes, "Thanks God, he doesn't have to . . ." Anywhere he turns among the ruling elite in Israel, there are fellows who understand him perfectly—they speak his language, they think his own thoughts. You could say they all come from the same old school—the general staff of the IDF.

Retired generals lead the three biggest political parties (even the National Religious Party)—with ex-generals below, scrambling up as leaders-in-waiting. And why not? In the last half-dozen elections, the voters have installed as prime ministers *only* ex-generals (with the exception of poor Netanyahu—a mere ex-colonel, but from an elite unit).

Ex-generals people the cabinet—not just the "security" jobs—the trend reaches down, now, to Minister of Transport . . . Tourism . . . Science, Culture and Sport. It's a rather new trend—another big change that happened in Israel. It didn't become a common practice till after the '67 War, exactly co-incident with the occupation. And it's not an imported trend—there is no other "Western democracy" with an ex-general in the P.M.'s chair. And there is no country with any pretension to civilian control over the military that would move a *serving* general directly from the top army job (Chief of the General Staff) into the cabinet as Minister of Defense. (Shaul Mofaz had just enough time to take off his uniform and buy a necktie.)

In practice, ex-generals, or former chiefs of intelligence (they hold the rank of general), or active generals (the Chief of Staff also sits in on cabinet discussions) wield all the power of government in Israel. They make the big decisions—which are mostly (or mostly discussed as) "security deci-sions." In addition, the big city mayors are generals, and governors of regions. The Jewish Agency is operated by a general. The water company, electric company, phone com-pany (all state-sponsored authorities, and powerful institu-tions)—all generals. And private companies—a lot of the big ones . . . in fact, a public company almost *needs* to put a gen-eral in the CEO's chair—it's good for the stock price. A top job in the IDF is the highest public evidence of toughness, smarts and zeal. It is Israel's Good Housekeeping seal.

My economics maven, Sever Plotzker, points out some

good and true reasons why the generals rise to the top—even in his bailiwick, the world of business. The army is Israel's finishing school—also its Harvard, MIT and Stanford. (In fact, half the generals seem to have *been* at Stanford—there's a splendid exchange program for them, there.) By the time a man makes general, he is, by definition, a practiced top manager, experienced at running a large operation. And, by the standards of corporate CEO-dom, you can also get them cheap—they, each and all, have a gorgeous army pension clattering into the till every month.

They have weaknesses, too, as Sever notes. They tend to give orders, perhaps more than they listen. They are tactical thinkers—goal oriented, they like to get the job done—but they may not be strategic. And then, too, they may know nothing about business. Some learn quick. It depends on the man. . . . Then, Sever makes another point—a point of particular pride here. Israeli generals aren't all of one stripe—in business or politics—there are lefties and righties.

And that's true, as far as it goes. In fact, these days, a general who's eyeing retirement may go shopping for a business—security? Arms sales? . . . Or cell phones? Or selling soap? . . . And at the same time, he may shop for a political home—Labour, Likud or one of the smaller parties—ideology may matter less than the opportunities each party has on offer. So they do end up on the right and the left—or what the papers call the right and the left. But how far does that go?

For there are some things these generals have in common. Of course, there are exceptions—but you could call it the general rule. It's a shared experience—by retirement age, it's a worldview. The cardinal ethic is to fight to a win—and never give up ground. For twenty years, at least, they have faced fear and inspired fear—it's what they know. Force has been their calling card, and the normal solution to problems they confronted. (There's an old army saying: "If force doesn't work, try more force.") And no one gets to general in the IDF without understanding that Arabs are the enemy. No one gets near a star on his collar without buying into the conflict. These fellows have all done well in the conflict. It made them the big guys they are.

It helps to explain why the governments change—Likud or Labour, in coalition with an ever-shifting cast of smaller parties—but the conflict goes on. It has a life of its own. It endures. It is a worldview. . . . It is the fear they know—in which they are masters. And without it, where would they be? Stripped of the purpose of their past, on uncharted ground—*there* is the fear they don't know.

There is always the hope that civilian life will alter this worldview—the predilection to force as first and final solution. New lives may erode it, or mix it alchemically with new experience . . . as a man learns to listen to the voters in politics . . . or learns to think outside the box in business. Maybe. But, these days politics is, more and more, about the old fear. . . .

And business? Well, half of that depends on the conflict, too. I don't mean just the companies that sell to the PA monopolies . . . and I don't mean just the arms business . . . or the security business (which is in clover—someone has to supply the thousands of guards in front of thousands of doors) . . . or the sleazy business (also making millions) of importing foreign workers to replace the Palestinians. . . . I mean, even normal business—clean, everyday consumer business.

That big wheel Yaakov Peri retired as head of the secret police and made a bang-up businessman—he was the go-getter CEO of Israel's largest cell phone firm. But would Peri have done as well if every Israeli parent did not fear enough to buy a new phone for every one of his kids? . . . (I honor Peri all the more for speaking out against the conflict, now.)

What about the guys who merely sell soap? (Jeez—that's got nothing to do with fear!) . . . Well, let's put it this way: There are five million Jews to sell soap to. And there are five million Arabs—four out of five in the captive market that the territories represent. So let's dream together. Can we even imagine . . . the day when our CEO-of-soap, the noted ex-general now commanding our business, convenes a meeting of the board to announce:

Gentlemen! I've thought long and hard about it. And I've decided that half of our market must go. It's wrong to keep it. And so, I shall bend my powers, and the vast powers of our company, to promote peace and a state for the Arabs—which will rid us of those extra customers. . . .

As I managed not to say to that sweet old *sulha* man in Gaza—don't hold your breath.

I know it's a fine time to tell you, now—but I'm always wrong about the Middle East. Of course, the Middle East will *make* you wrong. That's why it's a plum assignment for reporters— it preserves its capacity to shock. And—truth be told—a dyed- in-the-wool journalist doesn't mind, that much, being wrong. It's just another good story to explain why he was wrong.

Still, I wish I could say I was wrong on some details, on some wrinkle of history—or wrong for a few weeks, till events set me straight. But I can't say that. I've been wrong big and basic, and for years at a time.

For instance, twenty years ago, while Israel laid brutal siege to Beirut, I thought (and, alas, I said)—there would be one sure result from all that killing. Ariel Sharon was finished (said I). "They'll string him up by his thumbs!" . . . It was God's Humor to return me to Israel in time to witness Sharon's prime ministry—*and reelection.*

A bigger example: when I came home from the Middle East in the mid-1980s, people with a lot of time on their hands used to ask what I thought would happen in Israel. . . . *Peace* I thought would happen. I could make the case (as, alas, I said) that nothing else *could* happen. Because one thing was always true: Israel could only lose one war. The Arabs could lose a dozen—nothing changed. But if Israel lost once, that was God's finger on the Game Over button. And it was obvious, even twenty years ago, that the Arabs weren't getting any less numerous, any poorer, or stupider, or any friendlier to Israel. So, it seemed profoundly in Israel's self-interest to make a deal soon, while she held the cards—while she could still kick the PLO's butt into Jordan before lunchtime, if push came to shove.

All those things are still true. But peace doesn't seem near, now. In fact, it seems chimeric—was it ever really possible? . . . When most Israelis talk about a peace deal, now (even most of the majority that favors land-for-peace), it is with a somehow familiar admixture of fondness, remembrance and dismissiveness—like it was a suit left for years at the cleaners. Sure, it was a nice suit—they'd had some good times in that suit (and Sharon still wears something like it for visits to Washington) . . . but it just wouldn't fit anymore. And it's hopelessly out of style. Only a sucker would go back to the cleaners, now, and pay good money just to try it on . . . Israelis never want to feel like suckers.

On the Palestinian side, the prospects seem darker, too. Among the common folk, the justice of their cause, the hope for their nation, and the dream of a better, peaceful life still burn—but now like embers covered with a double load of ash. There is the occupation, which never gets easier. And there is the ash load of their own national leadership. Palestinians, still, will talk all night about the injustice of the present situation. That's easy—even safe, if the talk is private. But there are few who can promote with excitement any concrete proposals to change that situation. For one thing, it's too painfully apparent that no one on their side has the power to make a proposal stick. And anyone with a little power is getting rich in the status quo. Then, too, it's still not safe (or it doesn't seem safe enough—precious few will try) to condemn the martyr-bombers, the terror–warriors and their tactics, which have plunged Palestine into deeper woe.

What that means, in practice, is their cause is hostage to any ragtag group of morons who can persuade one kid to throw away his life. (And there are a million kids) . . . In the same way, the peace-majority of Jews is hostage to any moron settler who grabs up his gun (they all have guns) and straps on a couple of bandoliers of ammo, to shoot up a mosque and the faithful praying in it. (An incident just like that, ten years ago—the moron was named Baruch Goldstein—touched off the death-spiral in which we still whirl.) . . .

Which brings me to that good, new story I teased so shamelessly. I think I was wrong about the prospect for peace (at least for a deal—the start of peace), because I expected Israel to act in her national interest. What I didn't see, or failed to think about, was the breakup of Israel's national consensus—the atomization of the Jewish society. What Israel lost—apparently while I looked elsewhere—was precisely the capacity to act in the national interest. The interest of the nation was replaced by tribal interests—and, in a lot of cases I see now, by purely individual interest. Making money, for instance, or attaining personal position and power . . . things that were hidden, or at least subsumed under national imperatives, when I first knew and loved the place.

It seems to me a sad turn, and one that doesn't augur well. It seems to me a real loss. And as I've said (and shown,

as my powers permitted)—I blame the occupation. It is cor-
rosive.

It seems to me a bad bargain: trading the best—the
bright soul of the country—for some dry, rocky hills, which
are another people's home. And they are hills which—if
given away, gladly and with generosity—might purchase for
Israel the fondest dream of its founders . . . to make this little
land a place where Jews may live without fear.

Maybe it can still happen—or it's happening now, while I
look elsewhere. I have friends who are encouraged and excited by some recent signs. In the early autumn of 2003,
twenty-seven air force officers, both reservists and active-
duty pilots, signed a letter refusing to fly future missions that
targeted Palestinian cities. The pilots denounced the occupation and called the assassination bombings "illegal and immoral." Israel had many prior refuseniks—but this letter
caused a much greater stir. Pilots are the elite of the elite
among Israeli military forces.

About a month later, the current Chief of Staff, Lieutenant General Moshe Ya'alon, told three Israeli journalists
that he and other top brass in the IDF don't believe the occupation policies are working. The closures and curfews only
bring on more incidents—Israel is producing the terror that
she claims to be fighting. "In our tactical decisions, we are
operating contrary to our strategic interest." . . . Never before has the army's top dog made public such disagreement
with the orders of his government.

In the following month, the admirable Yaakov Peri, along with three other former chiefs of Shin Bet, the secret police, gave an interview that rocked the country again. In Israel's most popular daily, they brought their prestige and the cachet of their (general's) rank to bear against the policies of expropriation, violence and assassination. These are men who know—better than anyone else—where the bones are buried on both sides of the Green Line. And they united to announce that they fear for Israel, if current policies are not reversed.

Yet another hopeful sign: in December, an agreement was announced—actually a proposal for agreement—on a peace deal. It was called the Geneva Accord, because its architects got help from the Swiss Foreign Ministry, and mounted a notable "launching" ceremony in that famously peaceful Swiss city—host to past international accords that famously endured.

The architects of this proposal were two experienced pols—the former Israeli minister of justice Yossi Beilin, and the former PA minister of information Yasser Abed Rabbo. Both had served officially as negotiators for their nations, before. Now, as private citizens, they worked on this document for two-and-a-half years—and with that careful work and their own prestige, they put together impressive international support. (Even Colin Powell gave their effort a courtly nod.) The terms of the agreement? Well, of course, they are the terms that *everybody knows* must end up to be the terms of peace: the West Bank and Gaza for the Palestinians, and

Israel for the Jews, for once and for good. There would be no more Right of Return . . . there would be shared sovereignty in Jerusalem—the holy mosques for the Arabs, the Western Wall for the Jews. There would be mutual recognition . . . and no more war.

In the mind of the Israeli public, the Geneva Accord complemented (and perhaps supplanted) a similar, but sketchier "amateur agreement" that had been announced the year before. That one was drafted by the Palestinian aristocrat Sari Nusseibeh, and one of the old Shin Bet chiefs, Ami Ayalon. The public reaction had been hopeful. Seventy thousand Palestinians and a hundred thousand Israelis signed on as supporters, by petition and Web site. And the reaction to the new Geneva Accord was just as encouraging. In a poll commissioned by the Baker Institute (remember Bush the Elder's designated hitter, Jimmy Baker III?), a majority of Palestinians and a majority of Israelis endorsed the terms of the new agreement.

I can see why my friends are excited. It's wonderful to read about peace in the news again. . . . But I can't see myself, or them, dancing in the end zone any time soon. Maybe I'm just a come-lately curmudgeon, trying to make up for my dewy-eyed past. But I don't see the path forward for all or any of these protests and proposals for peace.

The protests? Well, the pilots were immediately relieved of duty and drummed out of their units. A few of the reserve guys had to recant, because they were about to lose their jobs in civilian life—like one pilot who flew for El Al. (Did

I mention that the national airline is also run by an ex-general?) . . . And the Chief of Staff? Well, perhaps he should start shopping for a business and a political home. . . .

The proposals? Well, they're beautiful—brave and just— a credit to their drafters . . . and they make me a little sad. Because when I look at them, what I see are men of standing and mature political judgment—men who, each and all, live under governments that profess to want peace . . . men who, nevertheless, looked at the facts, and decided . . . they had a better chance to stop the killing without their governments than with them.

And they were right. The negotiations of Abed Rabbo got a weak little blessing from Yassir Arafat. (Abed Rabbo probably figured, it might not be healthy to proceed without it.) But once the Geneva Accord was announced, Arafat dummied up, and issued not one word of support. As for Arik Sharon—he did not disappoint. He immediately branded Yossi Beilin a traitor, acting behind the government's back. . . . Somehow, I can't see peace, on the Geneva terms, looming on the near horizon.

But to borrow an old movie line (as the children keep saying in *Angels in the Outfield*) . . . "It *could* happen!"

Maybe there will come along an impeccably tough (and electable) ex-general in Israel who is willing to use all his smarts and zeal to secure that peace which would end Israel's wars. Someone like Yitzhak Rabin. (I didn't think his proposal would actually bring peace—but he was serious, and not afraid of his foes.) . . . It *could* happen!

Maybe Arafat will get hit by a bus! That could happen! (More likely, a tank.) . . .

Or perhaps there will come along an American president who actually means to use his vast power here—not because it will do him any good, or get him votes, or money, or new friends among Israelis, or among the American zionists, or the American Christian right. But just because it *is* right. . . . Even that *could* happen.

It's just, right now, I don't see how. You could take that as another good sign. I won't be offended. . . . In this case, I would love to be wrong again.

Glossary

Agudat Yisrael: in Israel, an ultra-Orthodox movement (originally opposed to the Zionist state) that became a political party. Now part of a coalition party called United Torah Judaism, it represents the ultra-religious Ashkenazim.

AIPAC: American Israeli Public Affairs Committee, a pro-Israel lobby based in Washington, D.C.

Allah hu akbar: Arabic phrase (the central assertion of Islam) meaning "God is most great."

Ashkenazi: European Jew. The plural is ashkenazim.

Bagatz: Hebrew acronym for Israeli High Court of Justice—equivalent to our Supreme Court.

Baksheesh: Arabic word meaning "gratuity," or "tip." It's a little pay-off.

Bar mitzvah: Jewish boy's coming of age ceremony, when he turns thirteen. (The ceremony for a girl is called *bat mitzvah*.)

Bupkiss: Yiddish word meaning "nothing."

Conservative Judaism: a branch of Judaism whose members are committed to Jewish laws and customs. At the same time, they believe that Jewish law is not static but evolves in response to historic conditions.

Declaration of Principles: first document signed September 13, 1993, on the White House lawn by Yassir Arafat and Yitzhak Rabin as part of the Oslo Peace Accords. The Palestinians formally recognized Israel and renounced terrorism. In exchange, Israel committed to withdrawing its army from the West Bank and Gaza, and recognized the hitherto outlawed Palestinian Liberation Organization (and its chairman, Yassir Arafat) as the legitimate leader of the Palestinian people.

Diaspora: dispersion of Jews outside of Israel.

Dinar: the name for the currency, both in Iraq and the Kingdom of Jordan.

Dome of the Rock: great mosque built in Jerusalem between A.D. 687 and 691 on the site of the Second Temple, which was destroyed by the Romans in A.D. 70. Part of a complex of religious sites that Arabs call Al-Haram al-Sharif, the Noble Sanctuary (which includes the Al-Aqsa Mosque), it is one of the best-known landmarks in Jerusalem and has become a symbol of Palestinian resistance.

Druze: an Arab minority group in Israel, living mostly in small mountain villages, members of an eleventh-century Islamic reform movement. They are not considered Muslim (by other Muslims) and have their own holy book and believe in reincarnation. They sided with the Jews during the War of Independence and are the only Arabs who serve in Israel's army.

Dunam: Hebrew (derived from Turkish) for the standard land measurement in Israel and Palestine—about a quarter-of-an-acre.

Duvdevan: an elite Israeli commando unit.

Eretz Yisrael: Hebrew for "land of Israel," used by many zionists to describe the land they believe was granted them by God. Some hard-liners think it includes not only the original (1948) State of Israel, along with the West Bank and Gaza, but also parts of Lebanon, Syria and Jordan. The hardest of hard-liners define it simply—"From the Nile to the Euphrates"—i.e., from the middle of Egypt to the middle of Iraq.

Fatah: a secular underground movement founded in 1959 by Yassir Arafat to encourage the liberation of Palestine from Israeli occupation by force. It is still the dominant Palestinian political party.

Fellahin: Arabic word (a plural) for peasants or farm laborers, sometimes used as an epithet, like bumpkins.

Galabeya: a traditional Arab peasant garment—usually cotton, and always long-sleeved and ankle-length. It may be worn by both men and women.

G-d: a method of writing the word "God" employed by traditional religious Jews to observe the prohibition against naming the deity.

Givati Brigade: a revered Israeli army brigade whose exploits date back to the War of Independence, when it was organized to defend the Negev and the isolated settlements of southern Israel.

Golani Brigade: the most highly decorated infantry unit in the IDF, also formed in 1948 during the War of Independence to defend northern Israel.

Goy, or *Goyim* (the plural), or *Goyishe* (the adjective): sometimes derogatory Hebrew and Yiddish words for non-Jew, non-Jews and non-Jewish, respectively. The noun literally translates as "nation."

Greater Israel: *see Eretz Yisrael.*

Green Line: 1949 armistice line, which remained Israel's eastern border until the Six Day War and the occupation of new territories.

Gush Emunim: "Bloc of the Faithful," movement of Israeli religious settlers.

Gush Shalom: "Peace Bloc," an activist group (named in conscious reference to Gush Emunim). It was founded in 1993 by former MK Uri Avnery to agitate against the occupation and for a Palestinian state.

Hadassah: the Women's Zionist Organization of America.

Hagadda: a sacred book containing the story of the Exodus and the ritual for the Seder, a feast celebrated during Passover that commemorates the exodus of the Jews from Egypt. The *Hagadda* is read aloud during the Passover Seder.

Haganah: the Jewish underground army that led the (1948) War of Independence and was predecessor to the IDF.

Hamas: the most popular and successful Islamic resistance group in Palestine, a 1987 outgrowth of the Muslim Brotherhood. It has been branded (and outlawed) as a terrorist organization by the U.S. and most allies. Its stated goal is an Islamic state in all of Palestine, supplanting Israel.

Haredim: Hebrew word for the ultra-Orthodox, literally "the fear-struck" (equivalent to our "God-fearing"). *Haredim* traditionally opposed the creation of a Jewish state and rejected the authority of Israel, because in their view, it would delay the Messiah. In recent years, they have shared the state's agenda.

Hasbarah: a Hebrew word meaning "explanation." We might call it PR, or spin.

Hegira: a journey to escape danger, originally the flight of Muhammad from Mecca to Medina in A.D. 622, marking the beginning of the Muslim era.

Herut: the right-wing party founded in 1948 by Menachem Begin. It espoused Vladimir Jabotinsky's Revisionist Zionism, calling for the immediate establishment of a Jewish state in all of *Eretz Yisrael.* Herut became the main component of the Likud coalition, which governs Israel today. And a new Herut party supports expansion of the settlements and the forcible transfer of Arabs out of Palestine.

Hezbollah: "Party of God." A militant Islamic party and militia organized in Lebanon by a group of clerics in 1982 to drive Israeli troops out of their country. It later took up the Palestinian cause and sponsors suicide attacks on Israelis.

Like Hamas, it does not recognize Israel's right to exist and seeks to create an Islamic state in all of Palestine.

Histadrut: Israel's powerful national labor union. Founded in Palestine in 1920 to organize Jewish workers, it helped to create the Jewish state. Though its power in politics has diminished, it is still one of Israel's largest and richest organizations.

IAF: the Israeli Air Force, part of the IDF.

IDF: the Israeli Defense Forces, an acronym used as shorthand for the full military panoply of Israel.

Intifada: from the Arabic word meaning "shaking off," this is the name used for the Palestinian uprisings against Israeli occupation that began in 1987 ("the First *Intifada*") and in 2000 ("the Al-Aqsa *Intifada*," named for the great mosque facing the Dome of the Rock).

Irgun: Jewish terrorists (full name Irgun Zeva'i Le'umi or "National Military Organization") who split off from the Haganah in 1931 in opposition to the mainstream policy of "restraint." The Irgun targeted both the British and Arabs, and blew up Jerusalem's King David Hotel in 1946. It was also blamed for massacres in Arab villages during the 1948 War of Independence.

Islamic Jihad: a small terrorist organization based in Damascus (Syria) and committed to the creation of an Islamic Palestinian state and the destruction of Israel.

Israel Lands Authority: powerful agency responsible for administering the ninety-three percent of Israeli lands that are in the public domain, including land owned by the

Jewish National Fund. "Owning" real estate in Israel usually means leasing lands from the ILA.

Izzedine al Qassam Brigade: the military arm of Hamas, named for a popular Palestinian resistance leader who died fighting the zionists and the British in 1935.

Jewish Agency: the executive arm of the World Zionist Organization. It represented the Jewish community in Palestine under the British Mandate and played a key role in the immigration of Jewish refugees. Today, it recruits and assists Jews throughout the world to settle in Israel.

Judea: *see* West Bank.

Kahane, Meir: a controversial rabbi born in Brooklyn in 1932 who founded the Jewish Defense League and called for forcibly deporting all Arabs from Greater Israel, establishing a theocratic Jewish state and banning marriage between Jews and non-Jews. In Israel, he founded the militantly anti-Arab Kach party and served as its leader in the Knesset. Kahane was assassinated by an Egyptian militant in 1990. After Kach member Baruch Goldstein massacred thirty-four Muslims praying in a Hebron mosque in 1994, the party was outlawed as a terrorist organization.

Keren Kayemeth Le'israel: the Jewish National Fund, established by the Fifth Zionist Congress in 1901 to raise money in Jewish communities to buy land in Palestine. Still, it owns about twelve-and-a-half percent of the land in Israel, second only to the state. Charged with planting trees and otherwise "reclaiming the land."

Kibbutz, or Kibbutzim (the plural), or Kibbutznik (a member of a kibbutz): the cooperative farming settlement was the backbone of the Labour Zionist movement. It derived from the socialist cooperative farm, but in the case of kibbutzim, the members were both the workers and owners of the enterprise. Over the years, the kibbutzim contributed many of Israel's best and most ideologically motivated leaders.

Knesset: the one-hundred-twenty member parliament of Israel.

Koran: the holy book of Islam.

Kosher: in compliance with Jewish dietary laws.

Labour: the center-left political party of Israel's founders. It dominated Israeli politics until the mid-1970s.

Land-for-peace: the idea that underlies all mainstream proposals for permanent peace deals between Israelis and Arabs. The phrase goes in and out of vogue, but the idea that Israel would trade conquered lands back to the Arabs in exchange for recognition and peaceful coexistence has persisted since Israel's triumph in the (1967) Six Day War.

Law of Return: the Israeli law allowing every Jew to immigrate with the full benefits of citizenship.

Likud: the right-wing Israeli political coalition that first came to power in 1977 under the leadership of Menachem Begin. With Ariel Sharon now in leadership, it is still the dominant party in Israel.

machsom: Hebrew for "checkpoint."

Mandatory Palestine: Palestine under British control, as

mandated by the League of Nations, after World War I. The Mandate lasted until 1948, when the Brits withdrew, the United Nations granted Israel statehood and war with the Arabs ensued.

Meretz: a left-wing Israeli party (affiliated with Peace Now) that supports the evacuation of the settlements in the occupied lands, the withdrawal of the IDF and creation of a Palestinian state.

Mitzvah: Hebrew for "commandment." Any of six hundred and thirteen righteous acts which Jews are commanded to perform. The word is used to describe any religious obligation or good deed.

MK: an abbreviation—modeled on the British MP—that is used as a title for a member of the Knesset, or parliament.

Moazzin: Arabic for the crier who calls the Muslim faithful to the mosque for prayer, five times a day.

Mukhtar: mayor or village leader, Arabic word for "chosen one."

Muqata: Yassir Arafat's compound and PA headquarters in the West Bank city of Ramallah.

National Religious Party: ultra-nationalist Israeli political party, voice of the settler movement, holds that Israel should be the only state from the Jordan River to the Mediterranean Sea. Also works to change state laws to conform to Jewish law.

Negev: desert area of southern Israel.

Occupied territories: West Bank and Gaza Strip, both captured by Israel in the (1967) Six Day War. This term is never used by Israeli hawks, who consider all the conquered lands to be part of *Eretz Yisrael*—i.e., part of God's grant to the Jews.

Orthodox Judaism: a range of Jewish movements, including Hasidic, Ultra-Orthodox and Modern Orthodox, that espouse a fundamentalist approach to Jewish teachings, and exhibit varying degrees of acceptance (or nonacceptance) of modernity, including modern academic approaches to history and the analysis of religious texts.

Oslo Peace Process: a series of agreements signed by Yassir Arafat of the PLO and Israeli Prime Minister Yitzhak Rabin, beginning in Sept. 1993. The Oslo Accords granted limited autonomy to the Palestinians under an Arafat regime, in exchange for his promise to crack down on terrorists and recognize the state of Israel.

Palestinian Authority or Palestinian National Authority (PA or PNA): the governing body created under the Oslo agreements to be staffed by the PLO (under its chairman, Yassir Arafat) to administer the occupied West Bank and Gaza, and to provide security for Israel.

Palestinian Legislative Council (PLC): a legislative body created by the Oslo agreements.

Palestinian Liberation Organization (PLO): the nationalist organization founded in 1964 under the auspices of the Arab League, dedicated at inception to the destruction of Israel. Later, it formally changed its aim to the establishment of an independent Palestinian state.

Parve: in kosher law, neither milk nor meat; foods that can be eaten with either.

Passover (or in Hebrew, *Pesach*): the springtime holiday celebrating the Jewish exodus from Egypt.

Peace Now (or in Hebrew, Shalom Akhshav): self-described "zionist peace movement" founded in 1978 by three hundred forty-eight soldiers and reserve officers to oppose the occupation. It quickly became the mainstream national organization for peace, often drawing tens of thousands of Israelis to its demonstrations.

Peyus: Yiddish for the long curling sideburns worn by many Orthodox Jewish men. Jewish law forbids cutting those hairs.

Pisher: A Yiddish endearment meaning "baby boy," a little squirt. The word is often used for anything undersized or of small consequence.

Pogrom: organized (and often officially promoted) persecution or massacre of a minority group. The word is used most commonly to describe Polish and Russian massacres of Jews.

Protekzia: Hebrew slang (from the Russian) for special protection, connections or "pull."

Purim: Jewish holiday that celebrates the foiling of a plot against the Jews by the wicked Haman. The Jewish heroine, Esther, bravely intercedes with her husband, King Ahashueras of Persia, and Haman, the evil advisor, is hanged.

Purity of Arms: the Israeli army's tradition of morality in warfare. It goes back to the Haganah, before the state was established, and encompasses a number of ideas, including protection of civilians, humane treatment of prisoners and the use of the minimum force required. The tradition also includes the right and duty of every Jewish soldier to refuse (and report) all illegal, immoral or indecent orders.

Putz: Yiddish word for "penis"—commonly a fool or a blackguard.

Qassam rockets: simple homemade steel rockets filled with explosives, they were developed by Hamas during the current *Intifada*. They are commonly used to bombard both settlements and towns inside Israel.

Qassami: *see* Izzedine al Qassam Brigade.

Reform Judaism (also Progressive or Liberal Judaism): this is the least restrictive branch of Judaism, which generally holds that it is up to the individual to determine which Jewish laws and traditions are relevant to contemporary life.

Refuseniks: Israeli draftees who refuse to go into the army for moral or political reasons. The word is also used for reservists who avoid further service on moral or political grounds.

Right of Return: the Palestinian assertion that their 1948 refugees should be able to return to their old homes in Israel.

Rimon: Hebrew for "pomegranate," which is soldier slang for "hand grenade"—as such it was the name of the secret assassination and dirty tricks unit under the command of Ariel Sharon, when he held the southern command in the early 1970s.

Sabras: Jews native to Israel, also the name of an indigenous cactus whose fruit is often compared to the native Israeli personality—tough and thorny on the outside, but sweet and soft within.

Samaria: *see* West Bank.

Schlemiel: Yiddish for bungler or dolt.

Schmear: Yiddish for "grease"—a word often used for an aggregate (the whole schmear), or a bribe.

Schlub: Yiddish for a person regarded as clumsy, stupid or unattractive.

Schnorrers, schnorring: Yiddish for freeloaders and freeloading.

Sephardim: Jews of Middle Eastern origin who trace their heritage and religious traditions back to a golden age in Spain, before the Inquisition in the fifteenth century.

Shabbas (in Hebrew, *Shabbat*): Yiddish for the Sabbath.

Shabbat Shalom: Hebrew greeting of goodwill on the Sabbath.

Shalom: Hebrew for "peace," the common greeting and good-bye in Israel.

Shas: Sephardi ultra-Orthodox party that split off from Agudat Yisrael in 1984. It soon became the dominant party among the Sephardim, even drawing non-Orthodox voters with its aggressive pursuit of benefits for the Sephardic population.

Shekel: biblical currency now used in Israel (NIS, New Israeli Shekel).

Shiksa: a non-Jewish woman.

Shin Bet (also, Shabak): Israel's domestic security and intelligence service. Commonly translated as the secret police.

Shinui: an Israeli political party founded in 1974, it was a big winner in the 2003 elections (third behind Likud and Labour). Under the leadership of Tommy Lapid, it promotes a stricter separation between the state and religion, repeal of Sabbath and kosher food laws, the legalization of civil marriage, and an end to government payments and draft deferrals for yeshiva students.

Shiva: seven days of mourning required by Jewish law.

Shtarker: Yiddish for "tough guy," a "muscleman."

Shtetl: a small Jewish community, largely agrarian, often tradition-bound and backward, once common in Eastern Europe.

Shul: Yiddish for "synagogue."

Six Day War (1967): Israel preempted attack by neighboring Arab countries and defeated them within a week. The name is credited to Moshe Dayan who meant to echo the biblical creation in six days. In battle, the Israelis took from the Egyptians both the Gaza Strip (which Egypt had administered) and the Sinai Peninsula (later returned to the Egyptians in the 1979 peace deal). From the Syrians the Israelis took the Golan Heights, which previously menaced the Jewish settlements of the upper Galilee. And from Jordan, the Israelis took the West Bank—all the land from the old Green Line to the Jordan River.

Sokhnut: Hebrew for the Jewish Agency.

Sukkot: Feast of Booths or Tabernacles. A joyous Jewish harvest festival that begins five days after Yom Kippur and lasts a week, it commemorates the forty years the Jews wandered in the desert. Celebrants build and eat or live in a *sukkah*, a booth or hut, to commemorate their ancestors' makeshift desert dwellings.

Sulha: the traditional Arab process of conflict resolution.

Torah: the five books of Moses (and the first five books of the Bible).

Tunisians: an epithet for Palestinian officials or VIPs who came to Palestine with Yassir Arafat when the Oslo Accords ended the PLO's exile in Tunis.

Unit 101: Ariel Sharon's old commando unit, famous or infamous for its bloody retaliatory strikes against Palestinians.

War of Independence (1948): war between the new nation of Israel and six surrounding Arab countries, all trying to kill off the new Jewish state before it could take hold on the land. By the war's end, Israel occupied seventy-eight percent of Mandatory Palestine. The Arabs who lived on that land mostly ran away or were driven away, and their refugee status (and their children's and grandchildren's) endures to this day. The Jews failed to conquer the shoreline of the Mediterranean near Gaza. That land, known thereafter as the Gaza Strip, was administered by Egypt for the next twenty years. And the army of Jordan managed to hold the west bank of the Jordan River. The land from that river to Jerusalem (commonly called the West Bank, thereafter) was annexed to the Kingdom of Jordan until the Six Day War.

West Bank: one section of the territories occupied in the (1967) Six Day War, it is east of Israel but west of the Jordan River. Most Jews revile the term West Bank because it harkens back to the day when the Kingdom of Jordan controlled both banks of the river. Israelis refer instead to "Judea and Samaria," which are names of the ancient Jewish kingdoms on that land in Bible-times.

Western Wall (*also* Wailing Wall): the last surviving remnant of the Second Temple destroyed by the Romans. After the destruction, the wall was the holiest of all places for Jews. For nearly 2,000 years, they have traveled from all over the world to pray at the Wall, begging God to return and "ingather" the Jews, so the Messiah might come at last. The Jews lost access to the site in the (1948) War of Independence and regained it almost twenty years later, in the Six Day War.

Yeshiva: a Jewish (usually Orthodox) school of religious studies.

Yiddish: a High German language, with borrowed Hebrew and Slavic words, used by Eastern European Jews.

Yiddishkeit: Yiddish culture from middle and Eastern Europe.

yofi: Hebrew word for "beautiful"—a common exclamation of approval.

Yom Kippur: the Day of Atonement for sins, especially in the year past. It occurs in autumn, one week after the turn of the year in the Hebrew calendar, and it is the highest of Jewish holy days.

Yom Kippur War (Also Ramadan or October War): In 1973, Anwar Sadat of Egypt attacked Israel (with help from Syria) on the holiday of Yom Kippur, ostensibly to regain territory lost in 1967. The attack took the Israeli army by surprise, and though they eventually prevailed in the three-week war, they suffered terrible casualties, shattering Israel's (previously near-absolute) faith in the probity and prowess of its government and army.

zionism: the belief that Jews should or must return to the Holy Land to fulfill God's promise in the Bible. In the late nineteenth century, the plight of Jews in Europe sparked a Jewish national movement, which quickly appropriated zionist belief as its foundation and fuel. Within a couple of decades, Jewish nationalism and zionism were considered one and the same. Jewish organizations all over the world backed the effort to colonize and create a state in Palestine—an effort which bore fruit, the State of Israel, in 1948.

Author's Note and Acknowledgments

Every working reporter spends a fair bit of time explaining to his sources his "ground rules." What he's trying to make clear is how he will use the information that's about to be passed from the source to the notebook. Will the published work name the source? Will it pin to that source any direct quotations?

In some towns, like Washington, this discussion of the ground rules is a lawyerly business that can take more time than the interview itself. It's more meaningful than the information transmitted—because the ground rules (in their delicious particularity and onerousness) indicate the source's *importance*, the explosive sensitivity of his or her knowledge. . . . Jerusalem isn't half that bad. And in the rest of Israel and Palestine, things are positively old-fashioned. Most people simply say what they mean—and spell their name, so you can get it right. For this brave candor I was always grateful.

Still, I found myself taking some time to explain to folks how I would use their information. I knew, going in, this book would be controversial. Anything about this topic is controversial. And over the years I have been made aware of how heretical my views may seem. I shaped my ground rules accordingly. What I mostly said was: "I don't use many quotes, and I probably won't quote you. If you say something really good, I'll likely just steal it."

That wasn't all joke. What I was asking them to do was make me understand. Then, I would tell the story in my own words, and on my own responsibility. What I meant to do was relieve the Israelis of the job of defending my heresies. Accordingly, I express my gratitude to many of them, by name, here—but none should be blamed for my nasty conclusions.

On the Palestinian side of the Green Line, things are much dicier. I have kept most source-names out of the text, and I shall hold to that caution in these acknowledgments. Alas, anyone who speaks the truth too loudly in the West Bank or Gaza could become a target for the Israelis *and* for the Palestinians. As I write, the PA is in shambles and for the most part incapable of making mischief, even for its own citizens. But even a broken clock is right twice a day—and if a single source of mine were jailed or tortured for the price of my pleasure at thanking the others, that would be a terrible bargain. So, anonymously, I thank them all, now, for their generosity and trust in me. In my house, they will never be nameless.

So, with those ground-rules-on-the-ground-rules established, I am grateful for aid and comfort, advice and friendship, conversation and laughter, honest outrage and a thousand kindnesses, a million coffees, too many meals, scores of introductions, occasional rides, incessant directions and—most of all—for good information . . . from Yusuf and Safa'a Abu Hamed, Yossi and Tami Aharon, Motti Aharonov, Meir Amit, Janet Aviad, Professor Shlomo Avineri, Bernie Avishai and Sidra Ezrachi, Uri Avnery, Yizhar Be'er, Ken Bode, Sherif Boraie, Dr. and Mrs. Avi Beigelman, Ron Ben-Yishai, Yossi Bernson, Shabtai Bilu, (my zionist rabbi) Zev Birger, Eli Biton, Gary Brenner, Professor Menachem Brinker, MK Roman Bronfman, Professor Amnon Brzezininski, Shmuli Calderon, Zev Chafets, Uri Cohen, Mohammad Darawshe, Professor Daniel Dor, Einat Eisenman, Rami and Nurit Peled El-Khanan, MK Gidon Ezra, Steve Franklin, Anschel Friedman, Rabbi Menachem Fruman, Eric Fusfield, Amos and Rivka Gitai, Abby Schechter Goral, Hillel Goral, Eitan Haber, Muki Hadar, Eleyakim Ha'etzni, Rafik Halaby, Josh Hammer, Aluf Hareven, Rina Harrison, Peter Hermann, Professor Ariel Hirschfeld, Elias Jabbour, Smadar Haran Kaiser and Yaacov Kaiser, Sayed Kashua, Yuval Katz, Dr. Anna Kazakhkova, Dave Keene, Dr. Ilan and Sue Kutz, Mayor Shlomo (Chich) Lahat, Yitzhak Laor, Nasr Mahamid, Lutfy and Vida Mash'our, Col. and Mrs. Benny Mativ, Dan Meridor, Yehuda Meshi-Zahav, Addisu Messele, Sami and Rachel Michael, Dalia Mistachki, Professor Arye Na'or, Liora Nir, Daniel Okev, Amir Oren, Professor Meir Pa'il, Yaakov Peri, Sever Plotzker, G. Jefferson Price III, Dov

Puder, Raiku Punamaki, Brig. Itzhak Pundak, Hagit Ra'anan, Rachel Rabin-Jacob, Talia Harris Ram, MK Mossi Raz, Danny Rubinstein, Robert Ruby, Edie Sabag, Yomtob Sabah, David Schechter, P. B. Schechter, Daniel Seaman, Gilead Sher, Professor Eitan Shiloni, Fr. Emil Shofani, Chaim Shur, Yishai and Mazal Shuster, Professor Arnon Soffer, Elisha Spiegelman, Professor Ramzi Suleiman, Bill Tonelli, Rachel Weinberg, Mayor Daniella Weiss, Itzhak Zak, Beate Zilversmidt, and Donald and Linda Zisquit.

I would never have reached most of those individuals (nor would I have understood what they told me) without the help of some splendid researchers, helpers and interpreters. They were partners and companions in this enterprise. In an act of friendship I shall never forget, my number-one interpreter from twenty-five years ago, Gideon Gitai, left his new life as a filmmaker in Finland and came back to Israel to help me. Both this book and the experience of learning for it were enriched by the grace and gifts of Michael Green. Ahmad Mashal kept me out of trouble in the West Bank. And Safwat Diab lent both bravery and brilliance to my adventures in Gaza. Ayelet Tamari and David Miron helped ably and generously as their schedules permitted.

And on that subject—one woman made my schedule each day and kindly bent her schedule to mine (no matter how many other demands her life presented). Ms. Pony Brzezinski beautifully served, from first to last, as my chief researcher, source-finder and project manager in Israel. Without her, this effort would have collapsed. With her, it never lost its fun. . . . And on *that* topic of fun—two other women became great pals to me and godmothers to this book: Deborah Harris and Batya Gur helped and humored me in every way. They lent wit and laughter to my days and nights. For months, they also lent me their great friend, Pony. . . . One more godparent to the book: the brrrilliant Shimon Yakira sliced, as is his habit in life, through all complications and obfuscations to help me make sense of what I learned. As befits a *padrino,* I owe him. . . . And one more fond salute: to Argentina Britvar, who first wakened me to the spice of life in Tel Aviv. Twenty-five years later, she was still wakening me to what was real. I would never have understood how to do this book without her.

This book would have been a thin soup without ladles-ful of fact from the press. The newspapers in Israel and the reporters who staff them are simply terrific. I read *Ha'aretz* and the *Jerusalem Post.* Whenever I could, I had read to me (by translators) stories from *Maariv* and *Yediot Ahronot.* I also tried not to miss the *Jerusalem Report,* and I sampled other periodicals (not well but widely) from the deep-think newsprint of *The New York Review of Books,* as far afield as the glossy and surprisingly deft *Hadassah* magazine. I was informed by the Voice of Israel, Galei Tsahal (Israel's Army Radio), and the BBC World Service; also by Channels One, Two and Ten in Israel, Jordanian TV, Al Jazeera and Al Arabiya. I learned from my compatriots' stories in *Newsweek,* the *L.A. Times, Baltimore Sun, Philadelphia Inquirer, Christian Science Monitor; Washington Post* and *The New York*

Times (especially the work of James Bennett). I also went to school on the British press (especially when it featured some new yarn from the *Guardian's* Jonathan Steele, or Robert Fisk in *The Independent.*) In addition, I derived great benefit from articles in publications and on the Web sites of Amnesty International, Human Rights Watch, the World Bank, the International Monetary Fund; also the Palestine Report (from the Jerusalem Media and Communications Center), the Electronic Intifada, Miftah, B'Tselem, Peace Now and Gush Shalom; also the Washington Report on Middle East Affairs and the Foundation for Middle East Peace. On the situation in the territories, I reserve for special mention three splendid sources, quite different from one another, but all original and valuable: the first is the anthropological work of Professor Sharif Kanaana, of Bir Zeit University; the second is the public opinion research and interpretation from Dr. Khalil Shikaki, at his Palestinian Center for Policy and Survey Research; the third is the groundbreaking economic analysis by Dr. Sara Roy, of Harvard University.

I was aided by a number of books—some for information, some for delight. I list them here by their author's names:

Mahmoud Abbas (Abu Mazen), *Through Secret Channels: The Road to Oslo* (Garnet Publishing, 1995).

Yigal Allon, *My Father's House: Israel's Foreign Minister*

Looks Back at the Heroic People, Heroic Country of His Youth (W.W. Norton, 1976).

Hannah Arendt, *Eichman in Jerusalem: A Report on the Banality of Evil* (Penguin, 1994).

Hanan Ashrawi, *This Side of Peace* (Simon & Schuster, 1995).

Roane Carey, ed., *The New Intifada: Resisting Israel's Apartheid* (Verso, 2001).

Jimmy Carter, *The Blood of Abraham: Insights into the Middle East* (Houghton Mifflin, 1986).

Zev Chafets, *Heroes and Hustlers, Hard Hats and Holy Men: Inside the New Israel* (William Morrow, 1986).

Noam Chomsky, *Fateful Triangle: The United States, Israel & the Palestinians* (South End Press, 1999).

Daniel Dor, *Intifada Hits the Headlines: How the Israeli Press Misreported the Outbreak of the Second Palestinian Uprising* (Indiana University Press, 2003).

Noah J. Efron, *Real Jews: Secular vs. Ultra-Orthodox and the Struggle for Jewish Identity in Israel* (Basic Books, 2003).

Amos Elon, *The Israelis: Founders and Sons* (Holt, Rinehart and Winston, 1971).

———, *A Blood-Dimmed Tide: Dispatches from the Middle East* (Columbia University Press, 1997).

———, *Flight into Egypt* (Pinnacle Books, 1981).

———, *Herzl* (Holt, Rinehart and Winston, 1975).

Yaron Ezrahi, *Rubber Bullets: Power and Conscience in Modern Israel* (Farrar, Straus and Giroux, 1996).

Norman Finkelstein, *Image and Reality of the Israel-Palestine Conflict* (Verso, 1995).

David Fromkin, *A Peace to End All Peace: The Fall of the Ottoman Empire and the Creation of the Modern Middle East* (Henry Holt & Co., 1989).

David Grossman, *Death as a Way of Life: Israel Ten Years After Oslo* (Farrar, Straus and Giroux, 2003).

———, *The Yellow Wind* (Farrar, Straus and Giroux, 2002).

———, *Sleeping on a Wire: Conversations with Palestinians in Israel* (Farrar, Straus and Giroux, 2003).

Joshua Hammer, *A Season in Bethlehem: Unholy War in a Sacred Place* (Free Press, 2003).

David Hare, *Via Dolorosa & When Shall We Live* (Faber and Faber, 1998).

Dilip Hiro, *Sharing the Promised Land: A Tale of the Israelis and Palestinians* (Olive Branch Press, 1999).

David Phillip Horovitz, *A Little Too Close to God: The Thrills and Panic of a Life in Israel* (Alfred A. Knopf, 2000).

Albert Hourani, *A History of the Arab Peoples* (Harvard University Press, 1991).

Baruch Kimmerling and Joel S. Migdal, *The Palestinian People: A History* (Harvard University Press, 2003).

Walter Laqueur, *A History of Zionism* (Holt, Rinehart and Winston, 1972).

Walter Laqueur and Barry Rubin, eds., *The Israel-Arab Reader: A Documentary History of the Middle East Conflict,* sixth edition (Penguin, 2001).

Paul A. Mendes-Flohr, *A Land of Two Peoples: Martin Buber on Jews and Arabs* (Oxford University Press, 1983).

Benny Morris, *Righteous Victims: A History of the Zionist-Arab Conflict, 1881–2001* (Vintage Books, 2001).

———, *The Birth of the Palestinian Refugee Problem, 1947–1949* (Cambridge University Press, 1987).

Michael Oren, *Six Days of War: June 1967 and the Making of the Modern Middle East* (Oxford University Press, 2002).

Amos Oz, *In the Land of Israel*. Translated by Maurie Goldberg-Bartura (Harcourt Brace & Company, 1993).

Sara Roy, *The Gaza Strip: The Political Economy of De-development* (Institute for Palestine Studies, Washington, D.C., 1995).

Danny Rubinstein, *The Mystery of Arafat* (Steerforth Press, 1995).

Joe Sacco, *Palestine* (Jonathan Cape, 2003).

Edward Said, *The Politics of Dispossession: The Struggle for Palestinian Self-Determination, 1969–1994* (Vintage Books, 1995).

———, *The End of the Peace Process: Oslo and After* (Vintage Books, 2001).

———, *The Question of Palestine* (Vintage Books, 1992).

———, *Out of Place: A Memoir* (Alfred A. Knopf, 2000).

———, *Peace and Its Discontents: Essays on Palestine in the Middle East Peace Process* (Vintage Books, 1996).

Tom Segev, *1949: The First Israelis* (Henry Holt & Co., 1998).

————, *One Palestine, Complete: Jews and Arabs Under the British Mandate* (Little, Brown, 2000).

————, *The Seventh Million: The Israelis and the Holocaust* (Henry Holt & Co., 1991).

Irwin Shaw and Frank Capa, *Report on Israel* (Simon and Schuster, 1950).

Raja Shehadeh, *Strangers in the House: Coming of Age in Occupied Palestine* (Steerforth Press, 2002).

This book was dreamed up in a ratty delicatessen on Forty-seventh Street, New York, where my publisher, David Rosenthal, took me for lunch. It's no accident that the man who published this work is the only New York book bigwig who could turn an Official Author Lunch into a couple of kosher hot dogs. In both cases, the key word is *chutzpah*. I thank him for it, and for sending me back to the Middle East.

At Simon & Schuster, where he reigns, I was helped and supported by deputy bigwigs Melissa Possick and Walter Weintz, by the shortest big wheel in the business, Alice Mayhew, and chief of all, Carolyn Reidy. I have also benefited from the exemplary work of the art director Jackie Seow, managing editor Irene Kheradi, production manager John Wahler, chief counsel Elisa Rivlin, president of the sales division Larry Norton, and executive director of marketing Michael Selleck. The wonderful executive director of publicity, Victoria Meyer, showed once again she is the best reader in New York. The publicity director Aileen Boyle gave valuable attention and advice. And they gave me a star to work with—Rachel Nagler. I was saved from many sins by my copy editor, Trent Duffy, and saved from unrepentance by Associate Director of Copyediting Gypsy da Silva. My quick and graceful editor, Ruth Fecych, made the book quicker, more graceful.

My agent, counsellor and chief of relations with the outside world, Flip Brophy, was best friend to me and this book, as always. In fact, she shared in its provenance by wangling me an invitation to the Jerusalem Book Fair in 2001—which got me thinking about the place again. She is, as Anwar Sadat used to say, a full partner.

My friend of the heart, Joan Smith, took this book to her heart and became its secret weapon. She started with a normal American newspaper reader's knowledge and became a Middle East savant. Day by day, every day, she collected fact and opinion for me, and commiserated with me, or exulted. She spurred me on, always, and found for me whatever I was needing. I wrote for her.

My daughter, Ruby, brought real life back to me, when the book threatened to become life. She's a thirteen year old with a good soul, and surprising *sechel*. As always, I told her my stories, and when I saw she got it, I knew I had it. And she helped in a bigger way: My hunger for peace is all about her. So, to her this book is dedicated.

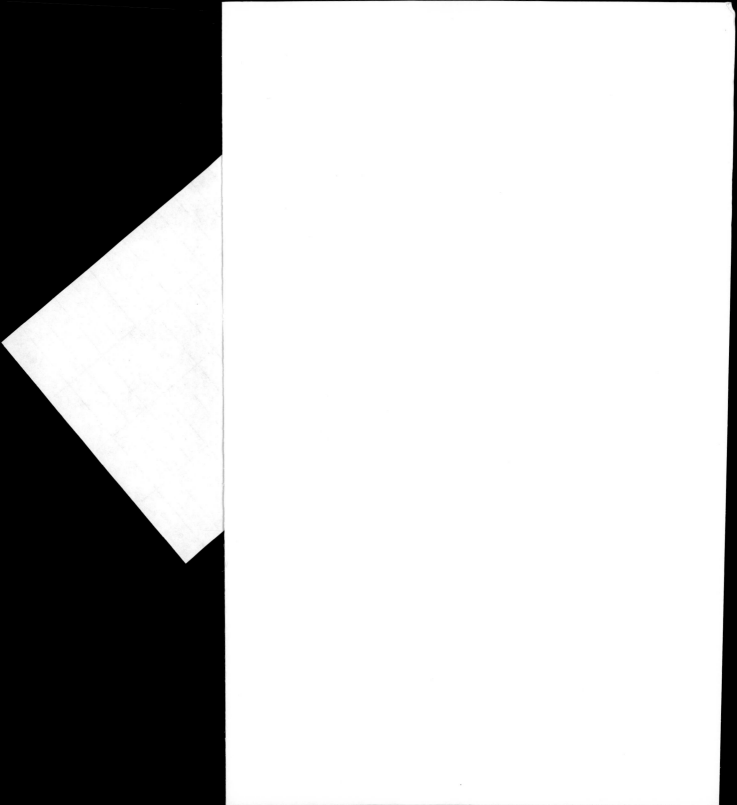

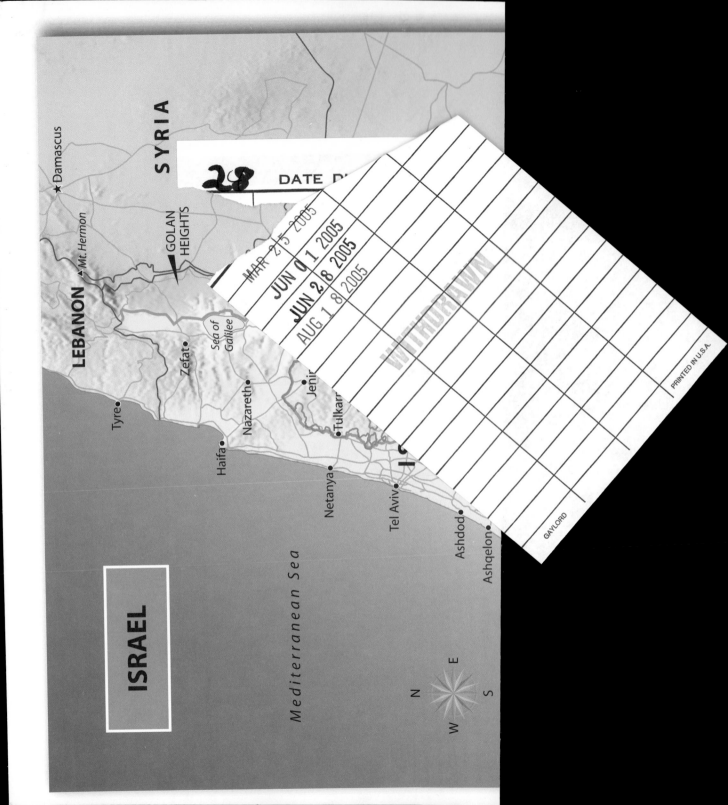